Construction Delays

- *Documenting Causes*
- *Winning Claims*
- *Recovering Costs*

Theodore J. Trauner, Jr., PE, PP
Illustrated by Carl W. Linde

Construction Delays

- *Documenting Causes*

- *Winning Claims*

- *Recovering Costs*

Theodore J. Trauner, Jr., PE, PP

R.S. MEANS COMPANY, INC.
CONSTRUCTION CONSULTANTS & PUBLISHERS
100 Construction Plaza
P.O. Box 800
Kingston, MA 02364-0800
(617) 585-7800

This book was edited by Mary Greene, Neil Smit and Julia Willard. Typesetting was supervised by Joan Marshman. The book and jacket were designed by Norman Forgit. Illustrations by Carl Linde.

Printed in the United States of America.

10   9   8   7   6   5   4   3   2
Library of Congress Cataloging in Publication Data
ISBN 0-87629-174-4

This book is dedicated to my wife, Dariel, whose encouragement, enthusiasm, support and understanding motivated me to take on this project.

Table of Contents

Foreword

When a construction project is delayed beyond the contract completion date or beyond the contractor's scheduled completion date, significant additional costs can be experienced by the contractor, the owner, or both. Because contract schedules are so important and delays can be so costly, more and more projects end up in arbitration, litigation, or some form of dispute concerning time-related questions. A judge, jurors, or arbitrators are then faced with the task of sorting out "who shot John" from a complex collection of facts and dates. Oftentimes, experts are required—both to perform an analysis of the delays that occurred, and to provide testimony to explain the analysis. One of the most difficult tasks of the expert is to educate the parties involved so that an understanding can be reached concerning the delays that occurred and who is responsible for them.

This book provides the background information necessary to understand delays. This understanding is not geared solely to the context of disputes, but rather provides a framework to help prevent disputes from occurring, and to resolve the questions of time as they arise during the project.

Chapter 1, "Types of Delays," explains the basic categories of excusable and non-excusable delays, and the subcategories of compensable and non-compensable delays. It addresses the concept of concurrency and also non-critical delays. This primer in delays prepares the reader for the specific issues covered in succeeding chapters.

Chapter 2 explains how to approach the analysis, including the starting points of as-planned and as-built schedules, and how one must compare the two in order to quantify the delays that have occurred. The question of liability is addressed separately, since this determination is made most expeditiously once the specific delays have been identified.

Chapters 3, 4, and 5 travel through the actual process of analyzing delays. Starting with the best case situation of having a detailed critical path method schedule (Chapter 3), the technique progresses through the more common occurrence of delay analysis using project bar charts (Chapter 4), and finally the worst case, a project with no as-planned schedule (Chapter 5). Recognizing that there are numerous approaches used in analyzing delays, Chapter 6 comments on some of the more common approaches used and the problems and pitfalls associated with them.

Damages to the owner and contractor are addressed in Chapters 7 through 11. Since inefficiency costs have become such a prevalent factor in many delay claims, they have been addressed separately in the hopes that some of the myth and magic that surrounds them may be cleared away. Similarly, the topic of damages associated with non-critical delays has been given special attention, since many projects experience these with little to no recognition of the problem.

Chapter 12, "Risk Management," could also be called "Prevention of Time-Related Problems," since it focuses on the delay-related risks of the various parties in a construction project. By maintaining this focus, each of the parties has a tendency to better control time and resolve delay problems as they occur.

This book has been written with the hope that a better understanding of delays, time extensions, and delay cost will help to prevent problems rather than foster and fuel the already litigious atmosphere that exists in construction.

Bear in mind that the methodology described herein can be applied to any type of project that (a) has a time constraint, and (b) is amenable to scheduling and the monitoring and control of time. This category could include supply contracts, manufacturing projects, and research and development projects, as well as traditional construction projects. The approach will be the same for all situations, given a logical and reasoned application within the context of the existing facts.

Acknowledgments

The author would like to acknowledge the following individuals for their capable assistance: Scott Lowe and Michael Payne, Esquire, whose review and suggestions were invaluable; and Lizanne Cotton, who spent innumerable hours typing, editing, assembling materials and coordinating this book. Special recognition must go to Mary Greene and Neil Smit, whose efforts in providing objective feedback and professional editing have been key to the quality of the final product.

Introduction

This book addresses the topic of construction delays and the resulting impacts and damages. This is a timely subject, since the construction industry has evolved such that failure to meet schedules can result in serious consequences, with unprecedented cost implications.

Recent years have seen a tremendous growth in the incidence of delays to projects and the number of delay damage claims which have come into dispute. The largest dollar value disputes almost always are delay related.

The financial significance of delays demands that the project owner, general contractor, construction manager, designer, and subcontractors be educated on damages. This book is designed to serve as a primer for that education process. All too many texts on this subject focus on the legal perspective, in legal language. This book is intended as a practical, hands-on guide to an area of construction that is not well understood.

All construction industry professionals should know the basic types of delays and understand the situations that give rise to entitlement for additional compensation. Most importantly, they should understand how a project schedule and ongoing project documentation can be used to determine whether a delay occurred, quantify the magnitude of the delay, and assess the cause of the delay. Furthermore, construction professionals should be able to assess the delay's impacts to the project, and quantify any costs or damages resulting from those impacts.

Many techniques are used to analyze delays. Some of these methods have inherent weaknesses and should be avoided. This book points out the shortcomings of these faulty methods and explains how a delay analysis *should* be performed. It then describes – specifically – how the analysis is done with CPM schedules. The discussion will include subtleties of the process, such as shifts in the critical path, and non-critical delays.

The subject of damages is covered in detail, including the major categories of extended field overhead and unabsorbed home office overhead. Likewise, the damages suffered by the owner, either actual or liquidated, are also explained.

Finally, a chapter is devoted to managing the risk of delays and time extensions from the viewpoints of the various parties to a construction project. A discussion of early completion schedules and constructive acceleration is also included.

The author's substantial experience in analyzing delays and quantifying damages provides the readers with numerous benefits, including:

- A clear, concise definition of the major types of delays
- A simple, practical explanation of how delays must be analyzed
- A detailed explanation of how delays are defined and quantified for projects with CPM schedules, bar charts, or no schedule at all
- A glimpse of some of the less obvious problems associated with delays, such as delays to non-critical activities
- An understanding of the shortcomings of some delay analysis methods that may not provide the desired results
- A detailed understanding of the various areas where costs can increase, how those areas are impacted, and how to calculate the costs
- An understanding of the risks delays present to various parties to the project, and how each of those parties can manage those risks

An explanation of delays and delay damages, presented in a straightforward, accessible manner, should be useful to public and private owners, construction managers, general contractors, subcontractors, designers, suppliers, and attorneys whose work involves them in the construction industry.

Chapter One

Types of Construction Delays

Chapter One

Types of Construction Delays

Before any discussion of delay analysis can begin, a clear understanding of the general types of delays is necessary. There are four basic ways to categorize delays:

- Excusable or Non-Excusable
- Concurrent or Non-Concurrent
- Compensable or Non-Compensable
- Critical or Non-Critical

All delays are either excusable or non-excusable. Both excusable and non-excusable delays can be defined as either concurrent or non-concurrent. Excusable delays are further broken down into compensable or non-compensable delays. Finally, before determining the impact of a delay on the project, the analyst must determine whether it is critical or non-critical. Figure 1.1 is an overview of the types of delays. This chapter addresses the distinctions among these types of delays.

Excusable and Non-Excusable Delays

Excusable Delays

In general, a delay is excusable if its cause is an unforeseeable event beyond the contractor's/subcontractor's control. Normally, delays resulting from the following events are considered excusable.

- General labor strikes
- Fires
- Floods
- Acts of God
- Owner-directed changes
- Errors and omissions in the plans and specifications
- Differing site conditions or concealed conditions
- Unusually severe weather
- Intervention by outside agencies (such as the EPA)
- Lack of action by government bodies, such as building inspection departments

The above conditions are reasonably unforeseeable and not within the contractor's control.

Before the analyst concludes that a delay is excusable based solely on the above definitions, he or she must refer to the construction contract documents. *Decisions concerning delays must be made within the context of the specific contract.* The contract should clearly define the factors it considers valid delays to the project, that justify extensions of the contract completion date. For example, a contract may not allow for any time extensions caused by weather conditions, regardless of how unusual, unexpected, or severe.

Non-Excusable Delays

Non-excusable delays are events within the contractor's control, or are foreseeable. Some examples of non-excusable delays are:

- Late performance of subcontractors
- Untimely performance by suppliers
- Faulty workmanship by the contractor or subcontractors
- A project-specific labor strike caused by either the contractor's unwillingness to meet with labor representatives or by unfair job practices

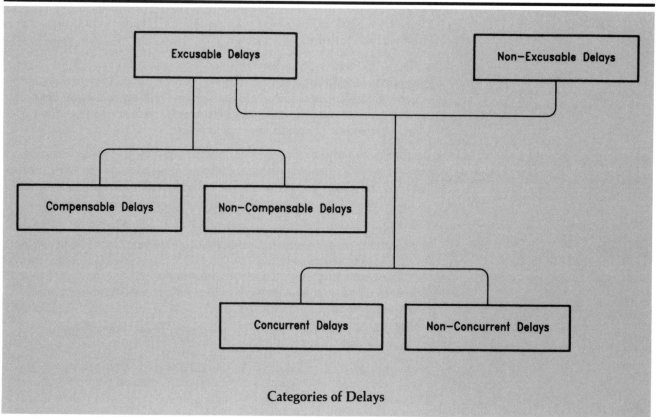

Categories of Delays

Figure 1.1

Again, the contract is the controlling document. For example, some contracts consider supplier delays excusable, if the contractor can prove the materials were requisitioned/ordered in a timely manner; others do not allow such delays. The owner and the designer/drafter of the contract must be sure the contract documents are clear and unambiguous. Similarly, before signing the contract, the contractor should fully understand what it considers excusable and non-excusable delays.

Compensable and Non-Compensable Delays

If a delay is compensable, the contractor is entitled to additional monetary compensation. Of course, the question of whether a delay is compensable or non-compensable means that it has already been determined an *excusable delay* (see Figure 1.1). A non-excusable delay warrants neither additional compensation nor a time extension.

Whether or not a delay is compensable depends primarily on the terms of the contract. In most cases, a contract specifically notes the kinds of delays which are *non-compensable*, for which the contractor does not receive any additional money, but may be allowed a time extension. Contracts distinguish between compensable and non-compensable delays in many ways, some of which are described in the following paragraphs.

Federal Contracts

Federal government contracts normally define strikes, floods, fires, acts of God, and unusually severe weather as excusable, but non-compensable, delays. All other forms of excusable delays are compensable, such as differing site conditions, owner-directed changes, and constructive changes that have a delay impact.

No Damage for Delay Clause

Some contracts are more restrictive in defining compensable delays. It is even quite common for a contract to use *exculpatory language* concerning delays. Exculpatory language is language that exculpates, or excuses, a party from some liability. The most general approach used in contracts concerning delays is the broad *no damage for delay* clause. The wording in this clause can take many forms. Figure 1.2 is an example of a broad *no damage for delay* clause. The wording in the clause in Figure 1.2 leaves little doubt that the contract does not allow compensation for delays, regardless of the cause.

There are many variations in contract clauses that address every possible situation on the compensability of delays. However, the broader the clause, the more likely it may not be enforceable. More specific clauses are more readily upheld by the courts.

Public contracts at the state and municipal level commonly contain specific *no damage for delay* clauses. Figure 1.3 is an example of a *no damage for delay* clause pertaining to work by utilities. Similarly, Figure 1.4 shows a *no damage for delay* clause covering work by other contractors. Finally, Figure 1.5 is a *no damage for delay* clause that specifically covers the review and return of shop drawings.

All parties to a project should clearly understand the clauses of the contract concerning delays and time extensions. If a contractor is considering signing a contract with such language, he/she should consult *qualified* counsel, familiar with construction litigation and the laws of the jurisdiction in which the clause applies.

When a contract identifies specific items in a contract as being non-compensable, it should clearly define each one. For example, if unusually severe weather is a non-compensable delay, the contract should clearly state the restriction. The contract may define *unusually severe weather* as weather not ordinarily expected for the specific time of year and region. The definition in the contract may further clarify *unusual weather* as that which exceeds the historical weather data recorded by the National Oceanic and Atmospheric Administration (NOAA) at a specific location. The Corps of Engineers has taken this one step further by specifying in their contracts the exact number of days of rain greater than 0.01 inches that the contractor can expect during each month of the project.

While the extent of detail provided by the Corps of Engineers may not be absolutely necessary, the owner should be sure the contract does not have ambiguous wording. Some contracts will list "inclement weather" as an excusable, non-compensable delay. "Inclement," however, can have many definitions. It is also possible that inclement weather may occur, but may not delay the project. Therefore, the owner should carefully draft the contract, and all signatories must carefully read and clearly understand the compensable and non-compensable delays specified in the contract.

No Damage for Delay Clause

If the contractor is delayed in completion of the work under the contract by any act or neglect of the owner or of any other contractor employed by the owner, or by changes in the work, or by any priority or allocation order duly issued by the federal government, or by any unforeseeable cause beyond the control and without the fault or negligence of the contractor, including but not restricted to, acts of God or of the public enemy, fires, floods, epidemics, quarantine restrictions, strikes, freight embargoes, and abnormally severe weather, or by delays of subcontractors or suppliers occasioned by any of the causes described above, or by delay authorized by the engineer for any cause which the engineer shall deem justifiable, then:

For each day of delay in completion of the work so caused, the contractor shall be allowed one day additional to the time limitation specified in the contract, it being understood and agreed that the allowance of same shall be solely at the discretion and approval of the owner.

No claim for any damages or any claim other than for extensions of time as herein provided shall be made or asserted against the owner by reason of any delays caused by the reasons hereinabove mentioned.

Figure 1.2

Figure 1.3

Cooperation with Utilities

It is understood and agreed that the contractor has considered in his bid all of the permanent and temporary utility facilities in their present and/or relocated positions, as shown on the plans and as revealed by his site investigation; is cognizant of the limited ability of the state to control the actions of the utilities; and in his bid has made allowance for the fact that no additional compensation will be allowed for any delays, inconvenience, or damage sustained by him due to any interference from the said utility facilities or the operation of moving them.

Figure 1.4

Cooperation Between Contractors

. . . Each Contractor involved shall assume all liability, financial or otherwise, in connection with his contract, and hereby waives any and all claims against the Department for additional compensation that may arise because of inconvenience, delay, or loss experienced by him because of the presence and operation of other contractors working within the limits of or adjacent to the Project.

Figure 1.5

Review of Shop Drawings

The Contractor should allow thirty (30) calendar days for the review of any shop drawings, samples, catalog cuts, etc. which are required to be submitted in accordance with the contract. This thirty (30) day time period will begin on the date the submission is received by the Architect/Engineer and terminate on the date it is returned by the Architect/Engineer. The Contractor should further allow thirty (30) calendar days for each resubmission of any rejected submission. Should any submission not be returned within the thirty (30) calendar days specified, it is understood and agreed that the sole remedy to the Contractor is an extension of the contract time. For each day of delay in completion of the overall project caused by the late return of submissions, the Contractor shall be allowed one day additional to the time limitation specified in the contract. No claim for any damages or any claim other than for extensions of time as herein provided shall be made or asserted against the Owner by reason of any delays caused by the reasons hereinabove mentioned.

Concurrent and Non-Concurrent Delays

If two delays occur at the same time, they are *concurrent*. If they do not occur at the same time, they are non-concurrent. While this may seem like a simple enough distinction, the courts and boards have had to make many decisions about concurrent delays. The weight of those decisions lends importance to the overall concept.

If a project experiences two concurrent delays, one of which is compensable and the other non-compensable, then the non-compensable one generally takes precedence over the compensable delay. For example:

> *A project has a delay from June 1 to June 30 because of a design problem. Simultaneously, the contractor experiences a general trade strike from June 1 to June 30.*

Clearly, the two delays are concurrent and run for the same period. Design delays are typically compensable. The union strike is a non-compensable delay. (A compensable delay entitles a contractor to both a time extension and additional monetary compensation. A non-compensable delay entitles a contractor to a time extension only.) In the example above, the contractor would receive a 30-day time extension, but no additional monetary compensation, because the non-compensable delay takes precedence over the compensable delay.

Figure 1.6 shows two additional case studies of concurrent delays.

If both compensable and non-compensable delays start on the same day but do not have the same duration, the courts and boards will make an apportionment between the two. For example, suppose that a project has a design-related delay from June 1 to June 30. Once again, the contractor simultaneously experiences a general trade strike from June 1 to June 27. The courts and boards may apportion the delays and award the contractor a 30-day time extension and three days of monetary compensation. This example is shown in case study 2 of Figure 1.6.

While this concept may appear clear-cut, there are complications. First, one must have a *clear* definition of compensable and non-compensable delays. Second, the analysis must be able to show specifically *when* the delays occur in order for the court or board to make a decision and/or apportionment. Also, past decisions of the courts and boards often fail to provide enough specifics on the delay facts for those cases.

From a scheduling and delay analysis perspective, one additional situation must be considered. Figure 1.7 portrays situations similar to those described in Figure 1.6. However, the outcome in these examples is different.

The Primacy of Delay

The conclusions in Figure 1.7 are based on a concept known as the *primacy of delay*. To understand this concept completely, one must have a thorough working knowledge of scheduling and, in particular, of the Critical Path Method. For the sake of simplicity, however, we offer the following brief explanation.

In the first case study on Figure 1.7, the owner's delay began before the contractor's delay. If the analyst updates the schedule to the 2nd or 3rd of June, it would show that the owner's issuance of a Stop Work Order caused a delay. It would also show that, because of the delay, every other activity yet to be performed would have additional time in which to be performed.

Therefore, the subcontractor's failure to perform never became critical and, thereby, never itself delayed the project.

In the second case study, the contractor's delay began before the owner's delay, and extended past the duration of the owner's delay. Hence, the owner's delay never became critical.

Concurrent Delays

Case Study 1:
   Delay 1: Owner stop work order.
      Effective date – June 1, 1990
      Order lifted   – June 30, 1990
      Total delay   – 30 days
   Delay 2: Labor strike.
      Effective date – June 1, 1990
      Strike lifted   – June 30, 1990
      Total delay   – 30 days

Outcome: Contractor entitled to 30 days time extension, but no additional compensation.

Case Study 2:
   Delay 1: Owner stop work order.
      Effective date – June 1, 1990
      Order lifted   – June 30, 1990
      Total delay   – 30 days
   Delay 2: Labor strike.
      Effective date – June 1, 1990
      Order lifted   – June 27, 1990
      Total delay   – 27 days

Outcome: Contractor entitled to a 30-day time extension and additional compensation for 3 days of delay.

Figure 1.6

Concurrent Delay Examples
Primacy of Delay

Case Study 1:
   Delay 1: Owner stop work order.
      Effective date – June 1, 1990
      Order lifted   – June 30, 1990
      Total delay   – 30 days
   Delay 2: Subcontractor does not report to site for work.
      Effective date – June 5, 1990
      Subcontractor begins work – June 25, 1990
      Total delay   – 20 days

Outcome: Contractor is entitled to a 30-day extension of time and additional compensation for 30 days of delay.

Case Study 2:
   Delay 1: Owner stop work order.
      Effective date – June 5, 1990
      Order lifted   – June 25, 1990
      Total delay   – 20 days
   Delay 2: Subcontractor does not report to site for work.
      Effective date – June 2, 1990
      Subcontractor begins work – June 30, 1990
      Total delay   – 28 days

Outcome: Contractor is entitled to neither a time extension nor any additional compensation.

Figure 1.7

Of course, valid arguments are raised against the primacy of delay. However, all of these generally fall into the "but for" arena, covered in Chapter 6, "Problematic Analysis Techniques." Briefly, the "but for" delay argument does not focus on *when* a delay begins. It asserts that as long as there is any overlap in time between delays, that period of time is concurrent. A "but for" approach for case study 1 (Figure 1.7) would allow a 30-day time extension and a 10-day monetary compensation. For case study 2 (also Figure 1.7), it would allow a time extension of 20 days. The major problem with the "but for" approach is that it ignores the dynamic nature of the critical path.

Critical Versus Non-Critical Delays

In any discussion of delays to a project, the inherent assumption is that the delay affects the progress of the entire project, or is critical to the project completion. However, many delays occur that do not delay the project completion date. These are non-critical delays. The determination of which activities truly control the project completion date depends on:

- The project itself
- The contractor's plan and schedule (particularly the critical path) to accomplish the work
- The requirements of the contract for sequence and phasing
- The physical constraints of the project – how to build the job from a practical perspective

Regardless of how one analyzes a project and the schedule to find the delays, there is one overriding concern: *the analysis must accurately reflect the contemporaneous information when the delays were occurring.* "Contemporaneous documents" refers to the daily reports, updated schedule, and any other job data available that show the circumstances at the time of the delay(s). Proper research and documentation virtually eliminates the "but for's" and any other hypotheses contrived to advance predisposed conclusions or desired results.

Methodology of Analyzing Delays

Chapter Two
Methodology of Analyzing Delays

Because every project is unique, the analysis technique performed on each delay situation may also have subtle differences. Nevertheless, some basic approaches can be established for performing delay analyses. This chapter presents the overall concept of how one approaches a delay analysis. It then describes how to identify and quantify delays. The last step in the process is identifying the cause of, or the liability for, the delay.

As-Planned Schedule

As its name implies, the as-planned schedule is the schedule created before construction begins. Most projects have some form of as-planned schedule. It is most often the contractor's original schedule submitted in accordance with the contract documents.

Forms of As-Planned Schedules

The as-planned schedule can take many forms. It may be a detailed Critical Path Method (CPM) schedule or a simple bar chart. A sample CPM schedule appears in Figure 2.1. This sample is an activity-on-arrow network diagram. It shows the logical sequence of construction, the activity name or description, and the duration of the activity in workdays.

Figure 2.2 is a computerized calculation of the CPM schedule. This report lists the activities from Figure 2.1 in order of the numerical designation given by the nodes, or by an *I-J sort*. (I and J are the representative designators for the numbers used in the nodes at the beginning and the end of an activity in a network diagram.) The report in Figure 2.2 has also converted the workday durations to match the calendar for the project. It lists the start and finish dates by calendar date.

To facilitate the reader's understanding of the Critical Path Method (CPM) in the context of delay analysis, brief explanations accompany many of the technical terms used in this chapter. If the reader is not familiar with CPM scheduling, we recommend further study in this area. (Two good references on this subject are *Project Planning and Control for Construction*, by David R. Pierce, and *Means Scheduling Manual*, by F. William Horsley, both published by R.S. Means.)

Figure 2.3 is the same computer calculation for the project. However, this time, the activities are sorted by *float* in ascending order. For the sake of clarity, *float* is a term used with the Critical Path Method to indicate the difference between when an activity can start and when it *must* start.

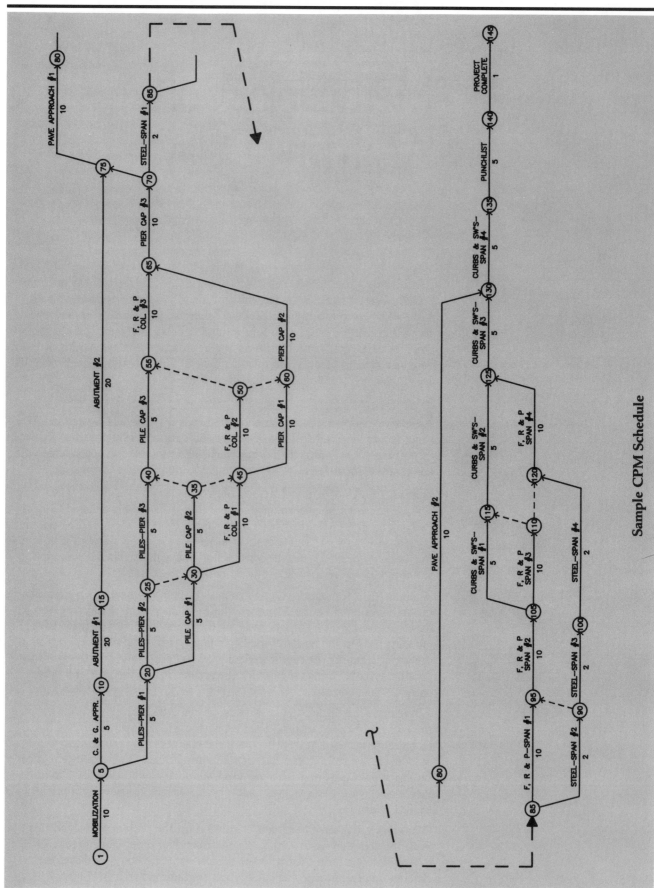

Sample CPM Schedule

Figure 2.1

ACME CONSTRUCTION, INC.   PRIMAVERA PROJECT PLANNER   WEST STREET BRIDGE

REPORT DATE 23OCT89 RUN NO. 2   WEST STREET BRIDGE - CPM SCHEDULE   START DATE 5MAY89 FIN DATE 20OCT89
           12:46

I-J SORT   DATA DATE 5MAY89 PAGE NO. 1

PRED	SUCC	ORIG DUR	REM DUR	CAL	%	CODE	ACTIVITY DESCRIPTION	EARLY START	EARLY FINISH	LATE START	LATE FINISH	TOTAL FLOAT
1	5	10	10	1	0		MOBILIZATION	5MAY89	18MAY89	5MAY89	18MAY89	0
5	10	5	5	1	0		CLEAR & GRUB APPROACHES	19MAY89	25MAY89	6JUL89	12JUL89	32
5	20	5	5	1	0		PILES - PIER #1	19MAY89	25MAY89	19MAY89	25MAY89	0
10	15	20	20	1	0		CONSTRUCT ABUTMENT #1	26MAY89	23JUN89	13JUL89	9AUG89	32
15	75	20	20	1	0		CONSTRUCT ABUTMENT #2	26JUN89	24JUL89	10AUG89	7SEP89	32
20	25	5	5	1	0		PILES - PIER #2	26MAY89	2JUN89	26MAY89	2JUN89	0
20	30	5	5	1	0		PILE CAP #1	26MAY89	2JUN89	26MAY89	2JUN89	0
25	30	0	0	1	0		DUMMY	5JUN89	2JUN89	5JUN89	2JUN89	0
25	40	5	5	1	0		PILES - PIER #3	5JUN89	9JUN89	19JUN89	23JUN89	10
30	35	5	5	1	0		PILE CAP #2	5JUN89	9JUN89	12JUN89	16JUN89	5
30	45	10	10	1	0		FORM, REIN. & POUR - COLUMN #1	5JUN89	16JUN89	5JUN89	16JUN89	0
35	40	0	0	1	0		DUMMY	12JUN89	9JUN89	26JUN89	23JUN89	10
35	45	0	0	1	0		DUMMY	12JUN89	9JUN89	19JUN89	16JUN89	5
40	55	5	5	1	0		PILE CAP #3	12JUN89	16JUN89	26JUN89	30JUN89	10
45	50	10	10	1	0		FORM, REIN. & POUR - COLUMN #2	19JUN89	30JUN89	19JUN89	30JUN89	0
45	60	10	10	1	0		PIER CAP #1	19JUN89	30JUN89	19JUN89	30JUN89	0
50	55	0	0	1	0		DUMMY	3JUL89	30JUN89	3JUL89	30JUN89	0
55	65	10	10	1	0		FORM, REIN. & POUR - COLUMN #3	3JUL89	17JUL89	3JUL89	17JUL89	0
60	65	10	10	1	0		PIER CAP #2	3JUL89	17JUL89	3JUL89	17JUL89	0
65	70	10	10	1	0		PIER CAP #3	18JUL89	31JUL89	18JUL89	31JUL89	0
70	75	0	0	1	0		DUMMY	1AUG89	31JUL89	8SEP89	7SEP89	27
70	85	2	2	1	0		STEEL - SPAN 1	1AUG89	2AUG89	1AUG89	2AUG89	0
75	80	10	10	1	0		PAVE APPROACH #1	1AUG89	14AUG89	8SEP89	21SEP89	27
80	130	10	10	1	0		PAVE APPROACH #2	15AUG89	28AUG89	22SEP89	5OCT89	27
85	90	2	2	1	0		STEEL - SPAN 2	3AUG89	4AUG89	15AUG89	16AUG89	8
85	95	10	10	1	0		FORM, REIN. & POUR - SPAN 1	3AUG89	16AUG89	3AUG89	16AUG89	0
90	95	0	0	1	0		DUMMY	7AUG89	4AUG89	17AUG89	16AUG89	8
90	100	2	2	1	0		STEEL - SPAN 3	7AUG89	8AUG89	11SEP89	12SEP89	24
95	105	10	10	1	0		FORM, REIN. & POUR - SPAN 2	17AUG89	30AUG89	17AUG89	30AUG89	0
100	120	2	2	1	0		STEEL - SPAN 4	9AUG89	10AUG89	13SEP89	14SEP89	24
105	110	10	10	1	0		FORM, REIN. & POUR - SPAN 3	31AUG89	14SEP89	31AUG89	14SEP89	0
105	115	5	5	1	0		CURBS & SIDEWALKS - SPAN 1	31AUG89	7SEP89	15SEP89	21SEP89	10
110	115	0	0	1	0		DUMMY	15SEP89	14SEP89	22SEP89	21SEP89	5
110	120	0	0	1	0		DUMMY	15SEP89	14SEP89	15SEP89	14SEP89	0
115	125	5	5	1	0		CURBS & SIDEWALKS - SPAN 2	15SEP89	21SEP89	22SEP89	28SEP89	5
120	125	10	10	1	0		FORM, REIN. & POUR - SPAN 4	15SEP89	28SEP89	15SEP89	28SEP89	0
125	130	5	5	1	0		CURBS & SIDEWALKS - SPAN 3	29SEP89	5OCT89	29SEP89	5OCT89	0
130	135	5	5	1	0		CURBS & SIDEWALKS - SPAN 4	6OCT89	12OCT89	6OCT89	12OCT89	0
135	140	5	5	1	0		PUNCHLIST	13OCT89	19OCT89	13OCT89	19OCT89	0
140	145	1	1	1	0		PROJECT COMPLETE	20OCT89	20OCT89	20OCT89	20OCT89	0

Figure 2.2

For example, if an activity can start as early as June 1, 1990, but must start by June 10, 1990, it has nine calendar days of float. Thus, the activity can start as late as June 10, 1990 and still not delay the project.

The reader should note that the list in Figure 2.3 begins with the activities with zero float and progresses upward to those with longer float times. Activities with zero float are the critical activities, or those which, if delayed, will delay the overall completion of the project.

The as-planned schedule could also be as simple as a bar chart. The project schedule presented in Figures 2.1, 2.2, and 2.3 appears in bar chart form in Figure 2.4. The bar chart does not show the interrelationships among the activities, nor does it have the same level of detail presented by the CPM schedule. Regardless of the form of the as-planned schedule, it is a valuable tool with which to measure delays.

Choose the Most Accurate Schedule

The analyst must carefully choose the schedule that best represents the project as-planned schedule. For example, the owner may have included a schedule with the bid documents as a guide for the contractors bidding the work, but it may be erroneous to use that version as the as-planned schedule for the project. Normally, the contractor's initial schedule submission serves as the project as-planned schedule. However, it is not uncommon for the owner's representative to send a schedule back to the contractor for changes or corrections. If the contractor submits the schedule a second and third time until it is finally accepted by the owner, chances are, the third schedule submission best represents the as-planned schedule for the project.

Review the As-Planned Schedule

After identifying the schedule that most reasonably represents the contractor's original planned sequence of work, the analyst reviews that schedule for logic and feasibility. A note of caution: Often the analyst, or the person assessing the project for delays, reviews the contractor's schedule and decides that it did not correctly portray (1) the logic of the project, or (2) the durations for the activities. The analyst might then change the schedule to reflect his or her judgment about the errors. The analyst should avoid this practice at all costs! If there are minor errors or inconsistencies in the contractor's as-planned schedule, they will be accounted for during the analysis of the delays. The decision as to whether or not the contractor's schedule was practicable is a highly subjective one. It is far better to give the contractor the benefit of the doubt than to disallow, ignore, or even change the schedule.

Narrative Schedule

In the worst case, neither a CPM schedule nor a bar chart schedule exists. In such cases, the next area to investigate is the existing project documents. A narrative description of the contractor's planned sequence of work may exist and could serve as the project as-planned schedule for the analysis.

Figure 2.5 is an example of correspondence the analyst could use to establish the contractor's as-planned sequence of work. The analyst could convert this information to a bar chart representation, as shown in Figure 2.6. This bar chart provides at least some form of as-planned schedule for the analysis. Analysis without a CPM or bar chart schedule is covered in detail in Chapter 5.

```
---------------------------------------------------------------------------------------------------------------------------------------------------
ACME CONSTRUCTION, INC.                    PRIMAVERA PROJECT PLANNER              WEST STREET BRIDGE

REPORT DATE 23OCT89  RUN NO.   3          WEST STREET BRIDGE - CPM SCHEDULE       START DATE  5MAY89  FIN DATE 20OCT89
             12:47
TOTAL FLOAT/ES                                                                    DATA DATE  5MAY89  PAGE NO.   1
```

PRED	SUCC	ORIG DUR	REM DUR	CAL	%	CODE	ACTIVITY DESCRIPTION	EARLY START	EARLY FINISH	LATE START	LATE FINISH	TOTAL FLOAT
1	5	10	10	1	0		MOBILIZATION	5MAY89	18MAY89	5MAY89	18MAY89	0
5	20	5	5	1	0		PILES - PIER #1	19MAY89	25MAY89	19MAY89	25MAY89	0
20	25	5	5	1	0		PILES - PIER #2	26MAY89	2JUN89	26MAY89	2JUN89	0
20	30	5	5	1	0		PILE CAP #1	26MAY89	2JUN89	26MAY89	2JUN89	0
25	30	0	0	1	0		DUMMY	5JUN89	2JUN89	5JUN89	2JUN89	0
30	45	10	10	1	0		FORM, REIN. & POUR - COLUMN #1	5JUN89	16JUN89	5JUN89	16JUN89	0
45	50	10	10	1	0		FORM, REIN. & POUR - COLUMN #2	19JUN89	30JUN89	19JUN89	30JUN89	0
45	60	10	10	1	0		PIER CAP #1	19JUN89	30JUN89	19JUN89	30JUN89	0
50	55	0	0	1	0		DUMMY	3JUL89	30JUN89	3JUL89	30JUN89	0
55	65	10	10	1	0		FORM, REIN. & POUR - COLUMN #3	3JUL89	17JUL89	3JUL89	17JUL89	0
60	65	10	10	1	0		PIER CAP #2	3JUL89	17JUL89	3JUL89	17JUL89	0
65	70	10	10	1	0		PIER CAP #3	18JUL89	31JUL89	18JUL89	31JUL89	0
70	85	2	2	1	0		STEEL - SPAN 1	1AUG89	2AUG89	1AUG89	2AUG89	0
85	95	10	10	1	0		FORM, REIN, & POUR - SPAN 1	3AUG89	16AUG89	3AUG89	16AUG89	0
95	105	10	10	1	0		FORM, REIN. & POUR - SPAN 2	17AUG89	30AUG89	17AUG89	30AUG89	0
105	110	10	10	1	0		FORM, REIN. & POUR - SPAN 3	31AUG89	14SEP89	31AUG89	14SEP89	0
110	120	0	0	1	0		DUMMY	15SEP89	14SEP89	15SEP89	14SEP89	0
120	125	10	10	1	0		FORM, REIN. & POUR - SPAN 4	15SEP89	28SEP89	15SEP89	28SEP89	0
125	130	5	5	1	0		CURBS & SIDEWALKS - SPAN 3	29SEP89	5OCT89	29SEP89	5OCT89	0
130	135	5	5	1	0		CURBS & SIDEWALKS - SPAN 4	6OCT89	12OCT89	6OCT89	12OCT89	0
135	140	5	5	1	0		PUNCHLIST	13OCT89	19OCT89	13OCT89	19OCT89	0
140	145	1	1	1	0		PROJECT COMPLETE	20OCT89	20OCT89	20OCT89	20OCT89	0
30	35	5	5	1	0		PILE CAP #2	5JUN89	9JUN89	12JUN89	16JUN89	5
35	45	0	0	1	0		DUMMY	12JUN89	9JUN89	19JUN89	16JUN89	5
110	115	0	0	1	0		DUMMY	15SEP89	14SEP89	22SEP89	21SEP89	5
115	125	5	5	1	0		CURBS & SIDEWALKS - SPAN 2	15SEP89	21SEP89	22SEP89	28SEP89	5
85	90	2	2	1	0		STEEL - SPAN 2	3AUG89	4AUG89	15AUG89	16AUG89	8
90	95	0	0	1	0		DUMMY	7AUG89	4AUG89	17AUG89	16AUG89	8
25	40	5	5	1	0		PILES - PIER #3	5JUN89	9JUN89	19JUN89	23JUN89	10
35	40	0	0	1	0		DUMMY	12JUN89	9JUN89	26JUN89	23JUN89	10
40	55	5	5	1	0		PILE CAP #3	12JUN89	16JUN89	26JUN89	30JUN89	10
105	115	5	5	1	0		CURBS & SIDEWALKS - SPAN 1	31AUG89	7SEP89	15SEP89	21SEP89	10
90	100	2	2	1	0		STEEL - SPAN 3	7AUG89	8AUG89	11SEP89	12SEP89	24
100	120	2	2	1	0		STEEL - SPAN 4	9AUG89	10AUG89	13SEP89	14SEP89	24
70	75	0	0	1	0		DUMMY	1AUG89	31JUL89	8SEP89	7SEP89	27
75	80	10	10	1	0		PAVE APPROACH #1	1AUG89	14AUG89	8SEP89	21SEP89	27
80	130	10	10	1	0		PAVE APPROACH #2	15AUG89	28AUG89	22SEP89	5OCT89	27
5	10	5	5	1	0		CLEAR & GRUB APPROACHES	19MAY89	25MAY89	6JUL89	12JUL89	32
10	15	20	20	1	0		CONSTRUCT ABUTMENT #1	26MAY89	23JUN89	13JUL89	9AUG89	32
15	75	20	20	1	0		CONSTRUCT ABUTMENT #2	26JUN89	24JUL89	10AUG89	7SEP89	32

Figure 2.3

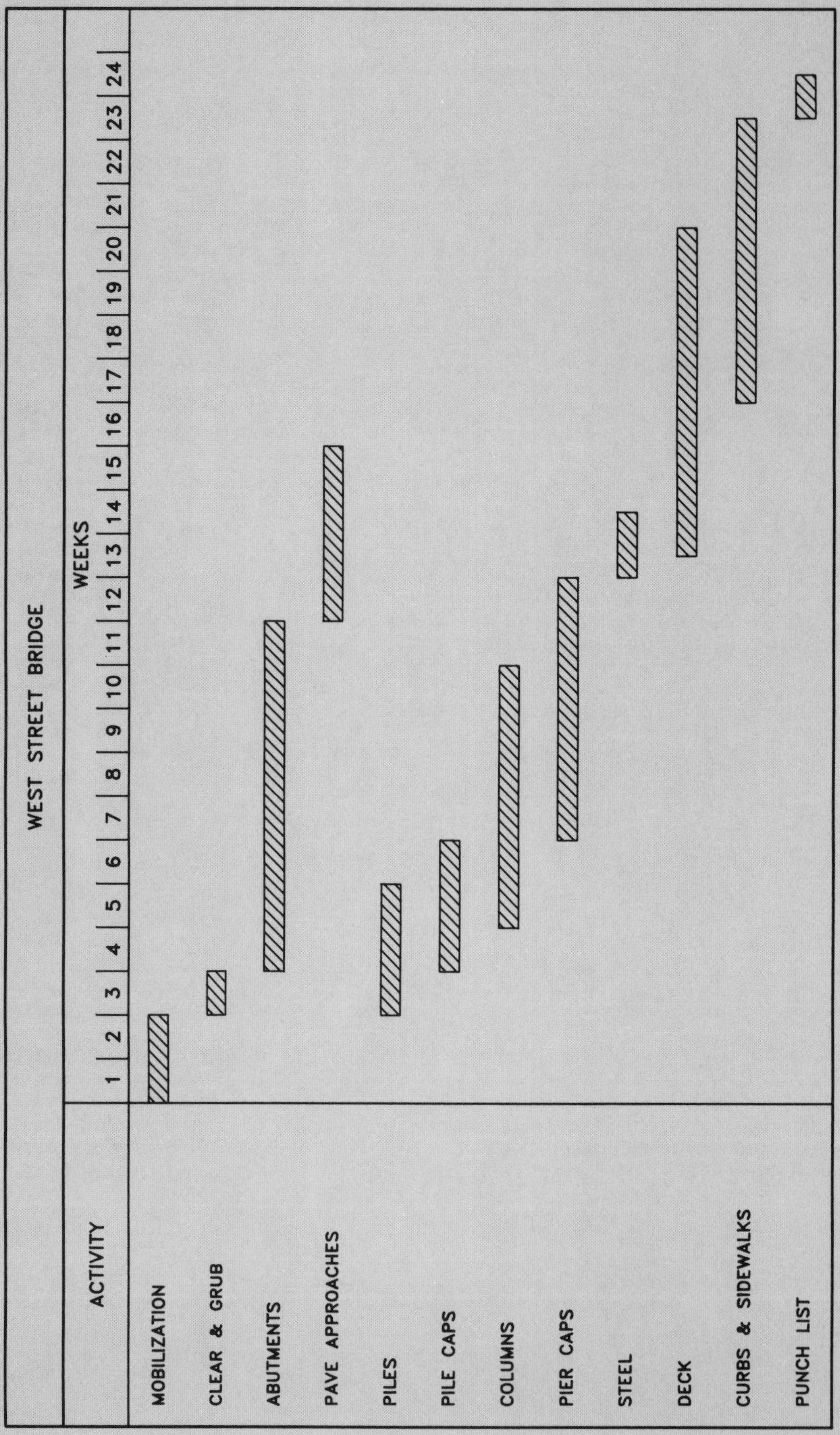

Bar Chart of Sample Project

Figure 2.4

18

ACME CONSTRUCTION, INC.

February 15, 1989

Archie Tech
Owner's Representative
Anywhere, USA 01111

Dear Archie:

Just to let you know how we plan the West Street Bridge, I
thought I would summarize our plan for you.

Initially we will mobilize and clear and grub the
approaches in the first three weeks. As soon as the
approaches are clear, we will start a crew on the abutments
and both of them should take about eight weeks. We will
begin the piles about the third week in the job and they
should take us about three weeks to do.

Once the pile driving crew is finished Pier #1, we will
start another crew on the caps, columns, and pier caps
which, all in all, should take about nine weeks to finish.

When all the piers are done, we will set the steel which
should take about two weeks. Just as soon as Span #1 steel
is in place, we will start the deck which will take about
eight weeks total. We will chase right behind the deck with
the curbs and sidewalks and punchlist. We should finish
that about three weeks after the deck is done.

I hope this is helpful to you.

Sincerely,

Joe Acme

Figure 2.5

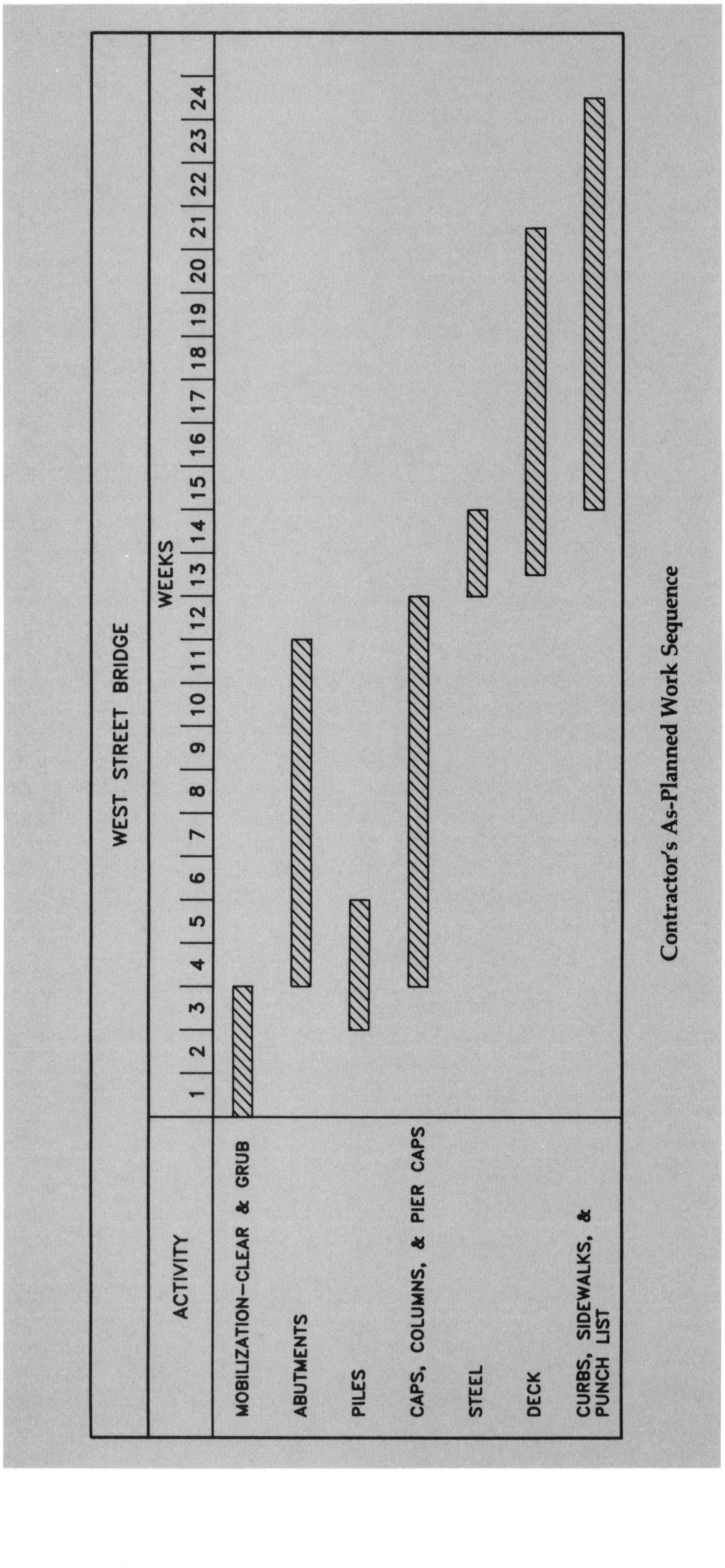

Contractor's As-Planned Work Sequence

Figure 2.6

As-Built Schedule

Once the analyst establishes the as-planned schedule, the next step is to prepare a project as-built schedule. Following are several ways to prepare an as-built schedule.

Use of Periodic Updates

In the best case, a CPM schedule is available for the project. Periodic updates of that schedule may well provide the necessary information for an as-built schedule. Normally, the updates record the dates specific activities start and finish. Based on this information, the analyst can readily create an as-built schedule.

Verify All Information

It is wise to verify all information in the updates, based on as many independent sources as possible. For example, the analyst might review the project daily reports to verify that specific activities started and finished on the dates indicated in the updates.

Missing Information in Updates

In some situations, the CPM updates may not record the actual start and finish dates of the activities. This may occur for two reasons. First, the individual preparing the updates may have suppressed or "dropped out" the activities as soon as they were completed. This is done to keep the updates from becoming cluttered with activities that are already finished. Second, some CPM computer programs automatically drop completed activities.

Use of Contemporaneous Documents

If the updates do not provide the information required, then the analyst has no alternative but to prepare his own as-built schedule, using the contemporaneous project documents. The documents that should be reviewed for possible sources of as-built information include:

- Project daily reports
- Project diaries
- Meeting minutes
- Pay requests/estimates
- Inspection reports by the designer, owner, lending institution, etc.
- Correspondence
- Memos to the file

Based on the information available, the analyst constructs as detailed an as-built schedule as possible. Figure 2.7 is an example of an as-built schedule created from the information above. The analyst lays out a calendar for the project, lists the identifiable activities, and notes the specific days that certain work was performed on these activities.

Merely because "no work" is noted for an activity during a specific day does not mean that no work was performed. It simply indicates that no work was *recorded* in the available documentation.

The detailed as-built schedule shown in Figure 2.7 may then be summarized into a more understandable chart, as shown in Figure 2.8.

Resist the Temptation to Summarize or Conclude

There is a tendency to summarize information from an as-built schedule or even to initially draw the as-built schedule by searching the documentation for the first recorded day for an activity and the last recorded day for the same activity. The analyst then connects the two points in time with a solid line representing a continuous activity. This practice can be misleading and can also misrepresent the facts, particularly when one attempts to ascertain the liability for delays (which will be discussed later in this chapter).

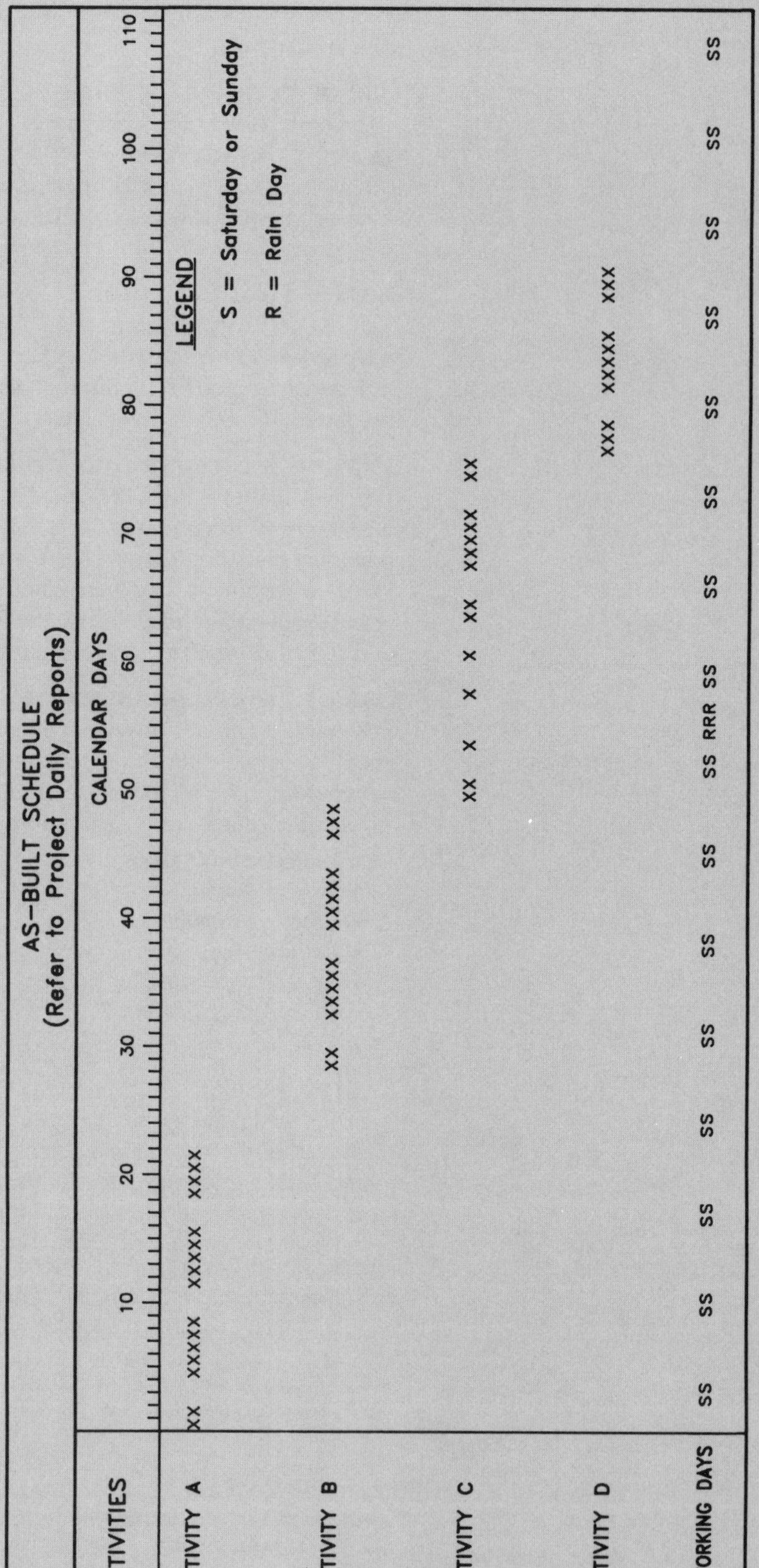

Figure 2.7

AS-BUILT SCHEDULE
(Refer to Project Daily Reports)

CALENDAR DAYS

ACTIVITIES	10	20	30	40	50	60	70	80	90	100	110
ACTIVITY A	xx xxxxx xxxxx xxxx										
ACTIVITY B			xx xxxxx xxxxx xxx								
ACTIVITY C					xx x x xx xxxxx xx						
ACTIVITY D								xxx xxxxx xxx			
NON-WORKING DAYS	SS SS	SS	SS	SS	SS RRR SS	SS	SS	SS	SS	SS	SS

LEGEND

S = Saturday or Sunday

R = Rain Day

As-Built Schedule Based on Daily Records

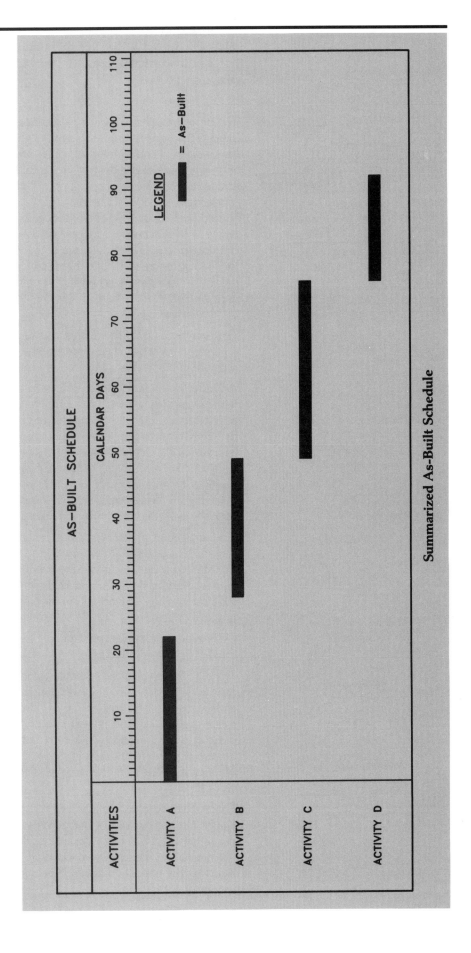

Figure 2.8

Summarized As-Built Schedule

The confidence one places in the accuracy of the as-built schedule depends on the level of detail of the supporting documentation. Once the preparation of the as-built schedule is complete, the process of analyzing and quantifying the delays can proceed.

Schedule Analysis / Quantifying the Delays

The process of analyzing the as-planned and as-built schedules is more difficult than one might first surmise. The normal inclination is to compare the as-planned and as-built schedules and draw conclusions about the causes and magnitude of the delays. This total comparison approach often leads to erroneous conclusions. For example, Figure 2.9 is a simplified bar chart of four activities that describe the critical path for a project. The activities are labeled A, B, C, and D for simplicity. Figure 2.10 is a bar chart representation of the as-built schedule for these same four activities. An overall comparison of the two schedules produces a schedule as shown in Figure 2.11. Reviewing Figure 2.11, one might conclude that activity D was delayed 43 days. It was originally scheduled to be complete on day 55, but did not end until day 98. A more correct step-by-step analysis would prove this conclusion incorrect.

To correctly analyze the delays, the analyst must assess each activity separately. As the analyst recognizes each delay, he or she must adjust the succeeding planned activities, taking these delays into account.

A further example, Figure 2.12, is a comparison of the as-planned schedule with the as-built schedule for activity A. It shows that the completion of activity A was delayed, and notes the magnitude of the delay. It further notes that activity A had an extended duration, meaning that the actual working duration of the activity was longer than scheduled. Based on the delay to the completion of activity A, the analyst must now adjust the remaining planned activities for that delay. Figure 2.13 depicts the adjusted as-planned schedule, reflecting the delays to the completion of activity A. Now the process can continue with the remaining activities.

The adjusted as-planned schedule is shown in Figure 2.14 with the as-built activity B. It notes that activity B in the adjusted as-planned schedule also experienced a twelve-day delay. In addition, the as-built schedule shows a *late start* for activity B, meaning activity B started later than its adjusted scheduled start date. Finally, the actual duration of activity B was six days longer than originally planned.

Once again, the as-planned schedule must be adjusted to reflect the delays to activity B. The adjusted as-planned schedule is shown in Figure 2.15.

The adjusted as-planned schedule with the actual duration of activity C appears in Figure 2.16. It shows that the start of activity C was delayed, and it would appear that activity C also had an extended duration. However, a careful review of the as-built information reveals that activity C actually did not have an extended duration, but instead had two interruptions. The more correct representation is shown in Figure 2.17. The number of days of delay is noted, as is the fact that activity C experienced an interrupted work flow.

The as-planned schedule adjusted for the delay to activity C is shown in Figure 2.18. It also shows that activity D clearly was not itself delayed, but rather was "bumped," because of the delays to the preceding activities (A, B, and C). The original conclusion that activity D delayed the project, based on the overall comparison of the as-planned and as-built schedules, was incorrect.

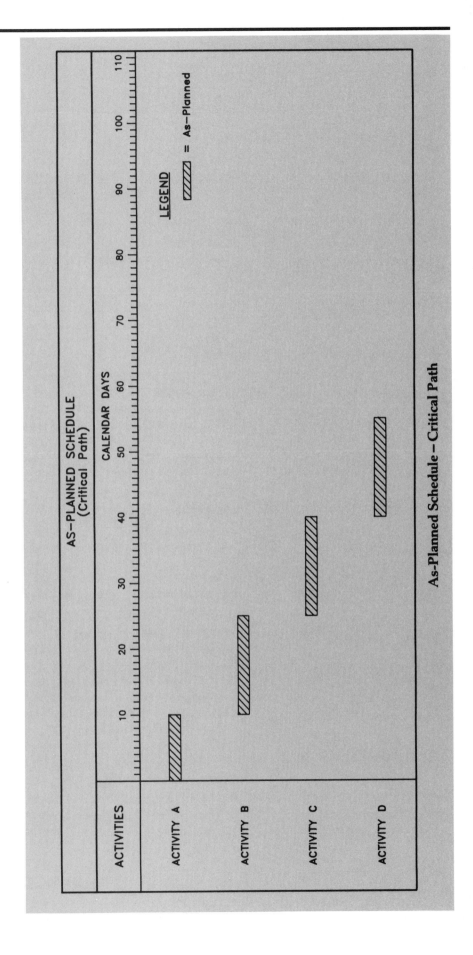

Figure 2.9

As-Planned Schedule – Critical Path

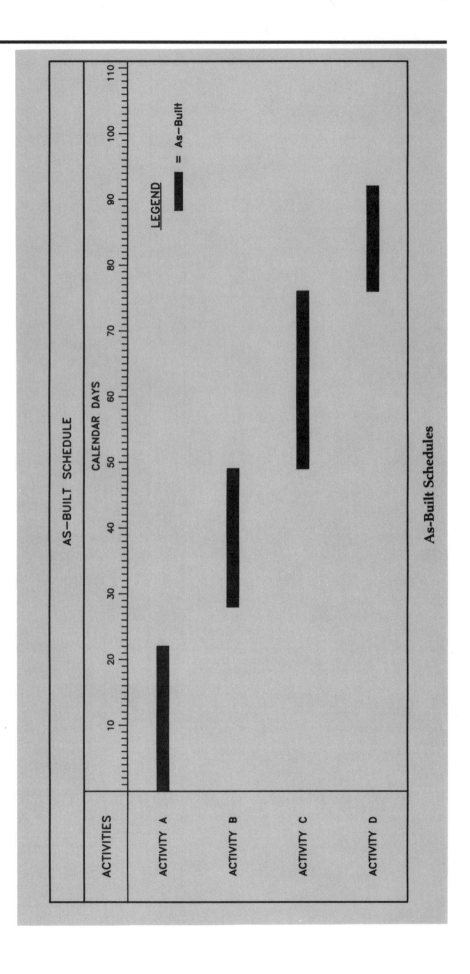

Figure 2.10

Figure 2.11

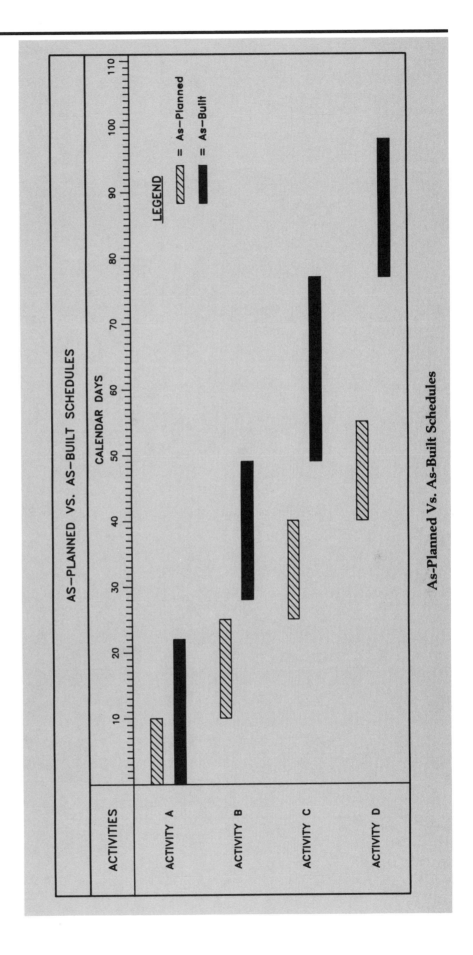

As-Planned Vs. As-Built Schedules

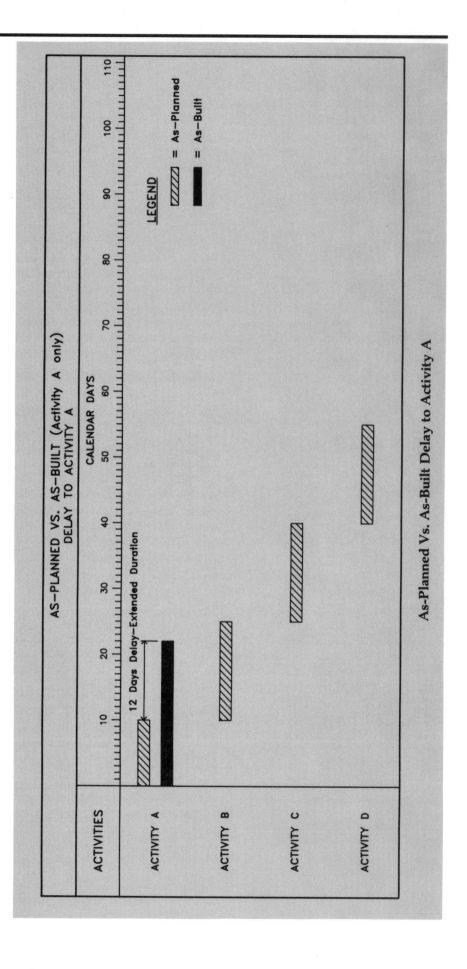

Figure 2.12

28

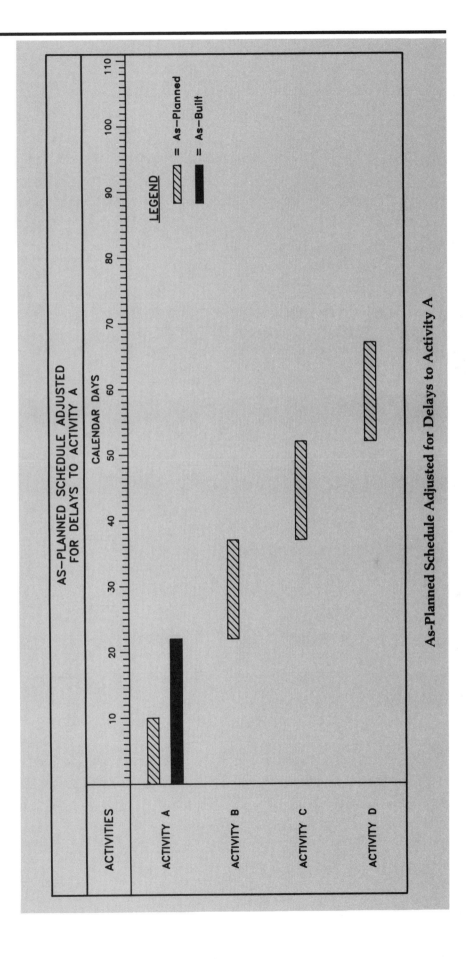

As-Planned Schedule Adjusted for Delays to Activity A

Figure 2.13

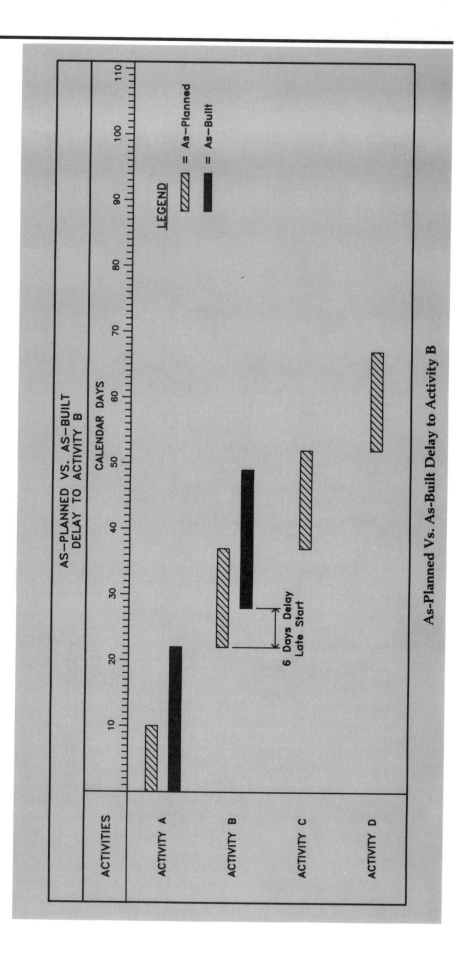

Figure 2.14

Figure 2.15

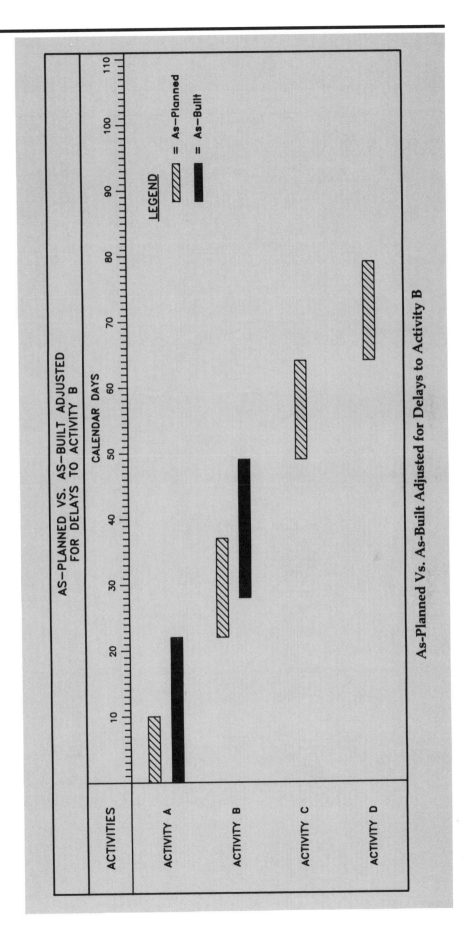

As-Planned Vs. As-Built Adjusted for Delays to Activity B

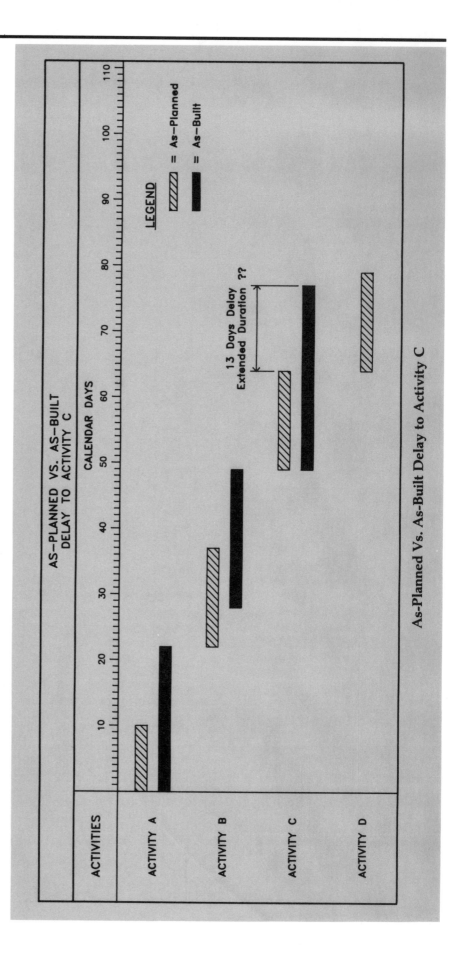

As-Planned Vs. As-Built Delay to Activity C

Figure 2.16

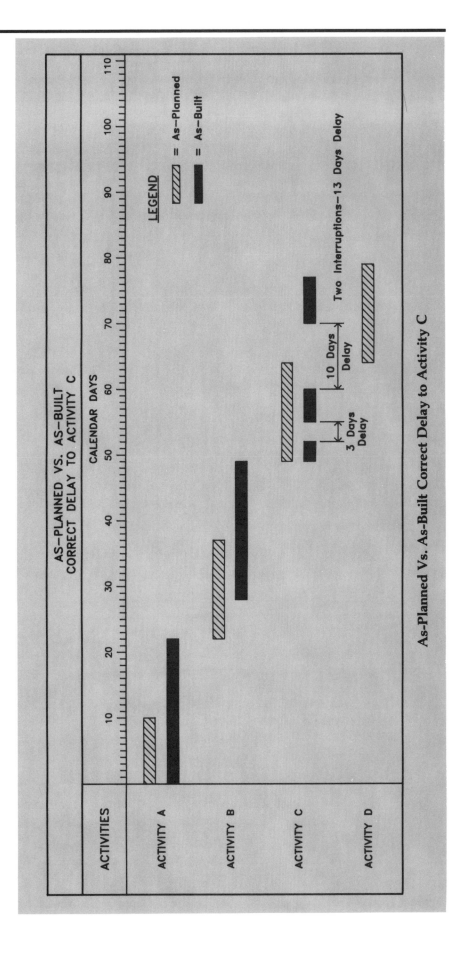

As-Planned Vs. As-Built Correct Delay to Activity C

Figure 2.17

33

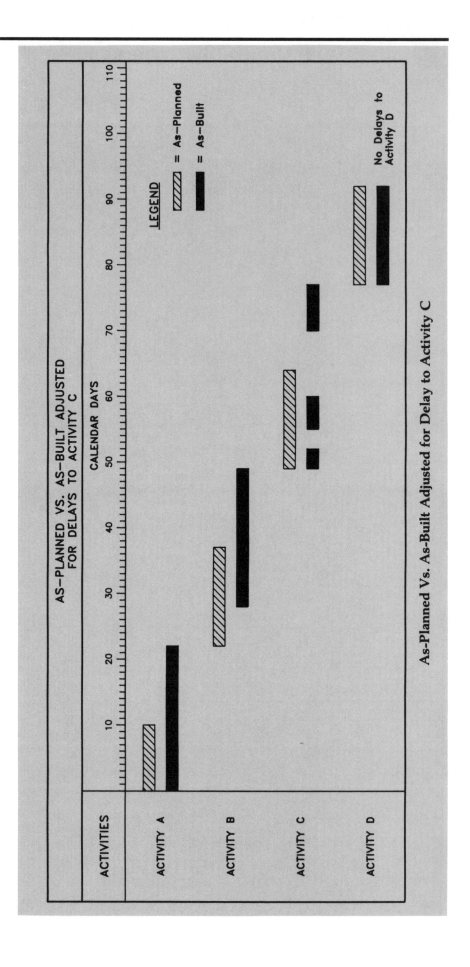

As-Planned Vs. As-Built Adjusted for Delay to Activity C

Figure 2.18

Wherever possible, the analyst should use this step-by-step approach for analyzing delays to reach the correct conclusions concerning delays and their causes. (Further examples of this process will be given in the next few chapters of this book.) The analyst must move back in time to the point when the actual delays were taking place to make an objective assessment of the delays and their causes. Ideally, such an assessment would have been made contemporaneously during the project as the schedule was updated each month. Unfortunately, this ideal situation is seldom realized.

Assessing Liability for the Delays

Once the analyst determines the activities that were delayed, the magnitude of the delays, and the general nature of the delays (extended duration, late start, etc.), he or she can then assess the liability for each delay.

Thorough Review of Documentation

The process of assigning liability for a delay requires a thorough review of all project documentation to find out what factors influenced the performance of the specific activity. In many cases, specific causes for the delay can be identified.

For example, the project daily reports may show that the contractor experienced an equipment breakdown on two separate occasions, which caused the interruptions to activity C noted during the delay analysis. Similarly, the analyst may discover that the late start of activity B was caused by the project designer's slow return of shop drawings.

In another example, the analyst finds that no documentation exists that reasonably explains why activity A had an extended duration. Without documentation, it would be reasonable to conclude that the extended duration was the contractor's liability. Either the scheduled duration was too optimistic, or inadequate resources were applied to the task to accomplish the work in the time scheduled. Unfortunately, project documentation seldom exists that will answer all the questions regarding the cause of delays for every activity.

Changes in the Critical Path

Throughout any delay analysis, the analyst must watch for any possible changes in the critical path of the project. Often the sole focus is on the original critical path without regard to what may have happened during the course of construction. To attain a true perspective on possible shifts in the project critical path, the analyst must review all activities during each step in the delay analysis process.

While some minor variations may occur in unique circumstances, any method other than the step-by-step approach to analyzing delays can result in incorrect conclusions and a distortion of the reality of time with respect to delays to each activity during the project.

Chapter Three

Delay Analysis with a CPM Schedule

Chapter Three
Delay Analysis with a CPM Schedule

This chapter explains how to perform a delay analysis with a Critical Path Method (CPM) schedule. Unfortunately, a detailed explanation of every nuance of a delay analysis for a CPM schedule is beyond the scope of this book. However, this chapter covers the basic principles.

Defining the As-Planned Schedule

As noted in the preceding chapter, the as-planned schedule is defined using the schedule submitted by the contractor before the project began. Normally, the owner requires some review, and possibly approval, of this schedule. Since the schedule submittal process can produce many different versions of the schedule, it is important to ensure that the *correct final approved schedule* is used for analysis.

Correcting Versus Leaving Errors

Next, the analyst reviews the schedule, looking for serious flaws in the logic or durations. Certain flaws in a schedule could render it inappropriate for analysis. For example, the schedule may show a sequence of activities that is not physically possible. For example, it might show erecting girders before supports are complete, starting roofing before the building is topped out, or following a sequence that directly conflicts with contract requirements, such as staging and phasing restrictions.

The analyst must resist the temptation to alter the schedule by adding or deleting activities. Similarly, the analyst must not change the logic or durations to produce a schedule that seems more representative of the schedule that *should have* been used on the project. This practice can produce a completely erroneous analysis. Furthermore, it will be demonstrated that there is no need to correct minor errors in logic or duration in the schedule, since the delay analysis process is self-correcting.

On the other hand, if the analyst notes serious errors in the logic of the schedule, he or she should consider not accepting the contractor's schedule as a valid tool with which to measure the delays. The validity of the schedule is subjective; therefore, the analyst should always seek help from a qualified scheduling consultant before making this determination. If, indeed, the schedule does not reflect the reality of the job progress, or does not reasonably represent the contractor's plan for performing the work, then it may be wiser to abandon the schedule and perform a delay analysis using the as-built schedule described in Chapter 5.

Upon reviewing the CPM schedule, the analyst may question the validity of the durations assigned to specific activities based on his or her own knowledge of the project, estimating skills, and experience. However, if the reviewer does not know the specific resources that the contractor planned to apply to the work, the durations in question should not be dismissed as erroneous. After all, an experienced and creative contractor can devise the most expedient method to build the project, and this may well require less time than one would normally estimate. In the same vein, the contractor may decide to apply fewer resources to particular activities and have durations longer than one might normally estimate. Neither of these decisions on the part of the contractor makes the schedule incorrect. Without specific contract language constraining the contractor's sequence or imposing milestone dates, the execution of the project is the contractor's responsibility.

Example   The project, a four-span bridge (scheduled in Figure 3.1), will be used to demonstrate the delay process throughout this chapter. The bridge has two reinforced concrete abutments and three piers. The piers have pile foundations, concrete pile caps, concrete pier columns, and concrete pier caps. The bridge has a steel superstructure, SIP metal deck forms, a reinforced concrete deck, curbs, and sidewalks.

Figure 3.1 is the logic diagram submitted by the contractor. A mathematical analysis of the schedule in *I-J sort* format is shown in Figure 3.2. A *total float sort* format of the same mathematical analysis appears in Figure 3.3. (See the beginning of Chapter 2, the section entitled, "Forms of As-Planned Schedules," for a definition of *I-J sort* and *total float sort*.

As can be seen in the example schedule, the contractor did not include any activities for procurement, or for shop drawing preparation, submission, or approval. Other than this oversight, the logic and durations for the remaining activities appear reasonable based on the information available to the analyst at this time.

The analyst may follow one of two courses of action.
1. Leave the schedule as is and allow the analysis to compensate for the lack of procurement and shop drawing activities.
2. Insert activities for the required procurement and shop drawing tasks.

Should the second course of action be chosen, there must be a sound basis in the project documents both for the insertion of the activities and for the durations used. For example, the contract may specifically define a time frame for review of shop drawings and submissions. Likewise, purchase orders with suppliers may provide information concerning fabrication and delivery durations.

If the analyst chooses to insert activities or durations, then the contemporaneous information that is available on that task must be used and should not be misapplied. For example, no activity is specified on the schedule for fabrication and delivery of steel for the project. However, the project documents show that the quotation by the steel supplier at the beginning of the project included a fabrication and delivery time of 120 days. The records also show that the actual fabrication and delivery time was 180 days. In this instance, the 120-day duration would be the appropriate number to use, since it reflects the planned duration known to the contractor at the beginning of the project. The 180-duration would be used in the as-built portion of the analysis.

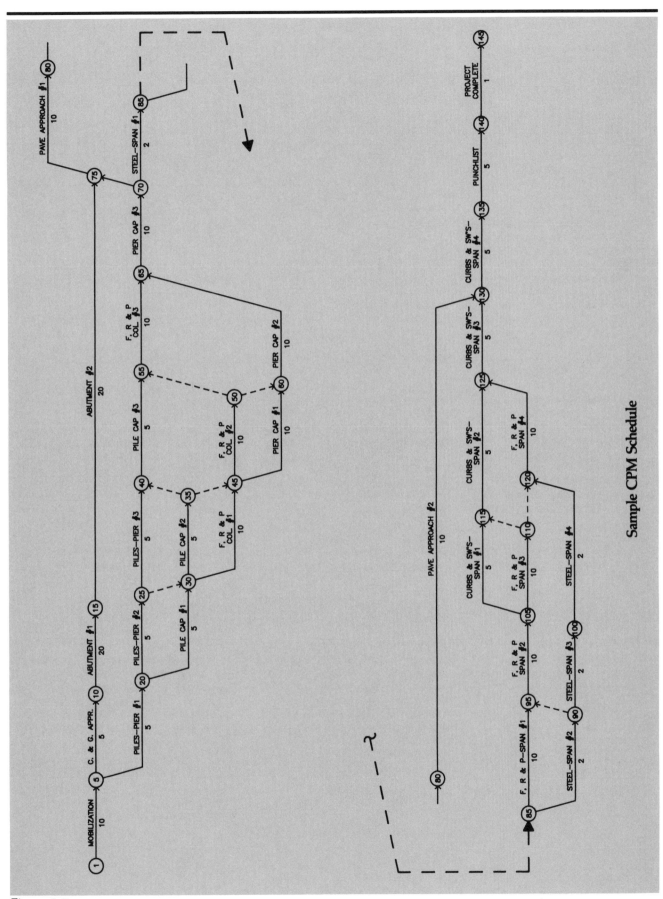

Sample CPM Schedule

Figure 3.1

PRED	SUCC	ORIG DUR	REM DUR	CAL	%	CODE	ACTIVITY DESCRIPTION	EARLY START	EARLY FINISH	LATE START	LATE FINISH	TOTAL FLOAT
1	5	10	10	1	0		MOBILIZATION	5MAY89	18MAY89	5MAY89	18MAY89	0
5	10	5	5	1	0		CLEAR & GRUB APPROACHES	19MAY89	25MAY89	6JUL89	12JUL89	32
5	20	5	5	1	0		PILES - PIER #1	19MAY89	25MAY89	19MAY89	25MAY89	0
10	15	20	20	1	0		CONSTRUCT ABUTMENT #1	26MAY89	23JUN89	13JUL89	9AUG89	32
15	75	20	20	1	0		CONSTRUCT ABUTMENT #2	26JUN89	24JUL89	10AUG89	7SEP89	32
20	25	5	5	1	0		PILES - PIER #2	26MAY89	2JUN89	26MAY89	2JUN89	0
20	30	5	5	1	0		PILE CAP #1	26MAY89	2JUN89	26MAY89	2JUN89	0
25	30	0	0	1	0		DUMMY	5JUN89	2JUN89	5JUN89	2JUN89	0
25	40	5	5	1	0		PILES - PIER #3	5JUN89	9JUN89	19JUN89	23JUN89	10
30	35	5	5	1	0		PILE CAP #2	5JUN89	9JUN89	12JUN89	16JUN89	5
30	45	10	10	1	0		FORM, REIN. & POUR - COLUMN #1	5JUN89	16JUN89	5JUN89	16JUN89	0
35	40	0	0	1	0		DUMMY	12JUN89	9JUN89	26JUN89	23JUN89	10
35	45	0	0	1	0		DUMMY	12JUN89	9JUN89	19JUN89	16JUN89	5
40	55	5	5	1	0		PILE CAP #3	12JUN89	16JUN89	26JUN89	30JUN89	10
45	50	10	10	1	0		FORM, REIN. & POUR - COLUMN #2	19JUN89	30JUN89	19JUN89	30JUN89	0
45	60	10	10	1	0		PIER CAP #1	19JUN89	30JUN89	19JUN89	30JUN89	0
50	55	0	0	1	0		DUMMY	3JUL89	30JUN89	3JUL89	30JUN89	0
55	65	10	10	1	0		FORM, REIN. & POUR - COLUMN #3	3JUL89	17JUL89	3JUL89	17JUL89	0
60	65	10	10	1	0		PIER CAP #2	3JUL89	17JUL89	3JUL89	17JUL89	0
65	70	10	10	1	0		PIER CAP #3	18JUL89	31JUL89	18JUL89	31JUL89	0
70	75	0	0	1	0		DUMMY	1AUG89	31JUL89	8SEP89	7SEP89	27
70	85	2	2	1	0		STEEL - SPAN 1	1AUG89	2AUG89	1AUG89	2AUG89	0
75	80	10	10	1	0		PAVE APPROACH #1	1AUG89	14AUG89	8SEP89	21SEP89	27
80	130	10	10	1	0		PAVE APPROACH #2	15AUG89	28AUG89	22SEP89	5OCT89	27
85	90	2	2	1	0		STEEL - SPAN 2	3AUG89	4AUG89	15AUG89	16AUG89	8
85	95	10	10	1	0		FORM, REIN, & POUR - SPAN 1	3AUG89	16AUG89	3AUG89	16AUG89	0
90	95	0	0	1	0		DUMMY	7AUG89	4AUG89	17AUG89	16AUG89	8
90	100	2	2	1	0		STEEL - SPAN 3	7AUG89	8AUG89	11SEP89	12SEP89	24
95	105	10	10	1	0		FORM, REIN. & POUR - SPAN 2	17AUG89	30AUG89	17AUG89	30AUG89	0
100	120	2	2	1	0		STEEL - SPAN 4	9AUG89	10AUG89	13SEP89	14SEP89	24
105	110	10	10	1	0		FORM, REIN. & POUR - SPAN 3	31AUG89	14SEP89	31AUG89	14SEP89	0
105	115	5	5	1	0		CURBS & SIDEWALKS - SPAN 1	31AUG89	7SEP89	15SEP89	21SEP89	10
110	115	0	0	1	0		DUMMY	15SEP89	14SEP89	22SEP89	21SEP89	5
110	120	0	0	1	0		DUMMY	15SEP89	14SEP89	15SEP89	14SEP89	0
115	125	5	5	1	0		CURBS & SIDEWALKS - SPAN 2	15SEP89	21SEP89	22SEP89	28SEP89	5
120	125	10	10	1	0		FORM, REIN. & POUR - SPAN 4	15SEP89	28SEP89	15SEP89	28SEP89	0
125	130	5	5	1	0		CURBS & SIDEWALKS - SPAN 3	29SEP89	5OCT89	29SEP89	5OCT89	0
130	135	5	5	1	0		CURBS & SIDEWALKS - SPAN 4	6OCT89	12OCT89	6OCT89	12OCT89	0
135	140	5	5	1	0		PUNCHLIST	13OCT89	19OCT89	13OCT89	19OCT89	0
140	145	1	1	1	0		PROJECT COMPLETE	20OCT89	20OCT89	20OCT89	20OCT89	0

Figure 3.2

ACME CONSTRUCTION, INC.   PRIMAVERA PROJECT PLANNER   WEST STREET BRIDGE

REPORT DATE 23OCT89 RUN NO.   7   WEST STREET BRIDGE - CPM SCHEDULE   START DATE 5MAY89 FIN DATE 20OCT89*
          12:41

TOTAL FLOAT/ES   DATA DATE   5MAY89 PAGE NO.   1

PRED	SUCC	ORIG DUR	REM DUR	CAL	%	CODE	ACTIVITY DESCRIPTION	EARLY START	EARLY FINISH	LATE START	LATE FINISH	TOTAL FLOAT
1	5	10	10	1	0		MOBILIZATION	5MAY89	18MAY89	5MAY89	18MAY89	0
5	20	5	5	1	0		PILES - PIER #1	19MAY89	25MAY89	19MAY89	25MAY89	0
20	25	5	5	1	0		PILES - PIER #2	26MAY89	2JUN89	26MAY89	2JUN89	0
20	30	5	5	1	0		PILE CAP #1	26MAY89	2JUN89	26MAY89	2JUN89	0
25	30	0	0	1	0		DUMMY	5JUN89	2JUN89	5JUN89	2JUN89	0
30	45	10	10	1	0		FORM, REIN. & POUR - COLUMN #1	5JUN89	16JUN89	5JUN89	16JUN89	0
45	50	10	10	1	0		FORM, REIN. & POUR - COLUMN #2	19JUN89	30JUN89	19JUN89	30JUN89	0
45	60	10	10	1	0		PIER CAP #1	19JUN89	30JUN89	19JUN89	30JUN89	0
50	55	0	0	1	0		DUMMY	3JUL89	30JUN89	3JUL89	30JUN89	0
55	65	10	10	1	0		FORM, REIN. & POUR - COLUMN #3	3JUL89	17JUL89	3JUL89	17JUL89	0
60	65	10	10	1	0		PIER CAP #2	3JUL89	17JUL89	3JUL89	17JUL89	0
65	70	10	10	1	0		PIER CAP #3	18JUL89	31JUL89	18JUL89	31JUL89	0
70	85	2	2	1	0		STEEL - SPAN 1	1AUG89	2AUG89	1AUG89	2AUG89	0
85	95	10	10	1	0		FORM, REIN. & POUR - SPAN 1	3AUG89	16AUG89	3AUG89	16AUG89	0
95	105	10	10	1	0		FORM, REIN. & POUR - SPAN 2	17AUG89	30AUG89	17AUG89	30AUG89	0
105	110	10	10	1	0		FORM, REIN. & POUR - SPAN 3	31AUG89	14SEP89	31AUG89	14SEP89	0
110	120	0	0	1	0		DUMMY	15SEP89	14SEP89	15SEP89	14SEP89	0
120	125	10	10	1	0		FORM, REIN. & POUR - SPAN 4	15SEP89	28SEP89	15SEP89	28SEP89	0
125	130	5	5	1	0		CURBS & SIDEWALKS - SPAN 3	29SEP89	5OCT89	29SEP89	5OCT89	0
130	135	5	5	1	0		CURBS & SIDEWALKS - SPAN 4	6OCT89	12OCT89	6OCT89	12OCT89	0
135	140	5	5	1	0		PUNCHLIST	13OCT89	19OCT89	13OCT89	19OCT89	0
140	145	1	1	1	0		PROJECT COMPLETE	20OCT89	20OCT89	20OCT89	20OCT89	0
30	35	5	5	1	0		PILE CAP #2	5JUN89	9JUN89	12JUN89	16JUN89	5
35	45	0	0	1	0		DUMMY	12JUN89	9JUN89	19JUN89	16JUN89	5
110	115	0	0	1	0		DUMMY	15SEP89	14SEP89	22SEP89	21SEP89	5
115	125	5	5	1	0		CURBS & SIDEWALKS - SPAN 2	15SEP89	21SEP89	22SEP89	28SEP89	5
85	90	2	2	1	0		STEEL - SPAN 2	3AUG89	4AUG89	15AUG89	16AUG89	8
90	95	0	0	1	0		DUMMY	7AUG89	4AUG89	17AUG89	16AUG89	8
25	40	5	5	1	0		PILES - PIER #3	5JUN89	9JUN89	19JUN89	23JUN89	10
35	40	0	0	1	0		DUMMY	12JUN89	9JUN89	26JUN89	23JUN89	10
40	55	5	5	1	0		PILE CAP #3	12JUN89	16JUN89	26JUN89	30JUN89	10
105	115	5	5	1	0		CURBS & SIDEWALKS - SPAN 1	31AUG89	7SEP89	15SEP89	21SEP89	10
90	100	2	2	1	0		STEEL - SPAN 3	7AUG89	8AUG89	11SEP89	12SEP89	24
100	120	2	2	1	0		STEEL - SPAN 4	9AUG89	10AUG89	13SEP89	14SEP89	24
70	75	0	0	1	0		DUMMY	1AUG89	31JUL89	8SEP89	7SEP89	27
75	80	10	10	1	0		PAVE APPROACH #1	1AUG89	14AUG89	8SEP89	21SEP89	27
80	130	10	10	1	0		PAVE APPROACH #2	15AUG89	28AUG89	22SEP89	5OCT89	27
5	10	5	5	1	0		CLEAR & GRUB APPROACHES	19MAY89	25MAY89	6JUL89	12JUL89	32
10	15	20	20	1	0		CONSTRUCT ABUTMENT #1	26MAY89	23JUN89	13JUL89	9AUG89	32
15	75	20	20	1	0		CONSTRUCT ABUTMENT #2	26JUN89	24JUL89	10AUG89	7SEP89	32

Figure 3.3

For this example, additional activities are inserted for the following reasons:
- To demonstrate the self-correcting nature of the delay analysis process.
- To avoid biasing the analysis (by using the most conservative approach).

The analyst accepts the schedule shown in Figures 3.1, 3.2, and 3.3 as the planned schedule for the example project.

Use of CPM Updates

Hopefully, the contractor will have updated the CPM schedule at intervals throughout the project. When CPM updates are available, the analyst can readily perform the delay analysis for the entire project. The example introduced in the previous section will be used to demonstrate the delay analysis process using CPM updates.

First Update

The first update of the CPM schedule for the example project is shown in Figure 3.4. This particular mathematical analysis is the *total float sort*, the easiest type of analysis report to use for determining what happened to the schedule since the last update (in this case, the original schedule).

As the schedule update shows, the project has fallen behind schedule by five workdays. One can recognize this by noting that the greatest negative float is five days. Since the schedule is calculated in workdays (in this case), that means the project is five workdays behind schedule.

Earlier, float was defined as the *difference between when an activity* **could** *start or finish and when the activity* **must** *start or finish*. In the original schedule (Figures 3.2 and 3.3), the critical path of the project has zero float. Thus, the activities with zero float *can* start/finish and *must* start/finish on the same day. These activities cannot experience delays without delaying the scheduled completion, or end, date of the project.

Negative float indicates that the activity is delayed and will start or finish at a date that will delay the overall project end date. When negative float appears in a schedule update, the critical path is the path of activities with the highest negative float. Therefore, in Figure 3.4, the activities with negative five workdays of float make up the critical path at the time of the update.

While the update clearly shows that the project is behind schedule by five workdays, it also shows the delay in calendar days. Refer to activity 140-145, "Project Complete," the last activity on the critical path. The scheduled late finish date for this activity is October 20, 1989. The update shows, however, that the early finish date is October 27, 1989. This represents the present projected completion date and, in this case, the delayed project completion date. The project is now seven calendar days behind schedule.

While the schedule update shows that the project has a five workday or seven calendar day delay, the analyst must also determine which specific activity or activities caused the delay.

By reviewing the completion dates of the finished activities and the status of each activity, and comparing the updated schedule to the original schedule, the analyst determines that activity 20−30, "Pile Cap # 1," has caused the delay. From the schedule in Figure 3.4, the analyst notes that all preceding activities on the critical path were finished either on or ahead of the original schedule. However, activity 20−30 has not yet started. Therefore, this is the controlling delay for the project for the period of this update.

ACME CONSTRUCTION, INC.   PRIMAVERA PROJECT PLANNER   WEST STREET BRIDGE

REPORT DATE 17OCT89 RUN NO.   20   WEST STREET BRIDGE - CPM SCHEDULE UPDATE #1   START DATE 5MAY89 FIN DATE 20OCT89*
             12:59
TOTAL FLOAT SORT   DATA DATE 5JUN89 PAGE NO.   1

----- ----- ---- ---- - --- ---------- --------------------------------------- -------- -------- -------- -------- -----
             ORIG REM   ACTIVITY DESCRIPTION   EARLY   EARLY   LATE   LATE   TOTAL
PRED SUCC   DUR DUR CAL %   CODE   START   FINISH   START   FINISH   FLOAT
----- ----- ---- ---- - --- ---------- --------------------------------------- -------- -------- -------- -------- -----

PRED	SUCC	ORIG DUR	REM DUR	CAL	%	CODE	ACTIVITY DESCRIPTION	EARLY START	EARLY FINISH	LATE START	LATE FINISH	TOTAL FLOAT
1	5	10	0	1	100		MOBILIZATION	5MAY89A	18MAY89A			
5	20	5	0	1	100		PILES - PIER #1	19MAY89A	25MAY89A			
20	30	5	5	1	0		PILE CAP #1	5JUN89	9JUN89	26MAY89	2JUN89	-5
30	45	10	10	1	0		FORM, REIN. & POUR - COLUMN #1	12JUN89	23JUN89	5JUN89	16JUN89	-5
45	50	10	10	1	0		FORM, REIN. & POUR - COLUMN #2	26JUN89	10JUL89	19JUN89	30JUN89	-5
45	60	10	10	1	0		PIER CAP #1	26JUN89	10JUL89	19JUN89	30JUN89	-5
50	55	0	0	1	0		DUMMY	11JUL89	10JUL89	3JUL89	30JUN89	-5
55	65	10	10	1	0		FORM, REIN. & POUR - COLUMN #3	11JUL89	24JUL89	3JUL89	17JUL89	-5
60	65	10	10	1	0		PIER CAP #2	11JUL89	24JUL89	3JUL89	17JUL89	-5
65	70	10	10	1	0		PIER CAP #3	25JUL89	7AUG89	18JUL89	31JUL89	-5
70	85	2	2	1	0		STEEL - SPAN 1	8AUG89	9AUG89	1AUG89	2AUG89	-5
85	95	10	10	1	0		FORM, REIN, & POUR - SPAN 1	10AUG89	23AUG89	3AUG89	16AUG89	-5
95	105	10	10	1	0		FORM, REIN. & POUR - SPAN 2	24AUG89	7SEP89	17AUG89	30AUG89	-5
105	110	10	10	1	0		FORM, REIN. & POUR - SPAN 3	8SEP89	21SEP89	31AUG89	14SEP89	-5
110	120	0	0	1	0		DUMMY	22SEP89	21SEP89	15SEP89	14SEP89	-5
120	125	10	10	1	0		FORM, REIN. & POUR - SPAN 4	22SEP89	5OCT89	15SEP89	28SEP89	-5
125	130	5	5	1	0		CURBS & SIDEWALKS - SPAN 3	6OCT89	12OCT89	29SEP89	5OCT89	-5
130	135	5	5	1	0		CURBS & SIDEWALKS - SPAN 4	13OCT89	19OCT89	6OCT89	12OCT89	-5
135	140	5	5	1	0		PUNCHLIST	20OCT89	26OCT89	13OCT89	19OCT89	-5
140	145	1	1	1	0		PROJECT COMPLETE	27OCT89	27OCT89	20OCT89	20OCT89	-5
20	25	5	4	1	20		PILES - PIER #2	30MAY89A	8JUN89		2JUN89	-4
25	30	0	0	1	0		DUMMY	9JUN89	8JUN89	5JUN89	2JUN89	-4
30	35	5	5	1	0		PILE CAP #2	12JUN89	16JUN89	12JUN89	16JUN89	0
35	45	0	0	1	0		DUMMY	19JUN89	16JUN89	19JUN89	16JUN89	0
110	115	0	0	1	0		DUMMY	22SEP89	21SEP89	22SEP89	21SEP89	0
115	125	5	5	1	0		CURBS & SIDEWALKS - SPAN 2	22SEP89	28SEP89	22SEP89	28SEP89	0
85	90	2	2	1	0		STEEL - SPAN 2	10AUG89	11AUG89	15AUG89	16AUG89	3
90	95	0	0	1	0		DUMMY	14AUG89	11AUG89	17AUG89	16AUG89	3
35	40	0	0	1	0		DUMMY	19JUN89	16JUN89	26JUN89	23JUN89	5
40	55	5	5	1	0		PILE CAP #3	19JUN89	23JUN89	26JUN89	30JUN89	5
105	115	5	5	1	0		CURBS & SIDEWALKS - SPAN 1	8SEP89	14SEP89	15SEP89	21SEP89	5
25	40	5	5	1	0		PILES - PIER #3	9JUN89	15JUN89	19JUN89	23JUN89	6
90	100	2	2	1	0		STEEL - SPAN 3	14AUG89	15AUG89	11SEP89	12SEP89	19
100	120	2	2	1	0		STEEL - SPAN 4	16AUG89	17AUG89	13SEP89	14SEP89	19
5	10	5	5	1	0		CLEAR & GRUB APPROACHES	5JUN89	9JUN89	6JUL89	12JUL89	22
10	15	20	20	1	0		CONSTRUCT ABUTMENT #1	12JUN89	10JUL89	13JUL89	9AUG89	22
15	75	20	20	1	0		CONSTRUCT ABUTMENT #2	11JUL89	7AUG89	10AUG89	7SEP89	22
70	75	0	0	1	0		DUMMY	8AUG89	7AUG89	8SEP89	7SEP89	22
75	80	10	10	1	0		PAVE APPROACH #1	8AUG89	21AUG89	8SEP89	21SEP89	22
80	130	10	10	1	0		PAVE APPROACH #2	22AUG89	5SEP89	22SEP89	5OCT89	22

Figure 3.4

Second Update

The second update for the project appears in Figure 3.5. This analysis is also a *total float sort*, and shows the present critical path with the highest negative float. In this update, the project is now an additional four workdays, or four calendar days, behind schedule, for a total project delay of nine workdays, or eleven calendar days.

5 workdays + 4 workdays = 9 workdays
(first update)   (second update)

7 calendar days + 6 calendar days = 13 calendar days
(first update)   (second update)

The analyst determines this delay by noting the nine days of negative float shown on the critical path, beginning with activity 30−45, "Form, Rein., and Pour Column # 2," and on the early and late finish dates of activity 140−145, "Project Complete."

The delay in this case had two causes:

(1) The first three workdays of delay were due to the late finish of activity 30−45, "Form, Rein., and Pour Column # 1."

(2) The last one workday of delay was caused by the lack of progress on activity 45−50, "Form, Rein., and Pour Column # 2."

The analyst reached these conclusions by referring to the projected finish date for activity 30−45 on the preceding update (Figure 3.4) − June 23, 1989. From Figure 3.5, the analyst sees that the actual finish date was June 28, 1989, three workdays later than scheduled on the preceding update. Likewise, an analysis of activity 45−50 shows that it started on June 29, 1989, but the progress recorded is only one workday, which is one workday behind the scheduled progress.

3 days (late finish) + 1 day (delay) = 4 days delay
(activity 30−45)   (activity 45−50)

Third Update

Figure 3.6 is the mathematical calculation for the third update for the project. As of this update, the project is now an additional twelve workdays, or eighteen calendar days behind schedule, for a total project delay of twenty-one workdays or thirty-one calendar days. The analyst reaches this conclusion by reviewing activities 70−85, "Steel−Span # 1," and 140−145, "Project Complete," as was done for the preceding updates. However, in this case, activity 70−85, "Steel−Span # 1," has not yet begun, despite the fact that the original scheduled start date was August 14, 1989.

A careful review of the documents shows a delay for this activity because the shop drawings for the material were not submitted and approved. This conclusion exemplifies the self-correcting mechanism of the delay analysis: The original schedule did not include activities for procurement or shop drawings. While the analyst did consider adding these items to the schedule, their omission becomes obvious without having to tamper with the original schedule.

The delay analysis for the remainder of the project would proceed using the same methodology shown on the first three updates.

REPORT DATE 17OCT89 RUN NO.   14   WEST STREET BRIDGE - CPM SCHEDULE UPDATE #2   START DATE 5MAY89 FIN DATE 20OCT89*
                13:02

TOTAL FLOAT SORT   DATA DATE   3JUL89 PAGE NO.   1

PRED	SUCC	ORIG DUR	REM DUR	CAL	%	CODE	ACTIVITY DESCRIPTION	EARLY START	EARLY FINISH	LATE START	LATE FINISH	TOTAL FLOAT
1	5	10	0	1	100		MOBILIZATION	5MAY89A	18MAY89A			
5	20	5	0	1	100		PILES - PIER #1	19MAY89A	25MAY89A			
20	25	5	0	1	100		PILES - PIER #2	30MAY89A	8JUN89A			
20	30	5	0	1	100		PILE CAP #1	5JUN89A	9JUN89A			
30	35	5	0	1	100		PILE CAP #2	12JUN89A	16JUN89A			
30	45	10	0	1	100		FORM, REIN. & POUR - COLUMN #1	12JUN89A	28JUN89A			
25	40	5	0	1	100		PILES - PIER #3	20JUN89A	26JUN89A			
25	30	0	0	1	100		DUMMY	3JUL89A	3JUL89A			
35	45	0	0	1	100		DUMMY	3JUL89A	3JUL89A			
45	50	10	9	1	10		FORM, REIN. & POUR - COLUMN #2	29JUN89A	14JUL89		30JUN89	-9
50	55	0	0	1	0		DUMMY	17JUL89	14JUL89	3JUL89	30JUN89	-9
55	65	10	10	1	0		FORM, REIN. & POUR - COLUMN #3	17JUL89	28JUL89	3JUL89	17JUL89	-9
65	70	10	10	1	0		PIER CAP #3	31JUL89	11AUG89	18JUL89	31JUL89	-9
70	85	2	2	1	0		STEEL - SPAN 1	14AUG89	15AUG89	1AUG89	2AUG89	-9
85	95	10	10	1	0		FORM, REIN, & POUR - SPAN 1	16AUG89	29AUG89	3AUG89	16AUG89	-9
95	105	10	10	1	0		FORM, REIN. & POUR - SPAN 2	30AUG89	13SEP89	17AUG89	30AUG89	-9
105	110	10	10	1	0		FORM, REIN. & POUR - SPAN 3	14SEP89	27SEP89	31AUG89	14SEP89	-9
110	120	0	0	1	0		DUMMY	28SEP89	27SEP89	15SEP89	14SEP89	-9
120	125	10	10	1	0		FORM, REIN. & POUR - SPAN 4	28SEP89	11OCT89	15SEP89	28SEP89	-9
125	130	5	5	1	0		CURBS & SIDEWALKS - SPAN 3	12OCT89	18OCT89	29SEP89	5OCT89	-9
130	135	5	5	1	0		CURBS & SIDEWALKS - SPAN 4	19OCT89	25OCT89	6OCT89	12OCT89	-9
135	140	5	5	1	0		PUNCHLIST	26OCT89	1NOV89	13OCT89	19OCT89	-9
140	145	1	1	1	0		PROJECT COMPLETE	2NOV89	2NOV89	20OCT89	20OCT89	-9
45	60	10	8	1	20		PIER CAP #1	28JUN89A	13JUL89		30JUN89	-8
60	65	10	10	1	0		PIER CAP #2	14JUL89	27JUL89	3JUL89	17JUL89	-8
35	40	0	0	1	0		DUMMY	3JUL89	30JUN89	26JUN89	23JUN89	-5
40	55	5	5	1	0		PILE CAP #3	3JUL89	10JUL89	26JUN89	30JUN89	-5
110	115	0	0	1	0		DUMMY	28SEP89	27SEP89	22SEP89	21SEP89	-4
115	125	5	5	1	0		CURBS & SIDEWALKS - SPAN 2	28SEP89	4OCT89	22SEP89	28SEP89	-4
85	90	2	2	1	0		STEEL - SPAN 2	16AUG89	17AUG89	15AUG89	16AUG89	-1
90	95	0	0	1	0		DUMMY	18AUG89	17AUG89	17AUG89	16AUG89	-1
105	115	5	5	1	0		CURBS & SIDEWALKS - SPAN 1	14SEP89	20SEP89	15SEP89	21SEP89	1
5	10	5	5	1	0		CLEAR & GRUB APPROACHES	3JUL89	10JUL89	6JUL89	12JUL89	2
10	15	20	20	1	0		CONSTRUCT ABUTMENT #1	11JUL89	7AUG89	13JUL89	9AUG89	2
15	75	20	20	1	0		CONSTRUCT ABUTMENT #2	8AUG89	5SEP89	10AUG89	7SEP89	2
75	80	10	10	1	0		PAVE APPROACH #1	6SEP89	19SEP89	8SEP89	21SEP89	2
80	130	10	10	1	0		PAVE APPROACH #2	20SEP89	3OCT89	22SEP89	5OCT89	2
90	100	2	2	1	0		STEEL - SPAN 3	18AUG89	21AUG89	11SEP89	12SEP89	15
100	120	2	2	1	0		STEEL - SPAN 4	22AUG89	23AUG89	13SEP89	14SEP89	15
70	75	0	0	1	0		DUMMY	14AUG89	11AUG89	8SEP89	7SEP89	18

Figure 3.5

ACME CONSTRUCTION, INC.   PRIMAVERA PROJECT PLANNER   WEST STREET BRIDGE

REPORT DATE 17OCT89 RUN NO.   8   WEST STREET BRIDGE - CPM SCHEDULE UPDATE #3   START DATE 5MAY89 FIN DATE 20OCT89*
            13:05

TOTAL FLOAT SORT   DATA DATE 30AUG89 PAGE NO.   1

PRED	SUCC	ORIG DUR	REM DUR	CAL	%	CODE	ACTIVITY DESCRIPTION	EARLY START	EARLY FINISH	LATE START	LATE FINISH	TOTAL FLOAT
1	5	10	0	1	100		MOBILIZATION	5MAY89A	18MAY89A			
5	20	5	0	1	100		PILES - PIER #1	19MAY89A	25MAY89A			
20	25	5	0	1	100		PILES - PIER #2	30MAY89A	8JUN89A			
20	30	5	0	1	100		PILE CAP #1	5JUN89A	9JUN89A			
30	35	5	0	1	100		PILE CAP #2	12JUN89A	16JUN89A			
30	45	10	0	1	100		FORM, REIN. & POUR - COLUMN #1	12JUN89A	28JUN89A			
25	40	5	0	1	100		PILES - PIER #3	20JUN89A	26JUN89A			
45	60	10	0	1	100		PIER CAP #1	28JUN89A	13JUL89A			
40	55	5	0	1	100		PILE CAP #3	29JUN89A	10JUL89A			
45	50	10	0	1	100		FORM, REIN. & POUR - COLUMN #2	29JUN89A	14JUL89A			
25	30	0	0	1	100		DUMMY	3JUL89A	3JUL89A			
35	45	0	0	1	100		DUMMY	3JUL89A	3JUL89A			
5	10	5	0	1	100		CLEAR & GRUB APPROACHES	5JUL89A	11JUL89A			
10	15	20	0	1	100		CONSTRUCT ABUTMENT #1	12JUL89A	8AUG89A			
60	65	10	0	1	100		PIER CAP #2	14JUL89A	27JUL89A			
50	55	0	0	1	100		DUMMY	17JUL89A	17JUL89A			
55	65	10	0	1	100		FORM, REIN. & POUR - COLUMN #3	17JUL89A	28JUL89A			
35	40	0	0	1	100		DUMMY	25JUL89A	25JUL89A			
65	70	10	0	1	100		PIER CAP #3	31JUL89A	11AUG89A			
15	75	20	0	1	100		CONSTRUCT ABUTMENT #2	10AUG89A	28AUG89A			
70	75	0	0	1	100		DUMMY	14AUG89A	14AUG89A			
70	85	2	2	1	0		STEEL - SPAN 1	30AUG89	31AUG89	1AUG89	2AUG89	-21
85	95	10	10	1	0		FORM, REIN, & POUR - SPAN 1	1SEP89	15SEP89	3AUG89	16AUG89	-21
95	105	10	10	1	0		FORM, REIN. & POUR - SPAN 2	18SEP89	29SEP89	17AUG89	30AUG89	-21
105	110	10	10	1	0		FORM, REIN. & POUR - SPAN 3	2OCT89	13OCT89	31AUG89	14SEP89	-21
110	120	0	0	1	0		DUMMY	16OCT89	13OCT89	15SEP89	14SEP89	-21
120	125	10	10	1	0		FORM, REIN. & POUR - SPAN 4	16OCT89	27OCT89	15SEP89	28SEP89	-21
125	130	5	5	1	0		CURBS & SIDEWALKS - SPAN 3	30OCT89	3NOV89	29SEP89	5OCT89	-21
130	135	5	5	1	0		CURBS & SIDEWALKS - SPAN 4	6NOV89	10NOV89	6OCT89	12OCT89	-21
135	140	5	5	1	0		PUNCHLIST	13NOV89	17NOV89	13OCT89	19OCT89	-21
140	145	1	1	1	0		PROJECT COMPLETE	20NOV89	20NOV89	20OCT89	20OCT89	-21
110	115	0	0	1	0		DUMMY	16OCT89	13OCT89	22SEP89	21SEP89	-16
115	125	5	5	1	0		CURBS & SIDEWALKS - SPAN 2	16OCT89	20OCT89	22SEP89	28SEP89	-16
85	90	2	2	1	0		STEEL - SPAN 2	1SEP89	5SEP89	15AUG89	16AUG89	-13
90	95	0	0	1	0		DUMMY	6SEP89	5SEP89	17AUG89	16AUG89	-13
105	115	5	5	1	0		CURBS & SIDEWALKS - SPAN 1	2OCT89	6OCT89	15SEP89	21SEP89	-11
90	100	2	2	1	0		STEEL - SPAN 3	6SEP89	7SEP89	11SEP89	12SEP89	3
100	120	2	2	1	0		STEEL - SPAN 4	8SEP89	11SEP89	13SEP89	14SEP89	3
75	80	10	10	1	0		PAVE APPROACH #1	30AUG89	13SEP89	8SEP89	21SEP89	6
80	130	10	10	1	0		PAVE APPROACH #2	14SEP89	27SEP89	22SEP89	5OCT89	6

Figure 3.6

Analysis Without CPM Updates

In many cases, a project begins with a reasonably accurate detailed CPM schedule, but the contractor does not update it consistently over the duration of the project. In fact, the schedule may not be updated at all, but instead allowed to "fall by the wayside" after the first submission. In either case, the analyst does not have the benefit of the updates with which to perform the analysis, as in the preceding example.

In this situation, an analysis is performed based on the original schedule submission, together with the as-built information on the project. In fact, the analysis can be performed in the same manner as was done with CPM updates but, in this case, the analyst must run the updates.

Example

Again, the contractor's original schedule submission (shown in Figures 3.1 through 3.3) is used. However, this time, no updates are available. Therefore, an as-built schedule is prepared from the daily reports on the project. This as-built schedule is shown in Figure 3.7.

In order to perform the analysis, the schedule is "updated" (retrospectively) at monthly intervals to: (1) determine which activities delay the project and (2) ensure that any changes in the critical path are detected. The first update in this example will be run as of June 5, 1989, one month after the project start date. The results of this update are the same as shown in Figure 3.4. The same analysis is run for each month of the project duration. Then, delays are pinpointed by comparing each schedule and the prospective versus the actual start and finish dates, as was done in the previous example.

The ability to update the schedule in this manner depends entirely on the availability and quality of the as-built information (daily reports, etc.). As the information becomes more sketchy, the analysis becomes more subjective.

Shifts in the Critical Path

Seldom does a project proceed through its entire duration and remain on the same critical path. This was noted to a small extent during the first analysis example in the beginning of this chapter. The critical path may shift several times during the construction process. The frequency of such shifts increases if the original schedule has several paths with small amounts of float. This occurs because it is easier for the small amounts of float to be more quickly consumed, thereby causing the critical path to shift.

Delay analysis would be relatively easy for the analyst to perform if the path shifted at approximately the same date as the data date of the monthly update. The data date is the calendar day on which the schedule is updated. For example, in Figure 3.6, the data date was August 30, 1989. All progress on each activity up to that date is incorporated into the schedule update.

However, a critical path shift at a data date occurs only when the analyst is extremely lucky. More often than not, the critical path shifts at some point between updates. The analyst must track back through the time between updates to determine exactly *when* the path shifted so that a correct determination of the activities delayed can be made. While not an easy task, it can be done.

The following example illustrates how to determine a shift in the critical path. For the sake of simplicity, the schedule in Figure 3.1 will also be used for this example.

To best illustrate the critical path shift, the update information is changed for the third update in this example. Figure 3.8 is a total float sort of the contractor's update as of August 30, 1989, almost two months after the second update (Figure 3.5) was performed (July 3).

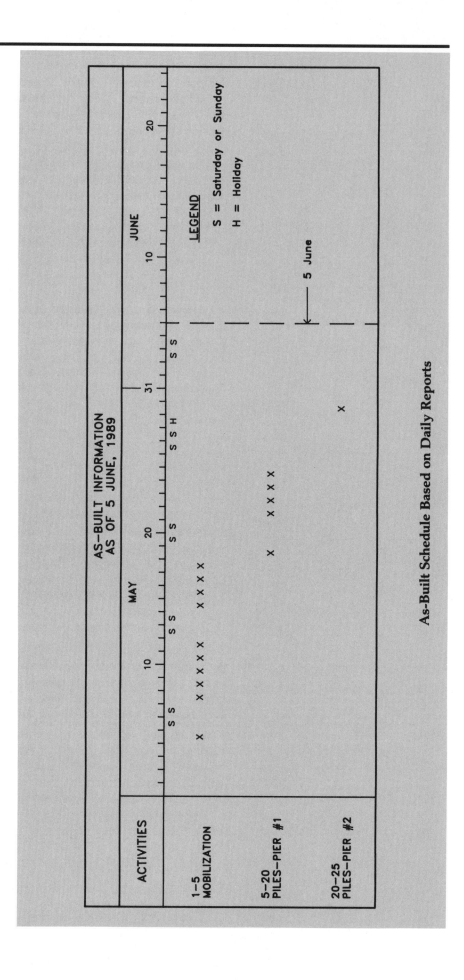

As-Built Schedule Based on Daily Reports

Figure 3.7

ACME CONSTRUCTION, INC.   PRIMAVERA PROJECT PLANNER   WEST STREET BRIDGE

REPORT DATE 10MAR89 RUN NO.   6   WEST STREET BRIDGE - CPM SCHEDULE UPDATE #3   START DATE 5MAY89 FIN DATE 20OCT89*

TOTAL FLOAT SORT   DATA DATE 30AUG89   PAGE NO.   1

PRED	SUCC	ORIG DUR	REM DUR	PCT	CODE	ACTIVITY DESCRIPTION	EARLY START	EARLY FINISH	LATE START	LATE FINISH	TOTAL FLOAT
1	5	10	0	100		MOBILIZATION	5MAY89A	18MAY89A			
5	20	5	0	100		PILES - PIER #1	19MAY89A	25MAY89A			
20	25	5	0	100		PILES - PIER #2	30MAY89A	8JUN89A			
20	30	5	0	100		PILE CAP #1	5JUN89A	9JUN89A			
25	30	0	0	100		DUMMY	3JUL89A	3JUL89A			
25	40	5	0	100		PILES - PIER #3	20JUN89A	26JUN89A			
30	35	5	0	100		PILE CAP #2	12JUN89A	16JUN89A			
30	45	10	0	100		FORM, REIN. & POUR - COLUMN #1	12JUN89A	28JUN89A			
35	40	0	0	100		DUMMY	25JUL89A	25JUL89A			
35	45	0	0	100		DUMMY	3JUL89A	3JUL89A			
40	55	5	0	100		PILE CAP #3	29JUN89A	10JUL89A			
45	50	10	0	100		FORM, REIN. & POUR - COLUMN #2	29JUN89A	14JUL89A			
45	60	10	0	100		PIER CAP #1	28JUN89A	13JUL89A			
50	55	0	0	100		DUMMY	17JUL89A	17JUL89A			
55	65	10	0	100		FORM, REIN. & POUR - COLUMN #3	17JUL89A	28JUL89A			
60	65	10	0	100		PIER CAP #2	14JUL89A	27JUL89A			
65	70	10	0	100		PIER CAP #3	31JUL89A	11AUG89A			
70	75	0	0	100		DUMMY	14AUG89A	14AUG89A			
5	10	5	5	0		CLEAR & GRUB APPROACHES	30AUG89	6SEP89	6JUL89	12JUL89	-39
10	15	20	20	0		CONSTRUCT ABUTMENT #1	7SEP89	4OCT89	13JUL89	9AUG89	-39
15	75	20	20	0		CONSTRUCT ABUTMENT #2	5OCT89	1NOV89	10AUG89	7SEP89	-39
75	80	10	10	0		PAVE APPROACH #1	2NOV89	15NOV89	8SEP89	21SEP89	-39
80	130	10	10	0		PAVE APPROACH #2	16NOV89	29NOV89	22SEP89	5OCT89	-39
130	135	5	5	0		CURBS & SIDEWALKS - SPAN 4	30NOV89	6DEC89	6OCT89	12OCT89	-39
135	140	5	5	0		PUNCHLIST	7DEC89	13DEC89	13OCT89	19OCT89	-39
140	145	1	1	0		PROJECT COMPLETE	14DEC89	14DEC89	20OCT89	20OCT89	-39
70	85	2	2	0		STEEL - SPAN 1	30AUG89	31AUG89	1AUG89	2AUG89	-21
85	95	10	10	0		FORM, REIN. & POUR - SPAN 1	1SEP89	15SEP89	3AUG89	16AUG89	-21
95	105	10	10	0		FORM, REIN. & POUR - SPAN 2	18SEP89	29SEP89	17AUG89	30AUG89	-21
105	110	10	10	0		FORM, REIN. & POUR - SPAN 3	2OCT89	13OCT89	31AUG89	14SEP89	-21
110	120	0	0	0		DUMMY	16OCT89	16OCT89	15SEP89	15SEP89	-21
120	125	10	10	0		FORM, REIN. & POUR - SPAN 4	16OCT89	27OCT89	15SEP89	28SEP89	-21
125	130	5	5	0		CURBS & SIDEWALKS - SPAN 3	30OCT89	3NOV89	29SEP89	5OCT89	-21
110	115	0	0	0		DUMMY	16OCT89	16OCT89	22SEP89	22SEP89	-16
115	125	5	5	0		CURBS & SIDEWALKS - SPAN 2	16OCT89	20OCT89	22SEP89	28SEP89	-16
85	90	2	2	0		STEEL - SPAN 2	1SEP89	5SEP89	15AUG89	16AUG89	-13
90	95	0	0	0		DUMMY	6SEP89	6SEP89	17AUG89	17AUG89	-13
105	115	5	5	0		CURBS & SIDEWALKS - SPAN 1	2OCT89	6OCT89	15SEP89	21SEP89	-11
90	100	2	2	0		STEEL - SPAN 3	6SEP89	7SEP89	11SEP89	12SEP89	3
100	120	2	2	0		STEEL - SPAN 4	8SEP89	11SEP89	13SEP89	14SEP89	3

Figure 3.8

Even a cursory glance at the third update shows that the critical path has changed. In the second update (Figure 3.5), the critical path was along the pier column work. As of the third update (Figure 3.8), the critical path is along the "Clear and Grub Approaches." During the construction process, the contractor did not pursue the clearing and grubbing work until it finally exceeded its available float and became critical. As of the third update, activity 5–10, "Clear & Grub Approaches" is thirty-nine workdays behind schedule. As of the preceding update, the project was only nine workdays behind schedule. Sometime in the intervening two months, the project fell behind schedule an additional thirty workdays and changed critical paths. The question that must be answered is which activities caused the thirty workdays of additional delay? To answer that question, the analyst must determine when the critical path switched.

Data date:	August 30	July 3
Update #:	3	2

Negative Float: 39 workdays — 9 workdays = 30 workdays additional delay occurred between July 3 and August 30

There are various ways to perform a delay analysis of the additional thirty workdays. First, the analyst can prepare additional intermediate updates based on the data given in the schedule updates and the as-built information. The analyst may have to produce two or more updates to demonstrate accurately how the project was delayed during the period. This method is probably the most demonstrative and the most easily understood by those not intimately familiar with CPM.

Before demonstrating this method, it is beneficial to consider how the analyst can determine the shift in the critical path based on the existing information. Based on the data given in the existing two updates, the analyst can determine exactly when the critical path shifted by reviewing the specific information for each of the activities.

For example, in update number 2, Figure 3.5, the critical path started with activity 45–50, "Form, Reinforce & Pour Column # 2." Its early finish date, considering the delay at that point, was July 14, 1989. According to the third update, it was actually completed on July 14, 1989. Therefore, activity 45–50 did not cause any additional delay. Activity 5–10, "Clear & Grub Approaches," had a late start date of July 6, 1989. It did not start by that date and as of July 6, 1989, this activity had zero float. However, the project at that point already had negative nine days of float.

If every other activity continued to make progress as planned and activity 5–10 made no progress, then in nine workdays it would catch up to the existing critical path, and on the tenth workday it would become critical. This, in fact, is what happened. By reviewing a calendar, one can see that ten workdays from the July 6 date is July 20. On that date, the critical path shifts to the "Clear and Grub" path of activities.

To further check this conclusion, the analyst can review the other activities completed or worked on during the period between the two updates. These include activities 45–50, 45–60, 55–65, 60–65, and 65–70. All of these activities actually finished without delaying the project. The simplest comparison is between the early start and early finish dates shown in Figure 3.5 and the actual start and finish dates shown in Figure 3.8.

Based on the previous manual analysis, the analyst (using a computerized scheduling program) can run an update as of July 20, 1989 and demonstrate the shift in the critical path. Thus, of the thirty workdays of additional delay, all thirty workdays are attributed to the delay in the work on activity 5−10. Figure 3.9 shows the status of float along both paths for the calendar period from July 3 to July 21. Since progress is being made on all other activities, the float remains at negative nine. However, the float along the "Clear and Grub" path decreases each workday by one day. (There is no change in the float for weekends or holidays, since the float is calculated in workdays.)

As the diagram illustrates, on July 20, the float is negative ten on the "Clear and Grub" path, and only negative nine on the other path. Figure 3.10 is a *total float sort* of an update with a data date of July 20. As can be seen, the critical path shifts to the "Clear and Grub" path of activities.

It is possible that the critical path can shift more than once during an update period. This is why meticulous analysis must be performed as described.

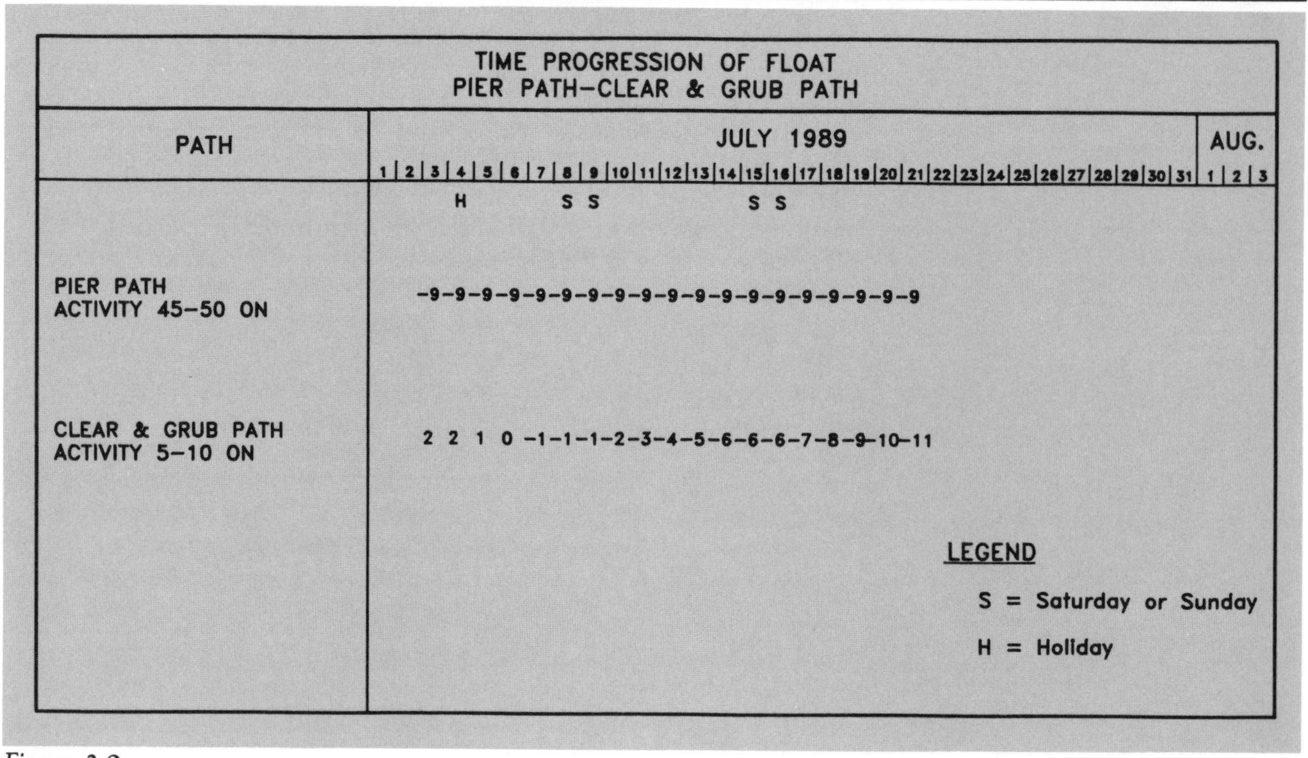
TIME PROGRESSION OF FLOAT
PIER PATH—CLEAR & GRUB PATH
PATH
JULY 1989
AUG.
1 2 3 4 5 6 7 8 9 10 11 12 13 14 15 16 17 18 19 20 21 22 23 24 25 26 27 28 29 30 31 1 2 3
H S S S S
PIER PATH
ACTIVITY 45–50 ON
-9-9-9-9-9-9-9-9-9-9-9-9-9-9-9-9-9-9-9-9
CLEAR & GRUB PATH
ACTIVITY 5–10 ON
2 2 1 0 -1-1-1-2-3-4-5-6-6-6-7-8-9-10-11
LEGEND
S = Saturday or Sunday
H = Holiday
Figure 3.9

ACME CONSTRUCTION, INC.   PRIMAVERA PROJECT PLANNER   WEST STREET BRIDGE

REPORT DATE 7DEC89 RUN NO.   25   WEST STREET BRIDGE - CPM SCHEDULE UPDATE I   START DATE 5MAY89 FIN DATE 20OCT89*
                 0:41
TOTAL FLOAT/ES   DATA DATE 20JUL89 PAGE NO.   1

PRED	SUCC	ORIG DUR	REM DUR	CAL	%	CODE	ACTIVITY DESCRIPTION	EARLY START	EARLY FINISH	LATE START	LATE FINISH	TOTAL FLOAT
1	5	10	0	1	100		MOBILIZATION	5MAY89A	18MAY89A			
5	20	5	0	1	100		PILES - PIER #1	19MAY89A	25MAY89A			
20	25	5	0	1	100		PILES - PIER #2	30MAY89A	8JUN89A			
20	30	5	0	1	100		PILE CAP #1	5JUN89A	9JUN89A			
25	30	0	0	1	100		DUMMY	3JUL89A	3JUL89A			
25	40	5	0	1	100		PILES - PIER #3	20JUN89A	26JUN89A			
30	35	5	0	1	100		PILE CAP #2	12JUN89A	16JUN89A			
30	45	10	0	1	100		FORM, REIN. & POUR - COLUMN #1	12JUN89A	28JUN89A			
35	45	0	0	1	100		DUMMY	3JUL89A	3JUL89A			
40	55	5	0	1	100		PILE CAP #3	29JUN89A	10JUL89A			
45	50	10	0	1	100		FORM, REIN. & POUR - COLUMN #2	29JUN89A	14JUL89A			
45	60	10	0	1	100		PIER CAP #1	28JUN89A	13JUL89A			
50	55	0	0	1	100		DUMMY	17JUL89A	17JUL89A			
5	10	5	5	1	0		CLEAR & GRUB APPROACHES	20JUL89	26JUL89	6JUL89	12JUL89	-10
10	15	20	20	1	0		CONSTRUCT ABUTMENT #1	27JUL89	23AUG89	13JUL89	9AUG89	-10
15	75	20	20	1	0		CONSTRUCT ABUTMENT #2	24AUG89	21SEP89	10AUG89	7SEP89	-10
75	80	10	10	1	0		PAVE APPROACH #1	22SEP89	5OCT89	8SEP89	21SEP89	-10
80	130	10	10	1	0		PAVE APPROACH #2	6OCT89	19OCT89	22SEP89	5OCT89	-10
130	135	5	5	1	0		CURBS & SIDEWALKS - SPAN 4	20OCT89	26OCT89	6OCT89	12OCT89	-10
135	140	5	5	1	0		PUNCHLIST	27OCT89	2NOV89	13OCT89	19OCT89	-10
140	145	1	1	1	0		PROJECT COMPLETE	3NOV89	3NOV89	20OCT89	20OCT89	-10
35	40	0	0	1	0		DUMMY	20JUL89	19JUL89	7JUL89	6JUL89	-9
55	65	10	7	1	30		FORM, REIN. & POUR - COLUMN #3	17JUL89A	28JUL89		17JUL89	-9
65	70	10	10	1	0		PIER CAP #3	31JUL89	11AUG89	18JUL89	31JUL89	-9
70	85	2	2	1	0		STEEL - SPAN 1	14AUG89	15AUG89	1AUG89	2AUG89	-9
85	95	10	10	1	0		FORM, REIN, & POUR - SPAN 1	16AUG89	29AUG89	3AUG89	16AUG89	-9
95	105	10	10	1	0		FORM, REIN. & POUR - SPAN 2	30AUG89	13SEP89	17AUG89	30AUG89	-9
105	110	10	10	1	0		FORM, REIN. & POUR - SPAN 3	14SEP89	27SEP89	31AUG89	14SEP89	-9
110	120	0	0	1	0		DUMMY	28SEP89	27SEP89	15SEP89	14SEP89	-9
120	125	10	10	1	0		FORM, REIN. & POUR - SPAN 4	28SEP89	11OCT89	15SEP89	28SEP89	-9
125	130	5	5	1	0		CURBS & SIDEWALKS - SPAN 3	12OCT89	18OCT89	29SEP89	5OCT89	-9
60	65	10	6	1	40		PIER CAP #2	14JUL89A	27JUL89		17JUL89	-8
110	115	0	0	1	0		DUMMY	28SEP89	27SEP89	22SEP89	21SEP89	-4
115	125	5	5	1	0		CURBS & SIDEWALKS - SPAN 2	28SEP89	4OCT89	22SEP89	28SEP89	-4
85	90	2	2	1	0		STEEL - SPAN 2	16AUG89	17AUG89	15AUG89	16AUG89	-1
90	95	0	0	1	0		DUMMY	18AUG89	17AUG89	17AUG89	16AUG89	-1
105	115	5	5	1	0		CURBS & SIDEWALKS - SPAN 1	14SEP89	20SEP89	15SEP89	21SEP89	1
90	100	2	2	1	0		STEEL - SPAN 3	18AUG89	21AUG89	11SEP89	12SEP89	15
100	120	2	2	1	0		STEEL - SPAN 4	22AUG89	23AUG89	13SEP89	14SEP89	15
70	75	0	0	1	0		DUMMY	14AUG89	11AUG89	8SEP89	7SEP89	18

Figure 3.10

Chapter Four

Delay Analysis with Bar Charts

Chapter Four

Delay Analysis with Bar Charts

The preceding chapter described how to perform a delay analysis in the ideal circumstances, when a detailed CPM schedule was created as the original as-planned schedule for the project. With a CPM schedule as a starting point, the analyst can perform the delay analysis with a reasonable level of confidence, whether or not periodic updates are available. In reality, many projects are scheduled using a bar chart. For projects with many interrelated activities, this method is not as desirable as a CPM schedule, but one can still perform a meaningful and accurate analysis using a bar chart. As the level of existing detail and the degree of information decrease, the delay analysis becomes more subjective. This chapter describes how one goes about performing a delay analysis when the project schedule is a bar chart.

Bar Charts Versus CPM Schedules

There is nothing inherently wrong with scheduling a project with a bar chart. Bar charts were in use long before the Critical Path Method was even created. As some professionals are quick to point out, the Empire State Building was scheduled with a bar chart and not the CPM. In fact, a *detailed* bar chart can provide almost as much information as a CPM schedule.

Figure 4.1 is the bar chart for the sample project referred to in the preceding chapters. This bar chart does not provide as much detail as the CPM schedule for the same project. Figure 4.2 is a detailed bar chart for this project, which more clearly defines the proposed work plan of the contractor. In this case, each major activity is broken down into the work on the respective piers and spans. This added information provides the analyst and the contractor/owner with a more detailed picture of the plan for construction.

With very little effort, the analyst can modify the bar chart (see Figure 4.2) to show the interrelationships among the activities (see Figure 4.3). Minimal study of this schedule shows that with the addition of nodes and perhaps a few dummies, one would produce the same CPM schedule for the project as is shown in Chapter 2, Figure 2.1.

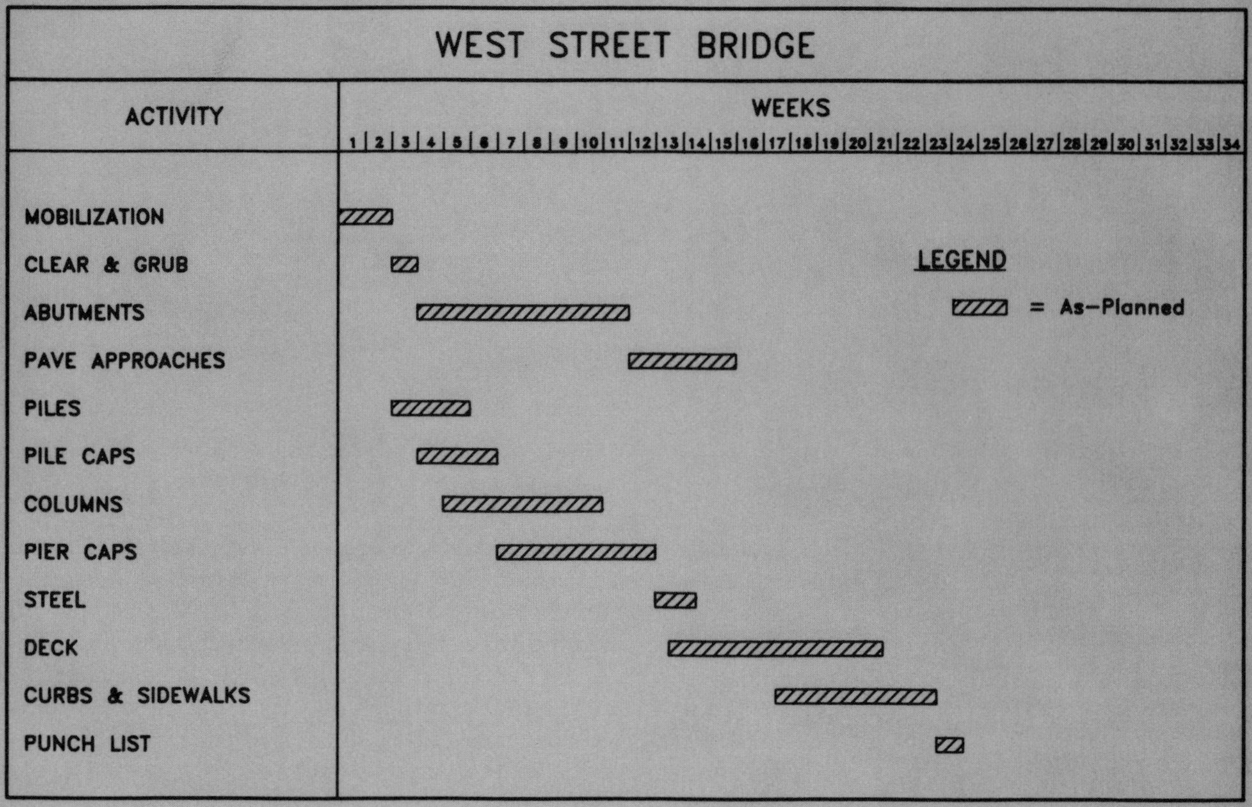

Bar Chart for Sample Project

Figure 4.1

WEST STREET BRIDGE

ACTIVITY	WEEKS
	1 2 3 4 5 6 7 8 9 10 11 12 13 14 15 16 17 18 19 20 21 22 23 24 25 26 27 28 29 30 31 32 33 34

ACTIVITY	Bar
MOBILIZATION	weeks 1–2
CLEAR & GRUB	week 2
ABUTMENT #1	weeks 3–7
ABUTMENT #2	weeks 7–10
PAVE APPROACH #1	weeks 12–13
PAVE APPROACH #2	weeks 14–15
PILES–PIER #1	week 1
PILES–PIER #2	week 2
PILES–PIER #3	week 3
PILE CAP #1	week 1
PILE CAP #2	week 2
PILE CAP #3	week 3
PIER COLUMN #1	weeks 4–5
PIER COLUMN #2	weeks 6–7
PIER COLUMN #3	weeks 8–9
PIER CAP #1	weeks 6–7
PIER CAP #2	weeks 8–9
PIER CAP #3	weeks 10–11
STEEL SPAN #1	week 13
STEEL SPAN #2	week 13
STEEL SPAN #3	week 13
STEEL SPAN #4	week 14
F, R, & P, SPAN #1	weeks 13–14
F, R, & P, SPAN #2	weeks 15–16
F, R, & P, SPAN #3	weeks 17–18
F, R, & P, SPAN #4	weeks 19–20
CURBS & SIDEWALKS, SPAN #1	week 17
CURBS & SIDEWALKS, SPAN #2	week 19
CURBS & SIDEWALKS, SPAN #3	week 22
CURBS & SIDEWALKS, SPAN #4	week 23
PUNCH LIST	week 24

LEGEND

▨▨▨ = As–Planned

Detailed Bar Chart for Sample Project

Figure 4.2

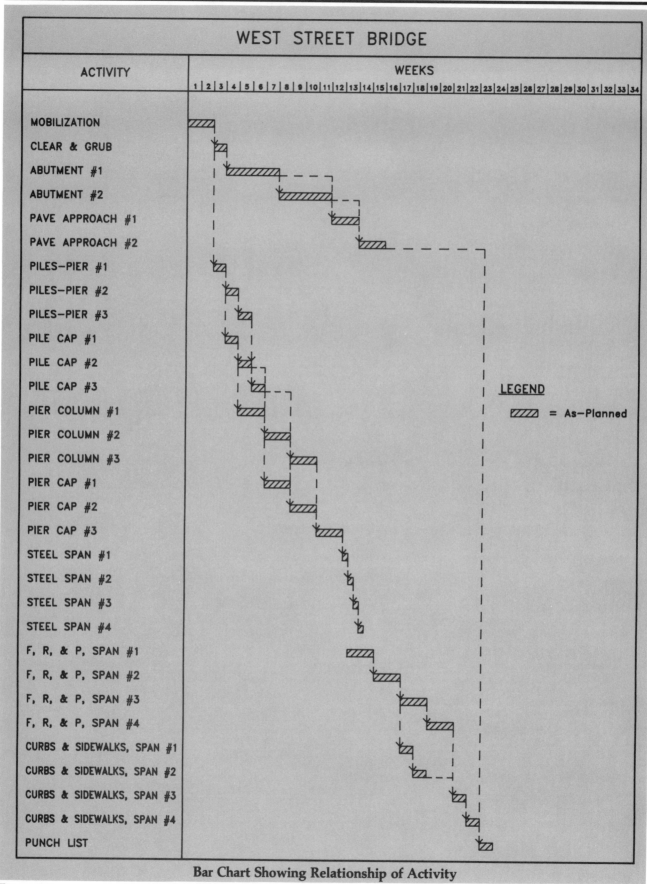

Bar Chart Showing Relationship of Activity

Figure 4.3

In fact, most bar charts for projects do not contain as much detail as that in Figure 4.3, and often not even as much as the bar chart in Figure 4.2. In general, most bar charts suffer from some major shortcomings that diminish their usefulness as a management tool and their effectiveness in measuring delays. Among their shortcomings are:

- Lack of detail—too few activities for the amount and complexity of the work
- No indication of the interrelationships among the activities
- No definition of the critical path of the project

Obviously, these weaknesses hamper the analyst performing a delay analysis, but they do not make it an impossible task. If nothing else, the bar chart is helpful in that it defines the plan for constructing the project and it can be used as the basis for the analysis.

Defining the Critical Path

The first step in analyzing a bar chart is to define the critical path. Every project has a critical path. Simply because a project does not have a CPM schedule, does not mean that it does not have a critical path. The following definitions illustrate this point.

Basic CPM

In CPM scheduling, the drafter of the schedule prepares a logic diagram or a network diagram. Once durations are assigned to the activities in the diagram, a critical path is calculated. This is a purely arithmetical process. The definition of the critical path is: *the longest path through the network diagram measured in time.* Thus, the path with the longest duration defines the shortest duration for the project. The project cannot finish until every path has been traversed. A delay to an activity on the critical path will delay the completion date of the project. Whether the critical path is defined in a CPM schedule or a bar chart, every project has a series of interrelated activities that will control the completion time.

Identifying the Critical Path on a Bar Chart

Having established the fact that a critical path exists in a bar chart schedule, the delay analyst should identify this critical path. The analyst must review the bar chart in detail for obvious conclusions about the sequence of work. These conclusions may be based on project documentation that might clarify the thought process that went into creating the bar chart or defining the planned work sequence. Documentation that can be helpful includes the contract documents (which may dictate staging or phasing), pre-construction meeting minutes, internal contractor memoranda, or project correspondence.

Practical knowledge of the type of project and the physical construction requirements is necessary to reach a reasonable conclusion about the project's critical path. For example, to analyze a bar chart of a high-rise structure, the analyst must know that interior finishes cannot start until the building is "dried-in," that the normal sequence of the progression of trades is from the bottom up, and that it is common for trades to follow behind each other as the building progresses upward, instead of waiting until the preceding trade completely finishes its work.

A note of caution: The analyst should resist the temptation to interpret the bar chart schedule based solely on his or her own experience. Merely because one has performed work in a particular sequence in the past does not mean that the contractor on this project has planned it the same way. Unless the bar chart is extremely brief, the analyst should be able to glean some indication of the overall plan and sequence of activities to determine the critical path.

Referring to Figure 4.2, we will define the critical path for the sample bridge project. The critical path starts with the mobilization activity, with a duration of two weeks. This is obvious, since no other activity is scheduled to occur during this period. The next two activities are the clear and grub activity and the piles at pier #1. In reviewing the sequence of activities, the clear and grub activity is related to the abutment and approach work. The abutment and approach work is scheduled to finish well before the end of the project and does not appear to be related to the schedule of activities on bridge construction. The analyst can determine from the contract documents that the approaches are not concrete as is the bridge deck; consequently, there is no physical reason to coordinate the concrete placement for the bridge with the approach construction. The only possible relationship could be the ability to move the concrete placing equipment onto the bridge superstructure. However, since the schedule reflects that the deck work is to start before workers complete either of the approaches, the analyst concludes that the equipment can be located independently of the approach work. Therefore, it appears that the abutment/approach path is not on the critical path for the project.

The critical path must move through the piles and piers. When viewing this bar chart, the analyst sees that the work is "stair-stepped" through the specific activities for each pier. Thus, the piles at pier #1 are complete and the piles at Pier #2 are starting, while the pile cap at pier #1 is concurrently constructed. Based on the graphic representation, the critical path appears to follow these activities:

    Piles – Pier #1
    Pile Cap #1
    Pier Column #1
    Pier Cap #1

At this point, the analyst recognizes that the pier columns and the pier caps each have two-week durations, and the next activity – steel erection – does not begin until all pier caps are complete. Therefore, all pier column and pier cap activities are most likely on the critical path, not just the first piles, piers, columns, and caps.

Using similar reasoning, the steel for span #1 is critical and then the path continues through deck placement for all spans. Next are the curbs and sidewalks for spans #3 and #4 and finally, the punch list work.

Thus, the overall critical path from the bar chart (Figure 4.3) is:

    Mobilization
    Piles – Pier #1
    Pile Cap #1
    Pier Column #1
    Pier Column #2
    Pier Cap #1
    Pier Column #3
    Pier Cap #2
    Pier Cap #3
    Steel Span #1
    F, R, & P Span #1
    F, R, & P Span #2
    F, R, & P Span #3
    F, R, & P Span #4
    Curbs & Sidewalks Span #3
    Curbs & Sidewalks Span #4
    Punch list

The analyst could reach a similar conclusion working with the less detailed bar chart alone (see Figure 4.1). This would, however, require that the analyst make more assumptions about the work on the separate piers. As was noted in the preceding discussion, contemporaneous documentation can help the analyst define the contractor's planned sequence in more detail. The less detailed the bar chart, the more assumptions required by the analyst to determine the project's critical path.

Quantifying the Delays

The process of quantifying the delays using a bar chart is similar to the process performed in the preceding chapter when a CPM schedule was available. Again, the analyst must prepare a detailed as-built schedule showing, as specifically as possible, the schedule of work performed.

Figure 4.4 is the as-built schedule for this project. Once the as-built has been prepared, the analysis can proceed.

As the as-built schedule (Figure 4.4) shows, the mobilization activity started on schedule (the first day of week one), and finished on schedule (by the end of week two). The remaining activities, however, did not proceed in the same manner as the as-planned schedule had predicted. Rather than analyze the entire project, the first three delays will be analyzed to demonstrate the delay analysis methodology that can be applied to the rest of the project (see Chapter 2 for a detailed methodology of delay analysis).

The pile driving at piers # 1, # 2, and # 3; the pile caps at piers # 1 and # 2, and pier column # 1 were accomplished as planned in the three weeks immediately following the mobilization activity. The clear and grub activity, however, did not proceed as planned, but instead started two weeks late and finished within one week (the planned duration). If the previous conclusions concerning the critical path were correct, the delay to the start of clearing and grubbing should not have resulted in a delay to the project. To check this conclusion, the analyst can "update" the bar chart as of the end of week five, as shown in Figure 4.5.

As can be seen in Figure 4.5, the project is still on schedule; however, the abutment and approach work has been moved over or "bumped" in time because of the delay to the clear and grub activity. As expected, there is no delay to the critical path. The adjusted schedule (Figure 4.5) shows the as-built condition for the first five weeks of the project and the adjusted as-planned activities for the remainder of the job.

Based on the as-built information, the analyst decides to "update" the schedule as of the end of week eleven. The as-built schedule (Figure 4.4) shows that the abutment/approach work has not yet begun and that the pier cap work has also not yet begun. Pier columns # 1, and # 2 were completed on schedule. Pier column # 3, however, took one week longer to complete than planned. The adjusted schedule for week eleven is shown in Figure 4.6.

Based on the updated and adjusted schedule presented in Figure 4.6, the analyst concludes that the project is now five weeks behind schedule. The delay was caused by the late start of pier cap # 1 work. Although pier column # 3 was late in finishing and was on the original critical path, once the pier cap # 1 activity did not start on time, the critical path shifted, to depend solely on the pier cap work. The pier column # 3 activity was effectively given float by virtue of the delay to the pier cap activity.

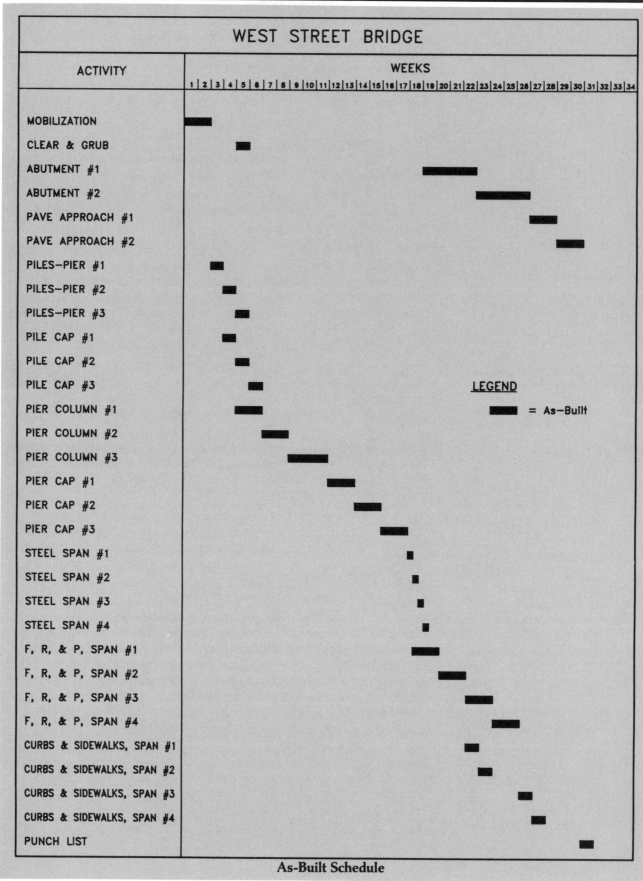

Figure 4.4

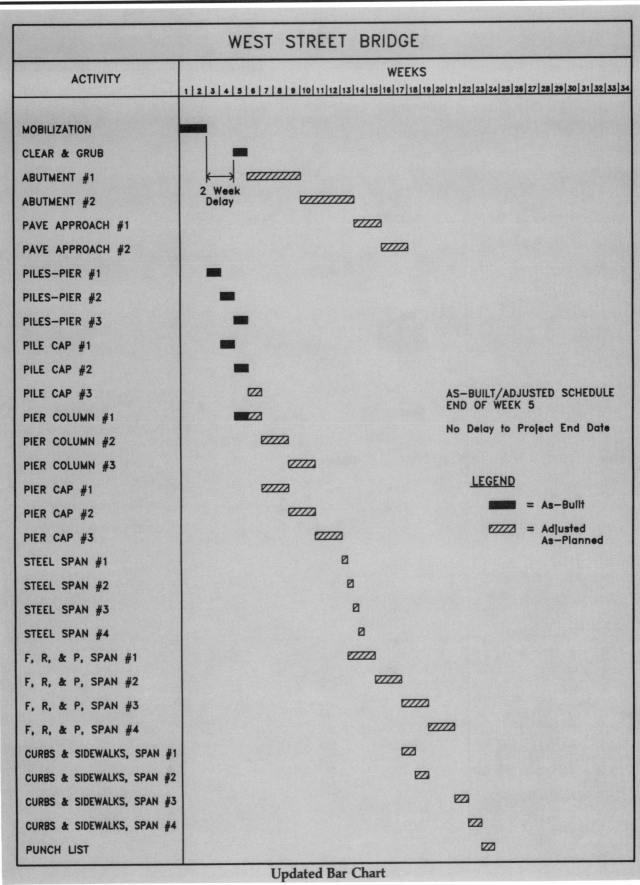

Figure 4.5

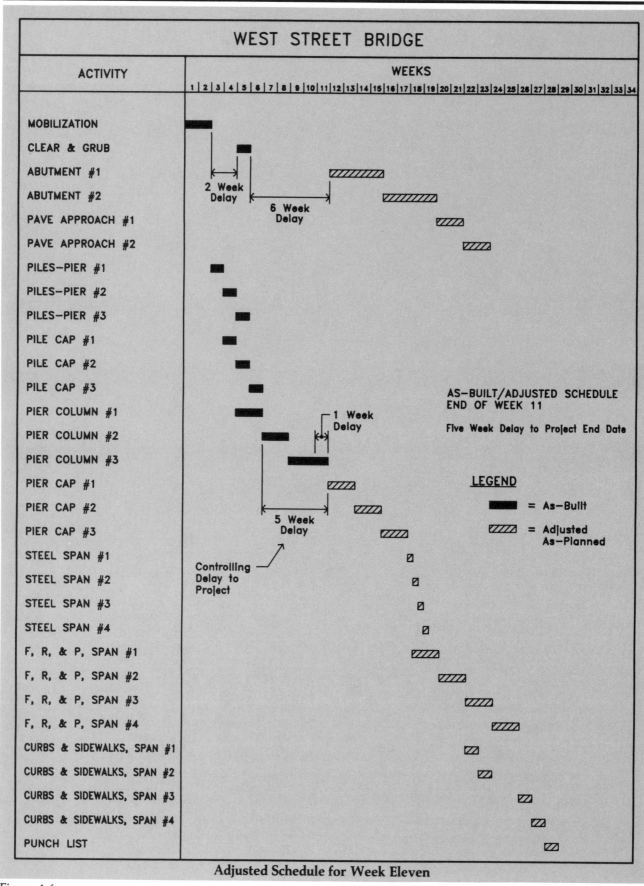

Figure 4.6

Next, the analyst decides to "update" the schedule at the end of week 18. This point is chosen because the activities along the pier/deck path continued in accordance with the adjusted schedule, but the abutment/approach work did not. It is in the middle of week fifteen that the critical path shifts. The as-built/adjusted as-planned schedule at the end of week eighteen is shown in Figure 4.7. Since the project had been delayed five weeks as of the last update, the additional delay since that update is two and one half weeks. The activities on the pier/deck path were not delayed any further since the last update. Therefore, the additional delay appears to be the result of a lack of progress on the abutment/approach path. Since this is an additional two and one half weeks, the critical path shifted two and one half weeks before this update, in the middle of week fifteen.

The example just given uses the same methodology described in Chapter 2. The analysis was made step-by-step at various points in time. The ability to perform the analysis and the accuracy of the results are dependent on the detail of the as-planned schedule and the available as-built information.

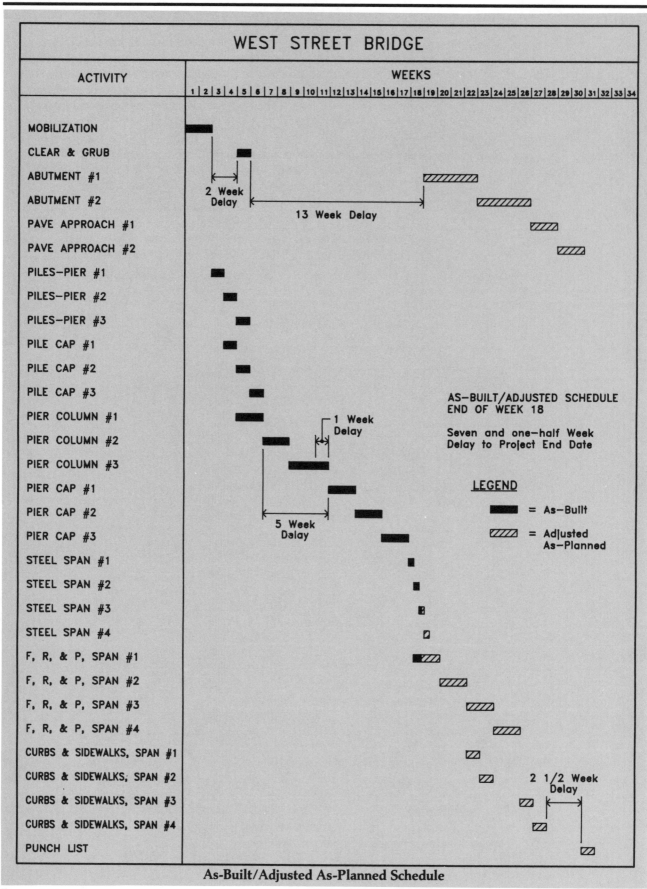

Figure 4.7

Chapter Five

Delay Analysis with No Schedule

Chapter Five
Delay Analysis with No Schedule

The preceding chapters discuss the performance of a delay analysis using a detailed CPM schedule (with and without updates), and a bar chart. This chapter addresses the "worst case" situation, the project with no as-planned schedule. This is the most difficult situation in which to perform a delay analysis. Again, as the available information decreases, the analyst must make more assumptions, and the analysis becomes more subjective. However, while this type of analysis is difficult, it is not impossible.

Contemporaneous Documents for Sequence and Timing

When there is no as-planned schedule, it is usually because the general contractor did not prepare any schedule for the project. In this situation, the analyst should begin by reviewing all available documentation to determine if any information exists that may provide some idea of a proposed sequence of the work or timing for specific activities. The analyst should investigate the following documents:

- The contract documents – for any specific sequence, phasing, or staging specified as a requirement on the project. (See Figure 5.1.)
- Correspondence between the general contractor and the owner or owner's representative – for references to sequence or timing, even if only for a portion of the project. (See Figure 5.2a & b)
- Subcontract agreements – to look for any sequence or timing dictated to the subcontractors by the general contractor concerning specific subcontract work.
- Correspondence with subcontractors – for any discussion concerning schedules, sequence, or timing. (See Figure 5.3.)
- Partial schedules produced during the project – these may describe any planned sequence or timing for portions of the project. (See Figure 5.4.)
- Meeting minutes – for any discussions concerning scheduling, particularly the preconstruction meeting minutes. (See Figure 5.5.)
- Daily log or diary entries by either the general contractor's personnel or the owner's representative. (See Figure 5.6.)
- Purchase orders with suppliers – these may show planned dates for delivery of materials or equipment.

The analyst should use all the available information to define some form of an as-planned schedule, or at least establish a general sequence for the work on the project, for different points or portions of the project.

Based on the sample information provided in Figures 5.1 through 5.6, the analyst is unable to determine an as-planned schedule. However, the following information can be determined:

1. The contract required that all abutment work be completed before any paving was performed on the approaches. The contract also required that completion of the project occur by the middle of the 24th week (from Figure 5.1).
2. The contractor planned to work from east to west, or from abutment # 1 to abutment # 2, and from pier # 1 to pier # 3 (from Figure 5.2a).
3. The owner's representative noted that the review and approval of the shop drawings for the reinforcing steel in the pier caps had taken longer than required and were not returned to the contractor until five weeks later than requested (from Figure 5.2b).
4. The contractor planned on erecting the steel at the beginning of the thirteenth week of the project (from Figure 5.3).
5. The contractor produced at least one ten-week "look-ahead" schedule that addressed the work on the piers and described the specific sequence for this work, including the piles, pile caps, pier columns, and pier caps (from Figure 5.4).
6. The contractor anticipated a two-week duration for the forming, reinforcing, and placing of each of the concrete deck spans (from Figure 5.5).
7. The contractor expected four-week durations for each of the abutments and two-week durations for each of the approaches (from Figure 5.6).

Based on the above information, the analyst can proceed with the analysis, despite the lack of a complete as-planned schedule.

When no schedule exists for a project, there is the strong temptation for the analyst to create an "after the fact" schedule, reasoning that it will allow the analysis to be more precise. Although the next chapter addresses this situation in more detail, note that it is best *not* to create such a schedule. This practice will bias the analysis and may not reflect the contractor's true planned sequence of work.

Special Conditions of the Contract – West Street Bridge – Section 1.01, paragraph 5.a:

In staging its work the contractor must complete all abutment construction activities prior to any paving of the approaches on both the east and west sides of the bridge.

Special Conditions of the Contract – West Street Bridge – Section 0.01, paragraph 3.b.:

TIME FOR COMPLETION: All contract work must be completed by the middle of the 24th week after the Notice to Proceed.

Figure 5.1

June 15, 1990

John Lewis
Owner's Representative
Job Trailer
West Street Bridge
Podunk, New York 00001

Dear Mr. Lewis:

As we discussed yesterday during our meeting, we plan to work our construction operations on the West Street Bridge from an east to west direction. In other words, we will construct abutment #1 first, and then abutment #2. Our paving of the approaches will follow the same sequence.

Similarly, our operations on the piers will progress from an east to west direction, starting with pier #1 and progressing through pier #3.

I trust this answers the question you raised, and you can notify the Township authorities accordingly so that they may effect the appropriate detours during the course of the project.

Sincerely,

Joe Super
Ace Construction

Figure 5.2a

August 20, 1990

Mr. Joe Super
Ace Construction
Job Trailer/West Street Bridge
Podunk, New York   00001

Dear Mr. Super:

Returned herein are the shop drawings submitted by Ace
Construction for the reinforcing steel for the pier caps.
As you will note, the drawings are approved as noted.
Fabrication of the reinforcing steel can begin in
accordance with the corrections noted.

I must note that these drawings are being returned to
you five weeks later than you requested. There are two
reasons why the return of the shop drawings is five weeks
beyond your requested date. First, you did not allow the
engineer adequate time to review the drawings. As a
minimum, the engineer requires three weeks to review
submissions. However, the timing of your submission allowed
only one week if they were to be returned within the time
frame requested. Second, the drawings were not prepared in
accordance with normal shop drawing practices and
consequently required much more time to review. As
submitted, the drawings were extremely difficult to
understand. While the engineer could have returned them
disapproved and required resubmission in the proper manner,
it was decided to take the extra time to correct them on
the first submission in order to expedite the process.

If you have any questions, please feel free to call.

Sincerely,

John Lewis
Owner's Representative

Figure 5.2b

June 25, 1990

Mr. Grey Ferrous
Ferrous Steel Erectors
Iron Street
Steeltown, New York 00002

Dear Mr. Ferrous:

In accordance with our previous conversations, Ace Construction will require the delivery and erection of the steel for the West Street Bridge to begin by the beginning of the 13th week of the project. Based on your present fabrication schedule, it appears that this should not be a problem.

Please be advised that time is of the essence on this contract. In the past, we have had problems with steel suppliers promising delivery dates and not adhering to them. Action such as this will not be tolerated on this project. Your delivery and erection of steel is critical to our timely completion of the project.

Sincerely,

Joe Super
Ace Construction

Figure 5.3

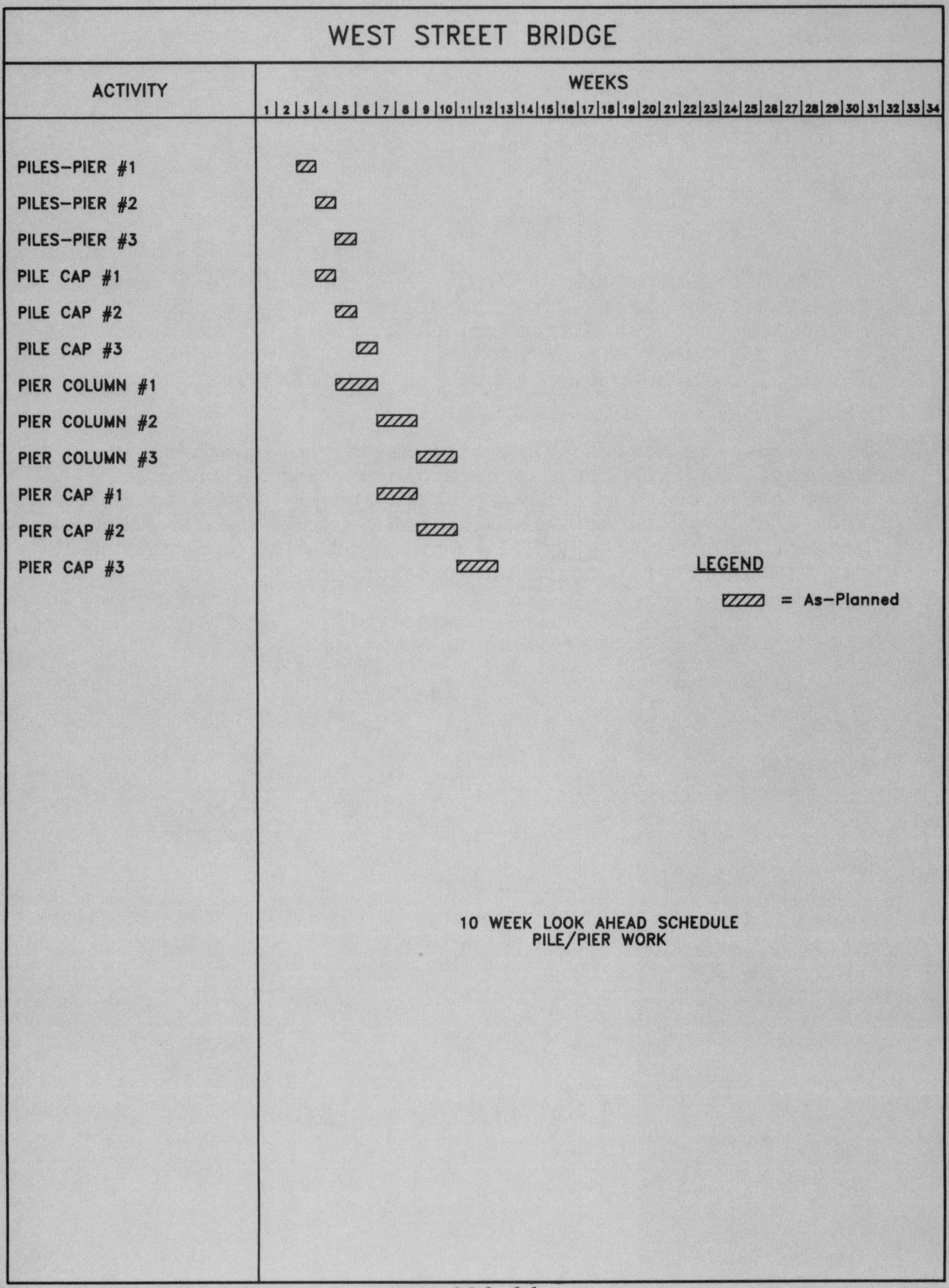

WEST STREET BRIDGE

ACTIVITY	WEEKS
	1 2 3 4 5 6 7 8 9 10 11 12 13 14 15 16 17 18 19 20 21 22 23 24 25 26 27 28 29 30 31 32 33 34
PILES—PIER #1	▨
PILES—PIER #2	▨
PILES—PIER #3	▨
PILE CAP #1	▨
PILE CAP #2	▨
PILE CAP #3	▨
PIER COLUMN #1	▨
PIER COLUMN #2	▨
PIER COLUMN #3	▨
PIER CAP #1	▨
PIER CAP #2	▨
PIER CAP #3	▨

LEGEND

▨ = As—Planned

10 WEEK LOOK AHEAD SCHEDULE
PILE/PIER WORK

Partial Schedule

Figure 5.4

Preconstruction Meeting Minutes

(Excerpt)

Contractor noted that the forming, reinforcing, and placing of the concrete deck spans will take two weeks per span. Contractor will proceed from east to west constructing span #1 through span #4.

Figure 5.5

Inspector's Daily Diary
(Excerpt)

During discussion today with Joe Super (Ace Construction), he noted that the abutment work would take about four weeks to perform for each abutment, and the paving of the approaches would take about two weeks for each side of the bridge. Joe noted that the existing abutment sills are acceptable as shown on the contract drawings. Therefore, they can accept the steel as is. The remainder of the work on the abutments can be performed either before the steel is in place or after it is set. He is going to try to have the abutments completed before he sets any steel, since the work will be easier that way. However, he is concerned about the lead time allowed for obtaining the epoxy material called for in the contract. He said that if necessary, he would set the steel so as not to delay the deck work which he feels controls his completion on the job.

Figure 5.6

As-Built Analysis

Although no as-planned schedule exists for this project, detailed daily reports do exist. Daily reports allow the analyst to prepare an as-built schedule for the job. The as-built schedule for the example project based on the daily reports appears in Figure 5.7.

In reviewing the as-built schedule, the first obvious conclusion is that the project was delayed seven and one half weeks. It was to be completed by the middle of the 24th week, but was not actually finished until the end of the 31st week. Therefore, the analyst must account for at least seven and one half weeks of delay. The delay could, in fact, be greater if the contractor had planned to finish the project early. However, no such plans were indicated in the project correspondence, so this assumption will not be made.

The as-built schedule also reveals that the contractor did work from east to west as planned.

Based on the letter to Ferrous Steel Erectors (Figure 5.3), the contractor planned to start steel erection at the beginning of the 13th week. The as-built schedule (Figure 5.7) shows that steel erection began at the beginning of the 18th week. A five-week delay can be identified for the start of the steel erection.

Following this conclusion, the analyst breaks down the activities that precede the start of steel erection. The analyst uses the ten-week "look-ahead" schedule from Figure 5.4 which the contractor produced at the end of the second week of the project. A comparison of this schedule with the as-built schedule for this portion of the project shows that a delay occurred to the construction of the pier caps. A delay also appears in the construction of pier column # 3, which took three weeks instead of two weeks to complete.

The comparison of the partial look-ahead schedule with the as-built portion is shown in Figure 5.8. Based on this comparison, it seems that the controlling delay was the delay to the start of the pier caps. This may have been the result of the five-week delay in approval of the shop drawings to which the owner's representative had referred in correspondence (Figure 5.2). It does not appear that the delay in the completion of pier column # 3 affected the completion of the project, since the flow of activities in the "look-ahead" schedule (and in the logical construction sequence) would have been in the stair-step fashion depicted.

The remainder of the work along the pier/deck path appears to have been performed in a logical, sequential fashion and does not indicate any further delay. There is, however, a gap between the completion of the curbs and sidewalks and the beginning of the punch list work. Based on the as-built schedule, the punch list work did not start until the abutments and approaches were completed. The abutment and approach work occurred in the sequence planned. However, it delayed the project an additional two and one half weeks, since this is the gap between the completion of the superstructure work and the start of the punch list work. Based on the information available, it can be determined that the abutment/approach work started later than planned, but was performed within the duration planned by the contractor.

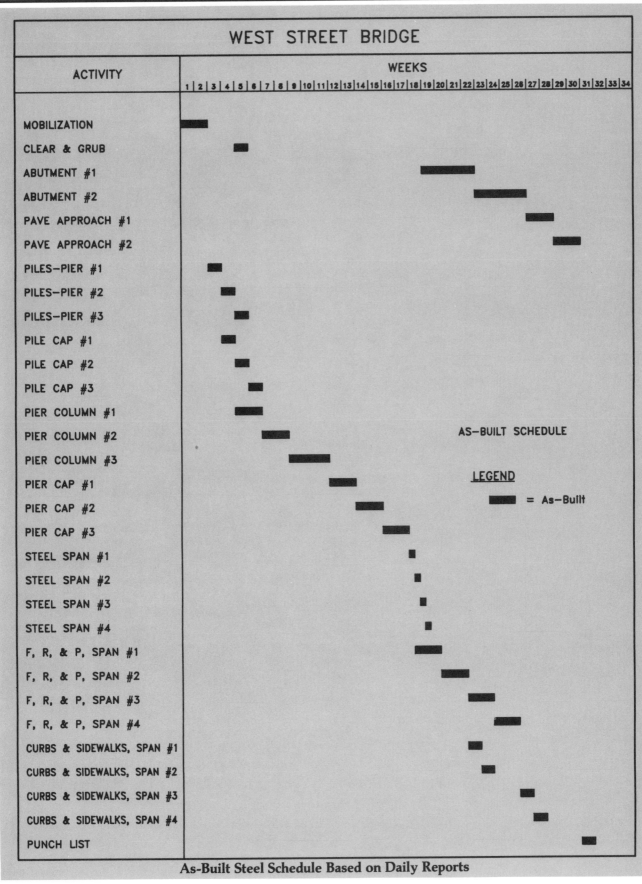

Figure 5.7

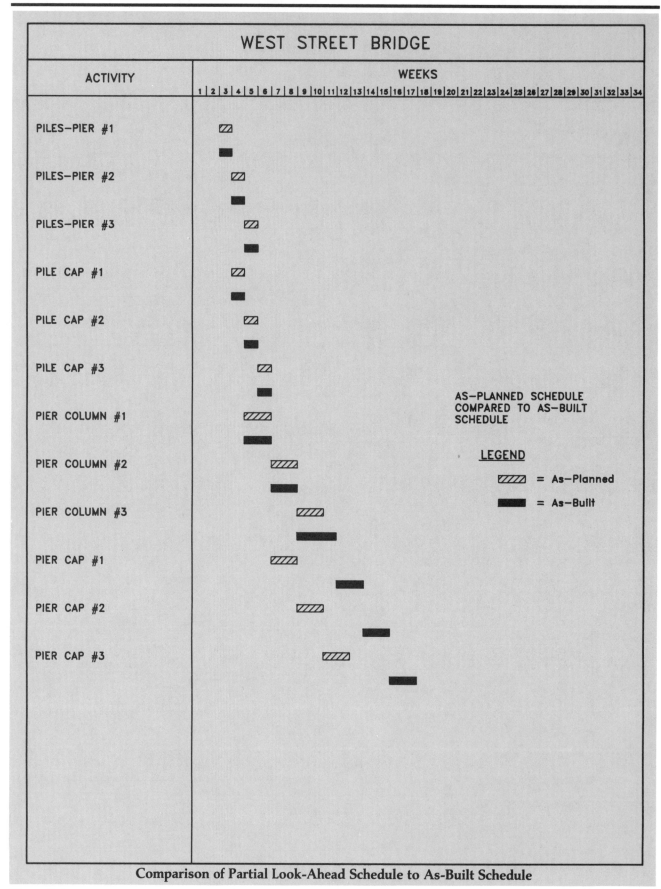

Comparison of Partial Look-Ahead Schedule to As-Built Schedule

Figure 5.8

A summary of the delays appears in Figure 5.9. The delay of seven and one half weeks is comprised of the following:

- Five weeks of delay to the start of the pier cap work.
- Two and one half weeks of delay to the start of the abutment/approach work.

At this point in the analysis, the analyst should again carefully review the project documentation to find out if any other supporting information is available to further substantiate the delay analysis. Also at this point, the analyst can begin to assess the reasons or causes for the delay, and thereby establish liability for the delays.

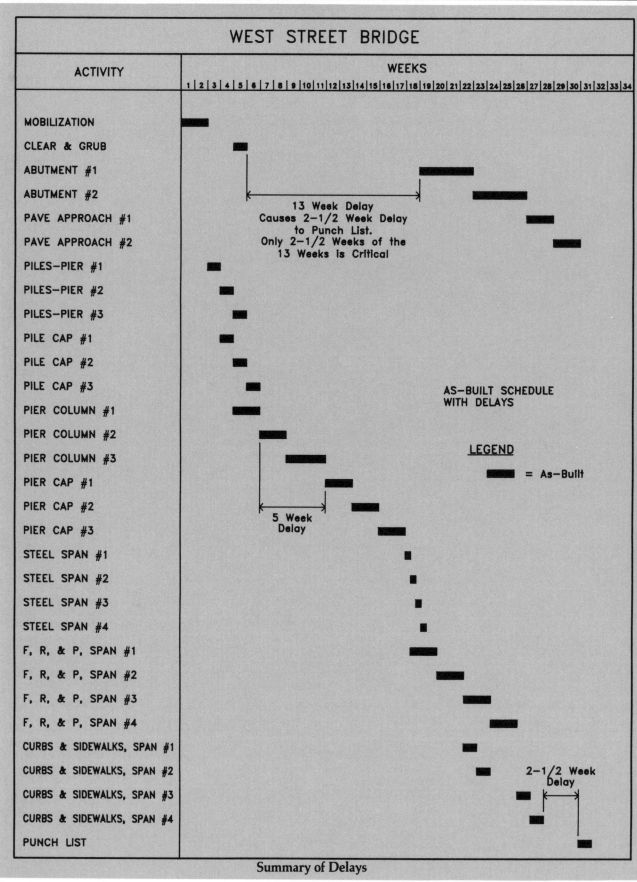

Figure 5.9

Chapter Six

Problematic Analysis Techniques

Chapter Six
Problematic Analysis Techniques

The preceding chapters have explained and demonstrated how a delay analysis *should* be performed. The fact is that analysts also use other techniques, in an attempt to quantify delays and justify time extensions and delay damages. This chapter addresses the more prevalent, but faulty, alternative approaches currently used to analyze delays. It is not recommended that any of these techniques be used, since they have shortcomings that may well render them useless. However, they are included because it is important that the reader understand the drawbacks of these methods, and why they should not be used or accepted.

Impacted As-Planned Analysis

Some analysts prefer to present a delay analysis in the form of an impacted as-planned analysis. In this approach, the analyst defines an as-planned schedule and then incorporates into this schedule the changes that have allegedly caused delays. The source for these changes is only the delays noted during construction that may have affected project time. This method does not update the schedule using actual as-built information, and there is no comparison of the "impacted" schedule with the actual as-built information. This is the major weakness of this type of analysis.

Clearly, if all the changes that affected the schedule are not put into the impacted schedule analysis, the results will be biased. Unfortunately, the analyst cannot always identify from the project documentation all circumstances that affected the schedule.

Events that are never mentioned in any project documentation can affect the schedule. For example, a specific activity might have a longer-than-planned duration. If this extended duration is not noted on the schedule as an "impact," then its effects will not be measured. In the methodology described in the preceding chapters, an extended duration would be accounted for by updating the schedule with the actual as-built durations (from contemporaneous documentation, such as the daily reports).

Some analysts like the impacted as-planned approach because it is simple and "clean." It allows them to present schedules showing one impact at a time so they can "demonstrate" how the project completion date is being delayed. They then proceed to each succeeding delay, inserting a new impact each time to show how the project end date is extended by each impact.

While this method is indeed "clean," it is also highly inaccurate. By using the first schedule, this method "freezes" the critical path at the beginning of the project, and thus, shifts in the critical path are not likely to be recognized. A simple project with a series of consecutive activities appears in Figure 6.1 to demonstrate this method.

Activities A through F must be performed in sequence, and are scheduled for the durations shown. Concurrently, but not until after the completion of activity B, there is another sequence of consecutive activities consisting of G through I with the respective durations shown.

The total project duration is thirty-five days. On day fifteen, the contractor modifies its work and adds another activity, J, immediately after activity I. Activity J has a duration of three days. This addition is shown in Figure 6.2. From the initial schedule perspective, the critical path has not changed; it still depends on activities A through F.

The project is actually completed in forty days—five days late. The as-built information for the project appears in Figure 6.3, plotted against the original as-planned schedule. A review of the as-built data shows that activity A started three days late. Activity C started six days early and out of sequence. Activity F took eight days longer to complete than planned. Activity J took four days longer than planned. All other activities started in sequence and were performed in the time frames originally scheduled.

The impacted as-planned approach would show the following results:

1. Figure 6.4—project delayed by three days because of the late start of activity A.
2. Figure 6.5—project ahead of schedule by three days because of the early start of activity C.
3. Figure 6.6—project delayed a total of five days due to the extended duration of activity F.

Therefore, the overall conclusion is that the project was delayed by five days, primarily because of the late finish of activity F. This conclusion is erroneous.

Using the analysis method presented in Chapter 2, the schedule is instead updated as of day fifteen, the day the contractor added activity J. The results appear in Figure 6.7. This update shows that the project is behind schedule by one day because of the delay to activity A, and that the critical path has shifted to the Phase II path of activities, G through J. This path then controls the remainder of the project and all five days of delay. The original critical path never becomes critical again.

In this case, the impacted as-planned approach for the entire project clearly leads to the wrong conclusion. The following additional example is presented to show how grossly inaccurate the impacted as-planned approach can be.

Example

The network diagram presented in Chapter 2 will again be used, and is shown in Figure 6.8. The original CPM mathematical calculation for this network is shown in Figures 6.9 and 6.10, which are the *I-J* and *total float sorts*.

In this example, the contractor is presenting a delay claim to the owner, using the impacted as-planned approach. In its claim, the contractor has noted two items that have allegedly delayed the job:

1. Late approval by the owner of the shop drawings for the reinforcing steel for the pier caps
2. A change in the design for the curbs and sidewalks

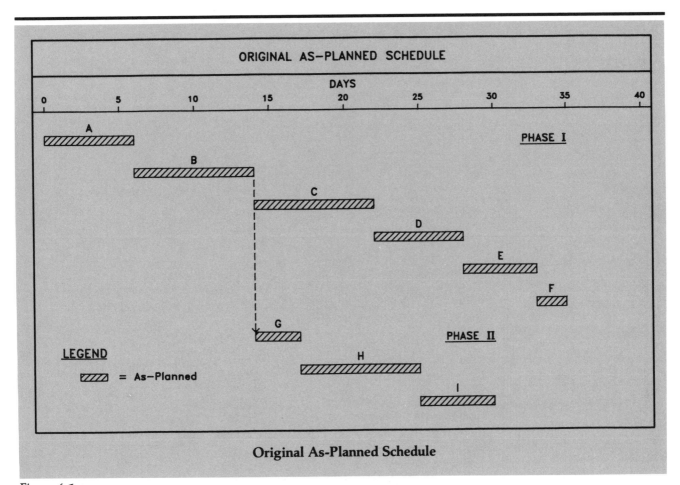

Original As-Planned Schedule

Figure 6.1

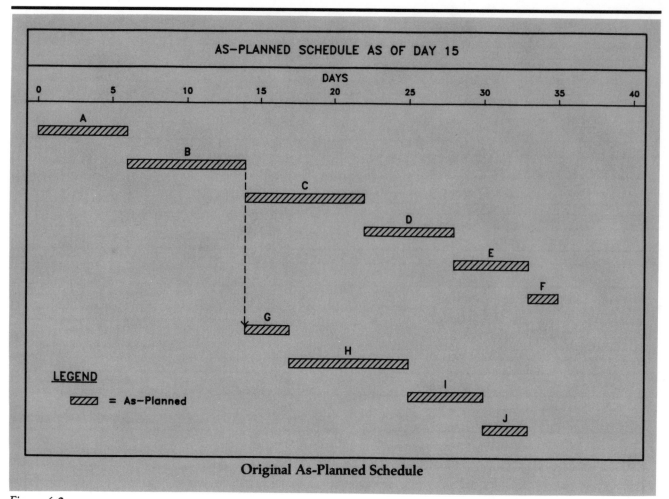

Original As-Planned Schedule

Figure 6.2

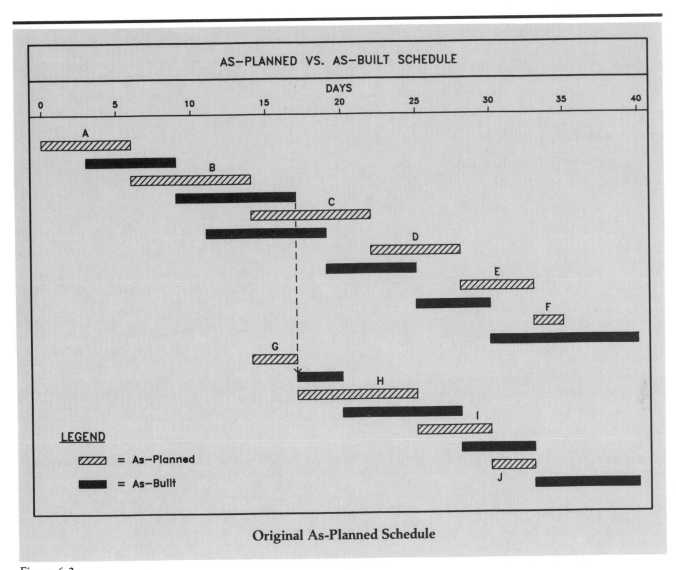

Original As-Planned Schedule

Figure 6.3

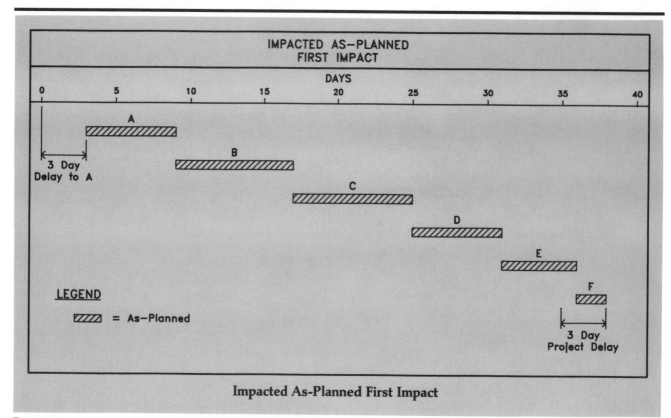

Figure 6.4

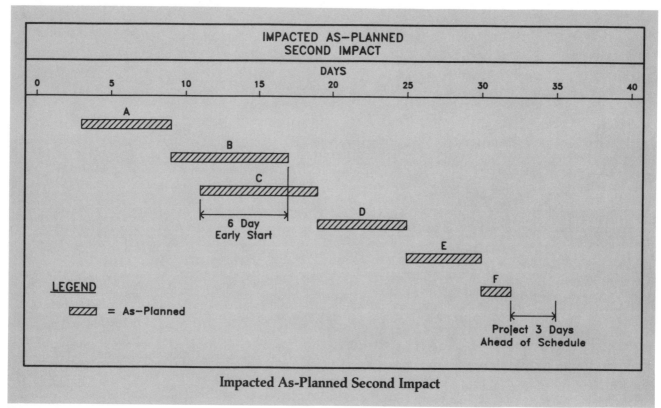

Figure 6.5

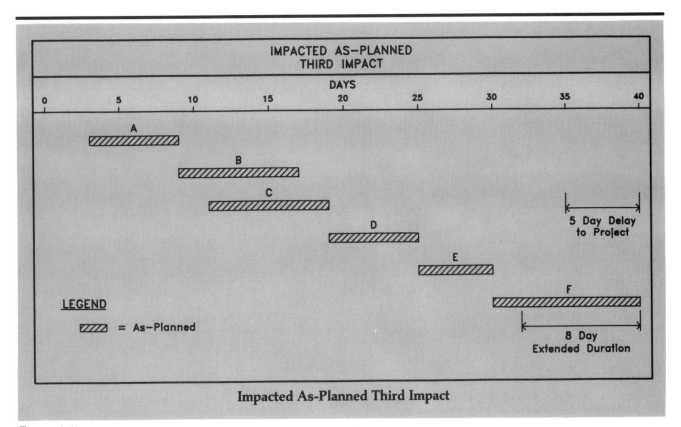

Impacted As-Planned Third Impact

Figure 6.6

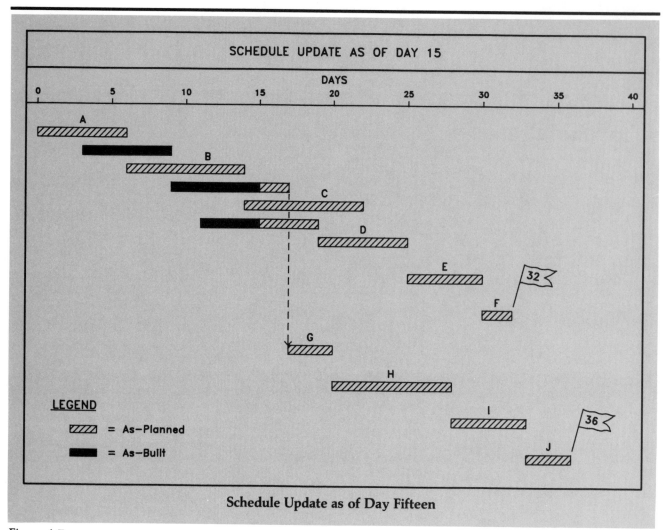

Schedule Update as of Day Fifteen

Figure 6.7

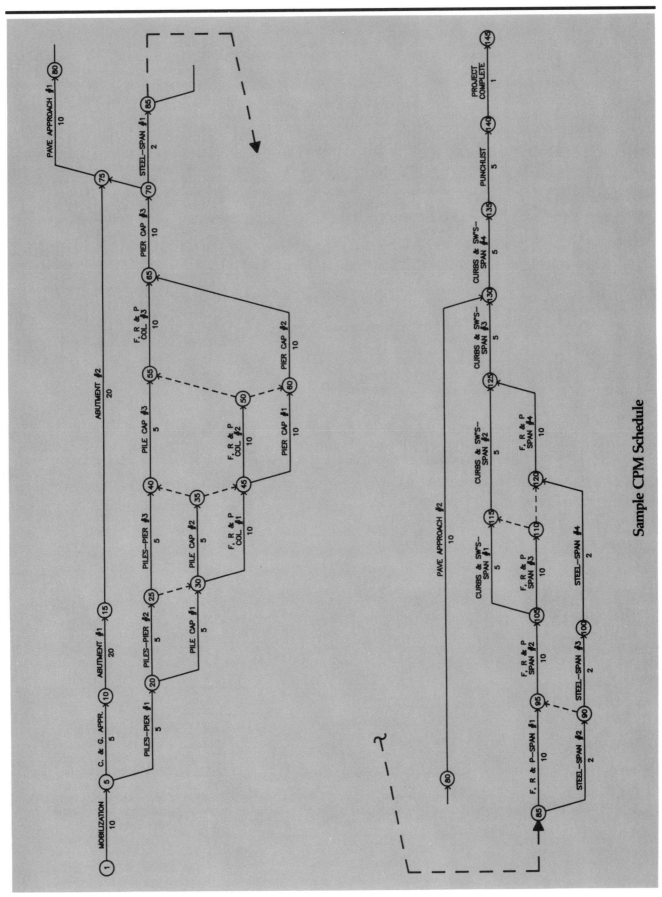

Figure 6.8

Sample CPM Schedule

ACME CONSTRUCTION, INC.   PRIMAVERA PROJECT PLANNER   WEST STREET BRIDGE

REPORT DATE 23OCT89 RUN NO.   6   WEST STREET BRIDGE - CPM SCHEDULE   START DATE 5MAY89 FIN DATE 20OCT89
                  12:49
I-J SORT   DATA DATE   5MAY89 PAGE NO.   1

PRED	SUCC	ORIG DUR	REM DUR	CAL	%	CODE	ACTIVITY DESCRIPTION	EARLY START	EARLY FINISH	LATE START	LATE FINISH	TOTAL FLOAT
1	5	10	10	1	0		MOBILIZATION	5MAY89	18MAY89	5MAY89	18MAY89	0
5	10	5	5	1	0		CLEAR & GRUB APPROACHES	19MAY89	25MAY89	6JUL89	12JUL89	32
5	20	5	5	1	0		PILES - PIER #1	19MAY89	25MAY89	19MAY89	25MAY89	0
10	15	20	20	1	0		CONSTRUCT ABUTMENT #1	26MAY89	23JUN89	13JUL89	9AUG89	32
15	75	20	20	1	0		CONSTRUCT ABUTMENT #2	26JUN89	24JUL89	10AUG89	7SEP89	32
20	25	5	5	1	0		PILES - PIER #2	26MAY89	2JUN89	26MAY89	2JUN89	0
20	30	5	5	1	0		PILE CAP #1	26MAY89	2JUN89	26MAY89	2JUN89	0
25	30	0	0	1	0		DUMMY	5JUN89	2JUN89	5JUN89	2JUN89	0
25	40	5	5	1	0		PILES - PIER #3	5JUN89	9JUN89	19JUN89	23JUN89	10
30	35	5	5	1	0		PILE CAP #2	5JUN89	9JUN89	12JUN89	16JUN89	5
30	45	10	10	1	0		FORM, REIN. & POUR - COLUMN #1	5JUN89	16JUN89	5JUN89	16JUN89	0
35	40	0	0	1	0		DUMMY	12JUN89	9JUN89	26JUN89	23JUN89	10
35	45	0	0	1	0		DUMMY	12JUN89	9JUN89	19JUN89	16JUN89	5
40	55	5	5	1	0		PILE CAP #3	12JUN89	16JUN89	26JUN89	30JUN89	10
45	50	10	10	1	0		FORM, REIN. & POUR - COLUMN #2	19JUN89	30JUN89	19JUN89	30JUN89	0
45	60	10	10	1	0		PIER CAP #1	19JUN89	30JUN89	19JUN89	30JUN89	0
50	55	0	0	1	0		DUMMY	3JUL89	30JUN89	3JUL89	30JUN89	0
55	65	10	10	1	0		FORM, REIN. & POUR - COLUMN #3	3JUL89	17JUL89	3JUL89	17JUL89	0
60	65	10	10	1	0		PIER CAP #2	3JUL89	17JUL89	3JUL89	17JUL89	0
65	70	10	10	1	0		PIER CAP #3	18JUL89	31JUL89	18JUL89	31JUL89	0
70	75	0	0	1	0		DUMMY	1AUG89	31JUL89	8SEP89	7SEP89	27
70	85	2	2	1	0		STEEL - SPAN 1	1AUG89	2AUG89	1AUG89	2AUG89	0
75	80	10	10	1	0		PAVE APPROACH #1	1AUG89	14AUG89	8SEP89	21SEP89	27
80	130	10	10	1	0		PAVE APPROACH #2	15AUG89	28AUG89	22SEP89	5OCT89	27
85	90	2	2	1	0		STEEL - SPAN 2	3AUG89	4AUG89	15AUG89	16AUG89	8
85	95	10	10	1	0		FORM, REIN, & POUR - SPAN 1	3AUG89	16AUG89	3AUG89	16AUG89	0
90	95	0	0	1	0		DUMMY	7AUG89	4AUG89	17AUG89	16AUG89	8
90	100	2	2	1	0		STEEL - SPAN 3	7AUG89	8AUG89	11SEP89	12SEP89	24
95	105	10	10	1	0		FORM, REIN. & POUR - SPAN 2	17AUG89	30AUG89	17AUG89	30AUG89	0
100	120	2	2	1	0		STEEL - SPAN 4	9AUG89	10AUG89	13SEP89	14SEP89	24
105	110	10	10	1	0		FORM, REIN. & POUR - SPAN 3	31AUG89	14SEP89	31AUG89	14SEP89	0
105	115	5	5	1	0		CURBS & SIDEWALKS - SPAN 1	31AUG89	7SEP89	15SEP89	21SEP89	10
110	115	0	0	1	0		DUMMY	15SEP89	14SEP89	22SEP89	21SEP89	5
110	120	0	0	1	0		DUMMY	15SEP89	14SEP89	15SEP89	14SEP89	0
115	125	5	5	1	0		CURBS & SIDEWALKS - SPAN 2	15SEP89	21SEP89	22SEP89	28SEP89	5
120	125	10	10	1	0		FORM, REIN. & POUR - SPAN 4	15SEP89	28SEP89	15SEP89	28SEP89	0
125	130	5	5	1	0		CURBS & SIDEWALKS - SPAN 3	29SEP89	5OCT89	29SEP89	5OCT89	0
130	135	5	5	1	0		CURBS & SIDEWALKS - SPAN 4	6OCT89	12OCT89	6OCT89	12OCT89	0
135	140	5	5	1	0		PUNCHLIST	13OCT89	19OCT89	13OCT89	19OCT89	0
140	145	1	1	1	0		PROJECT COMPLETE	20OCT89	20OCT89	20OCT89	20OCT89	0

Figure 6.9

ACME CONSTRUCTION, INC.   PRIMAVERA PROJECT PLANNER   WEST STREET BRIDGE

REPORT DATE 23OCT89 RUN NO.   5   WEST STREET BRIDGE - CPM SCHEDULE   START DATE 5MAY89 FIN DATE 20OCT89
            12:49
TOTAL FLOAT/ES   DATA DATE   5MAY89 PAGE NO.   1

PRED	SUCC	ORIG DUR	REM DUR	CAL	%	CODE	ACTIVITY DESCRIPTION	EARLY START	EARLY FINISH	LATE START	LATE FINISH	TOTAL FLOAT
1	5	10	10	1	0		MOBILIZATION	5MAY89	18MAY89	5MAY89	18MAY89	0
5	20	5	5	1	0		PILES - PIER #1	19MAY89	25MAY89	19MAY89	25MAY89	0
20	25	5	5	1	0		PILES - PIER #2	26MAY89	2JUN89	26MAY89	2JUN89	0
20	30	5	5	1	0		PILE CAP #1	26MAY89	2JUN89	26MAY89	2JUN89	0
25	30	0	0	1	0		DUMMY	5JUN89	2JUN89	5JUN89	2JUN89	0
30	45	10	10	1	0		FORM, REIN. & POUR - COLUMN #1	5JUN89	16JUN89	5JUN89	16JUN89	0
45	50	10	10	1	0		FORM, REIN. & POUR - COLUMN #2	19JUN89	30JUN89	19JUN89	30JUN89	0
45	60	10	10	1	0		PIER CAP #1	19JUN89	30JUN89	19JUN89	30JUN89	0
50	55	0	0	1	0		DUMMY	3JUL89	30JUN89	3JUL89	30JUN89	0
55	65	10	10	1	0		FORM, REIN. & POUR - COLUMN #3	3JUL89	17JUL89	3JUL89	17JUL89	0
60	65	10	10	1	0		PIER CAP #2	3JUL89	17JUL89	3JUL89	17JUL89	0
65	70	10	10	1	0		PIER CAP #3	18JUL89	31JUL89	18JUL89	31JUL89	0
70	85	2	2	1	0		STEEL - SPAN 1	1AUG89	2AUG89	1AUG89	2AUG89	0
85	95	10	10	1	0		FORM, REIN, & POUR - SPAN 1	3AUG89	16AUG89	3AUG89	16AUG89	0
95	105	10	10	1	0		FORM, REIN, & POUR - SPAN 2	17AUG89	30AUG89	17AUG89	30AUG89	0
105	110	10	10	1	0		FORM, REIN, & POUR - SPAN 3	31AUG89	14SEP89	31AUG89	14SEP89	0
110	120	0	0	1	0		DUMMY	15SEP89	14SEP89	15SEP89	14SEP89	0
120	125	10	10	1	0		FORM, REIN, & POUR - SPAN 4	15SEP89	28SEP89	15SEP89	28SEP89	0
125	130	5	5	1	0		CURBS & SIDEWALKS - SPAN 3	29SEP89	5OCT89	29SEP89	5OCT89	0
130	135	5	5	1	0		CURBS & SIDEWALKS - SPAN 4	6OCT89	12OCT89	6OCT89	12OCT89	0
135	140	5	5	1	0		PUNCHLIST	13OCT89	19OCT89	13OCT89	19OCT89	0
140	145	1	1	1	0		PROJECT COMPLETE	20OCT89	20OCT89	20OCT89	20OCT89	0
30	35	5	5	1	0		PILE CAP #2	5JUN89	9JUN89	12JUN89	16JUN89	5
35	45	0	0	1	0		DUMMY	12JUN89	9JUN89	19JUN89	16JUN89	5
110	115	0	0	1	0		DUMMY	15SEP89	14SEP89	22SEP89	21SEP89	5
115	125	5	5	1	0		CURBS & SIDEWALKS - SPAN 2	15SEP89	21SEP89	22SEP89	28SEP89	5
85	90	2	2	1	0		STEEL - SPAN 2	3AUG89	4AUG89	15AUG89	16AUG89	8
90	95	0	0	1	0		DUMMY	7AUG89	4AUG89	17AUG89	16AUG89	8
25	40	5	5	1	0		PILES - PIER #3	5JUN89	9JUN89	19JUN89	23JUN89	10
35	40	0	0	1	0		DUMMY	12JUN89	9JUN89	26JUN89	23JUN89	10
40	55	5	5	1	0		PILE CAP #3	12JUN89	16JUN89	26JUN89	30JUN89	10
105	115	5	5	1	0		CURBS & SIDEWALKS - SPAN 1	31AUG89	7SEP89	15SEP89	21SEP89	10
90	100	2	2	1	0		STEEL - SPAN 3	7AUG89	8AUG89	11SEP89	12SEP89	24
100	120	2	2	1	0		STEEL - SPAN 4	9AUG89	10AUG89	13SEP89	14SEP89	24
70	75	0	0	1	0		DUMMY	1AUG89	31JUL89	8SEP89	7SEP89	27
75	80	10	10	1	0		PAVE APPROACH #1	1AUG89	14AUG89	8SEP89	21SEP89	27
80	130	10	10	1	0		PAVE APPROACH #2	15AUG89	28AUG89	22SEP89	5OCT89	27
5	10	5	5	1	0		CLEAR & GRUB APPROACHES	19MAY89	25MAY89	6JUL89	12JUL89	32
10	15	20	20	1	0		CONSTRUCT ABUTMENT #1	26MAY89	23JUN89	13JUL89	9AUG89	32
15	75	20	20	1	0		CONSTRUCT ABUTMENT #2	26JUN89	24JUL89	10AUG89	7SEP89	32

Figure 6.10

The contractor and his consultant prepare an impacted as-planned analysis to illustrate the effects of these changes. They take the first alleged delay, which is the late approval of the shop drawings for the reinforcing steel for the pier caps, and insert that delay into the original as-planned CPM schedule. They note that pier cap # 1 should have started on June 19, 1989, but the shop drawing delay held up the delivery of the steel until June 23, 1989. Therefore, an "activity" called "Shop Drawing Delay" is inserted in the schedule. It is given node numbers 45–47, and the original pier cap # 1 activity is renumbered, 47–60. The duration of the new "activity" (shop drawing delay) is four workdays, from June 19 to June 23.

The CPM schedule can then be run on the computer to ascertain both the critical path and the new completion date of the project.

Figure 6.11 is the *I-J sort* and Figure 6.12 is the *total float sort* for this first impacted as-planned schedule. As the schedule indicates and as the contractor claims, the project was delayed four workdays, or six calendar days, by the delay to the shop drawings.

The contractor then inserts the second delay, allegedly due to the design changes for the curbs and sidewalks, which he claims prevented him from starting the curb and sidewalk construction on the originally scheduled date (September 15, 1989). The owner did not issue the new drawings for the curb and sidewalk detail until September 27, 1989. Even after the first impacted as-planned schedule, the late start date was still September 15, 1989.

To show the impact of this delay, the contractor restrains the start date of this activity and inserts the date of September 27, 1989. Again, the schedule is run on the computer to calculate the critical path and demonstrate the delay to the project. Figures 6.13 and 6.14 are the *I-J* and *total float sorts* for this second impacted as-planned schedule. As the update shows, the project is now eight workdays or twelve calendar days behind schedule, with a new completion date of November 1, 1989. This is an additional four workdays, or six calendar days of delay, attributed to the design change to the curbs and sidewalks.

While the above presentation certainly *appears* believable and seems convincing, it is actually quite erroneous. Recall that in previous examples with this same schedule, the schedule was updated with actual as-built information. The applicable updates appear in Figures 6.15 and 6.16. The alleged impacts had absolutely no effect on the project whatsoever and did not delay the critical path or the project completion date. The update of June 22, 1989 shows that the critical path is through Activity 30-45, "Form, Reinforce & Pour–Column # 1." The pier cap activity has an early start date of June 29, 1989. Therefore, no delay was caused by the shop drawing problem. The update of August 20, 1989 shows that "Curbs & Sidewalks–Span 1" (Activity 105–115) has an early start date of October 2, 1989, well after the September 27 alleged date of delay.

With the impacted as-planned approach, changes in the critical path are not likely to be discovered. There is also the risk that the impacted schedule does not reflect the reality of time on the project. The impacted as-planned approach may show delays on specific dates which are inconsistent with actual as-built information.

ACME CONSTRUCTION, INC.   PRIMAVERA PROJECT PLANNER   WEST STREET BRIDGE

REPORT DATE 17OCT89 RUN NO.   3   WEST STREET BRIDGE - CPM SCHEDULE   START DATE 5MAY89 FIN DATE 20OCT89*
                12:41
I-J SORT   DATA DATE   5MAY89 PAGE NO.   1

PRED	SUCC	ORIG DUR	REM DUR	CAL	%	CODE	ACTIVITY DESCRIPTION	EARLY START	EARLY FINISH	LATE START	LATE FINISH	TOTAL FLOAT
1	5	10	10	1	0		MOBILIZATION	5MAY89	18MAY89	1MAY89	12MAY89	-4
5	10	5	5	1	0		CLEAR & GRUB APPROACHES	19MAY89	25MAY89	6JUL89	12JUL89	32
5	20	5	5	1	0		PILES - PIER #1	19MAY89	25MAY89	15MAY89	19MAY89	-4
10	15	20	20	1	0		CONSTRUCT ABUTMENT #1	26MAY89	23JUN89	13JUL89	9AUG89	32
15	75	20	20	1	0		CONSTRUCT ABUTMENT #2	26JUN89	24JUL89	10AUG89	7SEP89	32
20	25	5	5	1	0		PILES - PIER #2	26MAY89	2JUN89	22MAY89	26MAY89	-4
20	30	5	5	1	0		PILE CAP #1	26MAY89	2JUN89	22MAY89	26MAY89	-4
25	30	0	0	1	0		DUMMY	5JUN89	2JUN89	30MAY89	26MAY89	-4
25	40	5	5	1	0		PILES - PIER #3	5JUN89	9JUN89	19JUN89	23JUN89	10
30	35	5	5	1	0		PILE CAP #2	5JUN89	9JUN89	6JUN89	12JUN89	1
30	45	10	10	1	0		FORM, REIN. & POUR - COLUMN #1	5JUN89	16JUN89	30MAY89	12JUN89	-4
35	40	0	0	1	0		DUMMY	12JUN89	9JUN89	26JUN89	23JUN89	10
35	45	0	0	1	0		DUMMY	12JUN89	9JUN89	13JUN89	12JUN89	1
40	55	5	5	1	0		PILE CAP #3	12JUN89	16JUN89	26JUN89	30JUN89	10
45	47	4	4	1	0		SHOP DRAWING DELAY	19JUN89	22JUN89	13JUN89	16JUN89	-4
45	50	10	10	1	0		FORM, REIN. & POUR - COLUMN #2	19JUN89	30JUN89	19JUN89	30JUN89	0
47	60	10	10	1	0		PIER CAP #1	23JUN89	7JUL89	19JUN89	30JUN89	-4
50	55	0	0	1	0		DUMMY	3JUL89	30JUN89	3JUL89	30JUN89	0
55	65	10	10	1	0		FORM, REIN. & POUR - COLUMN #3	3JUL89	17JUL89	3JUL89	17JUL89	0
60	65	10	10	1	0		PIER CAP #2	10JUL89	21JUL89	3JUL89	17JUL89	-4
65	70	10	10	1	0		PIER CAP #3	24JUL89	4AUG89	18JUL89	31JUL89	-4
70	75	0	0	1	0		DUMMY	7AUG89	4AUG89	8SEP89	7SEP89	23
70	85	2	2	1	0		STEEL - SPAN 1	7AUG89	8AUG89	1AUG89	2AUG89	-4
75	80	10	10	1	0		PAVE APPROACH #1	7AUG89	18AUG89	8SEP89	21SEP89	23
80	130	10	10	1	0		PAVE APPROACH #2	21AUG89	1SEP89	22SEP89	5OCT89	23
85	90	2	2	1	0		STEEL - SPAN 2	9AUG89	10AUG89	15AUG89	16AUG89	4
85	95	10	10	1	0		FORM, REIN. & POUR - SPAN 1	9AUG89	22AUG89	3AUG89	16AUG89	-4
90	95	0	0	1	0		DUMMY	11AUG89	10AUG89	17AUG89	16AUG89	4
90	100	2	2	1	0		STEEL - SPAN 3	11AUG89	14AUG89	11SEP89	12SEP89	20
95	105	10	10	1	0		FORM, REIN. & POUR - SPAN 2	23AUG89	6SEP89	17AUG89	30AUG89	-4
100	120	2	2	1	0		STEEL - SPAN 4	15AUG89	16AUG89	13SEP89	14SEP89	20
105	110	10	10	1	0		FORM, REIN. & POUR - SPAN 3	7SEP89	20SEP89	31AUG89	14SEP89	-4
105	115	5	5	1	0		CURBS & SIDEWALKS - SPAN 1	27SEP89*	3OCT89	15SEP89	21SEP89	-8
110	115	0	0	1	0		DUMMY	21SEP89	20SEP89	22SEP89	21SEP89	1
110	120	0	0	1	0		DUMMY	21SEP89	20SEP89	15SEP89	14SEP89	-4
115	125	5	5	1	0		CURBS & SIDEWALKS - SPAN 2	4OCT89	10OCT89	22SEP89	28SEP89	-8
120	125	10	10	1	0		FORM, REIN. & POUR - SPAN 4	21SEP89	4OCT89	15SEP89	28SEP89	-4
125	130	5	5	1	0		CURBS & SIDEWALKS - SPAN 3	11OCT89	17OCT89	29SEP89	5OCT89	-8
130	135	5	5	1	0		CURBS & SIDEWALKS - SPAN		24OCT89	6OCT89	12OCT89	-8
135	140	5	5	1	0		PUNCHLIST		31OCT89	13OCT89	19OCT89	-8
140	145	1	1	1	0		PROJECT COMPLETE		1NOV89	20OCT89	20OCT89	-8

Figure 6.11

ACME CONSTRUCTION, INC.   PRIMAVERA PROJECT PLANNER   WEST STREET BRIDGE

REPORT DATE 17OCT89 RUN NO.   8   WEST STREET BRIDGE - CPM SCHEDULE   START DATE 5MAY89 FIN DATE 20OCT89*
             12:52
TOTAL FLOAT SORT   DATA DATE   5MAY89 PAGE NO.   1

PRED	SUCC	ORIG DUR	REM DUR	CAL	%	CODE	ACTIVITY DESCRIPTION	EARLY START	EARLY FINISH	LATE START	LATE FINISH	TOTAL FLOAT
1	5	10	10	1	0		MOBILIZATION	5MAY89	18MAY89	1MAY89	12MAY89	-4
5	20	5	5	1	0		PILES - PIER #1	19MAY89	25MAY89	15MAY89	19MAY89	-4
20	25	5	5	1	0		PILES - PIER #2	26MAY89	2JUN89	22MAY89	26MAY89	-4
20	30	5	5	1	0		PILE CAP #1	26MAY89	2JUN89	22MAY89	26MAY89	-4
25	30	0	0	1	0		DUMMY	5JUN89	2JUN89	30MAY89	26MAY89	-4
30	45	10	10	1	0		FORM, REIN. & POUR - COLUMN #1	5JUN89	16JUN89	30MAY89	12JUN89	-4
45	47	4	4	1	0		SHOP DRAWING DELAY	19JUN89	22JUN89	13JUN89	16JUN89	-4
47	60	10	10	1	0		PIER CAP #1	23JUN89	7JUL89	19JUN89	30JUN89	-4
60	65	10	10	1	0		PIER CAP #2	10JUL89	21JUL89	3JUL89	17JUL89	-4
65	70	10	10	1	0		PIER CAP #3	24JUL89	4AUG89	18JUL89	31JUL89	-4
70	85	2	2	1	0		STEEL - SPAN 1	7AUG89	8AUG89	1AUG89	2AUG89	-4
85	95	10	10	1	0		FORM, REIN. & POUR - SPAN 1	9AUG89	22AUG89	3AUG89	16AUG89	-4
95	105	10	10	1	0		FORM, REIN. & POUR - SPAN 2	23AUG89	6SEP89	17AUG89	30AUG89	-4
105	110	10	10	1	0		FORM, REIN. & POUR - SPAN 3	7SEP89	20SEP89	31AUG89	14SEP89	-4
110	120	0	0	1	0		DUMMY	21SEP89	20SEP89	15SEP89	14SEP89	-4
120	125	10	10	1	0		FORM, REIN. & POUR - SPAN 4	21SEP89	4OCT89	15SEP89	28SEP89	-4
125	130	5	5	1	0		CURBS & SIDEWALKS - SPAN 3	5OCT89	11OCT89	29SEP89	5OCT89	-4
130	135	5	5	1	0		CURBS & SIDEWALKS - SPAN 4	12OCT89	18OCT89	6OCT89	12OCT89	-4
135	140	5	5	1	0		PUNCHLIST	19OCT89	25OCT89	13OCT89	19OCT89	-4
140	145	1	1	1	0		PROJECT COMPLETE	26OCT89	26OCT89	20OCT89	20OCT89	-4
45	50	10	10	1	0		FORM, REIN. & POUR - COLUMN #2	19JUN89	30JUN89	19JUN89	30JUN89	0
50	55	0	0	1	0		DUMMY	3JUL89	30JUN89	3JUL89	30JUN89	0
55	65	10	10	1	0		FORM, REIN. & POUR - COLUMN #3	3JUL89	17JUL89	3JUL89	17JUL89	0
30	35	5	5	1	0		PILE CAP #2	5JUN89	9JUN89	6JUN89	12JUN89	1
35	45	0	0	1	0		DUMMY	12JUN89	9JUN89	13JUN89	12JUN89	1
110	115	0	0	1	0		DUMMY	21SEP89	20SEP89	22SEP89	21SEP89	1
115	125	5	5	1	0		CURBS & SIDEWALKS - SPAN 2	21SEP89	27SEP89	22SEP89	28SEP89	1
85	90	2	2	1	0		STEEL - SPAN 2	9AUG89	10AUG89	15AUG89	16AUG89	4
90	95	0	0	1	0		DUMMY	11AUG89	10AUG89	17AUG89	16AUG89	4
105	115	5	5	1	0		CURBS & SIDEWALKS - SPAN 1	7SEP89	13SEP89	15SEP89	21SEP89	6
25	40	5	5	1	0		PILES - PIER #3	5JUN89	9JUN89	19JUN89	23JUN89	10
35	40	0	0	1	0		DUMMY	12JUN89	9JUN89	26JUN89	23JUN89	10
40	55	5	5	1	0		PILE CAP #3	12JUN89	16JUN89	26JUN89	30JUN89	10
90	100	2	2	1	0		STEEL - SPAN 3	11AUG89	14AUG89	11SEP89	12SEP89	20
100	120	2	2	1	0		STEEL - SPAN 4	15AUG89	16AUG89	13SEP89	14SEP89	20
70	75	0	0	1	0		DUMMY	7AUG89	4AUG89	8SEP89	7SEP89	23
75	80	10	10	1	0		PAVE APPROACH #1	7AUG89	18AUG89	8SEP89	21SEP89	23
80	130	10	10	1	0		PAVE APPROACH #2	21AUG89	1SEP89	22SEP89	5OCT89	23
5	10	5	5	1	0		CLEAR & GRUB APPROACHES	19MAY89	25MAY89	6JUL89	12JUL89	32
10	15	20	20	1	0		CONSTRUCT ABUTMENT #1	26MAY89	23JUN89	13JUL89	9AUG89	32
15	75	20	20	1	0		CONSTRUCT ABUTMENT #2	26JUN89	24JUL89	10AUG89	7SEP89	32

Figure 6.12

PRED	SUCC	ORIG DUR	REM DUR	CAL	%	CODE	ACTIVITY DESCRIPTION	EARLY START	EARLY FINISH	LATE START	LATE FINISH	TOTAL FLOAT
1	5	10	10	1	0		MOBILIZATION	5MAY89	18MAY89	1MAY89	12MAY89	−4
5	10	5	5	1	0		CLEAR & GRUB APPROACHES	19MAY89	25MAY89	6JUL89	12JUL89	32
5	20	5	5	1	0		PILES – PIER #1	19MAY89	25MAY89	15MAY89	19MAY89	−4
10	15	20	20	1	0		CONSTRUCT ABUTMENT #1	26MAY89	23JUN89	13JUL89	9AUG89	32
15	75	20	20	1	0		CONSTRUCT ABUTMENT #2	26JUN89	24JUL89	10JUL89	7SEP89	32
20	25	5	5	1	0		PILES – PIER #2	26MAY89	2JUN89	22MAY89	26MAY89	−4
20	30	5	5	1	0		PILE CAP #1	26MAY89	2JUN89	22MAY89	26MAY89	−4
25	30	0	0	1	0		DUMMY	5JUN89	2JUN89	30MAY89	26MAY89	−4
25	40	5	5	1	0		PILES – PIER #3	5JUN89	9JUN89	19JUN89	23JUN89	10
30	35	5	5	1	0		PILE CAP #2	5JUN89	9JUN89	6JUN89	12JUN89	1
30	45	10	10	1	0		FORM, REIN. & POUR – COLUMN #1	5JUN89	16JUN89	30MAY89	12JUN89	−4
35	40	0	0	1	0		DUMMY	12JUN89	9JUN89	26JUN89	23JUN89	10
35	45	0	0	1	0		DUMMY	12JUN89	9JUN89	13JUN89	12JUN89	1
40	55	5	5	1	0		PILE CAP #3	12JUN89	16JUN89	26JUN89	30JUN89	10
45	47	4	4	1	0		SHOP DRAWING DELAY	19JUN89	22JUN89	13JUN89	16JUN89	−4
45	50	10	10	1	0		FORM, REIN. & POUR – COLUMN #2	19JUN89	30JUN89	19JUN89	30JUN89	0
47	60	10	10	1	0		PIER CAP #1	23JUN89	7JUL89	19JUN89	30JUN89	−4
50	55	0	0	1	0		DUMMY	3JUL89	30JUN89	3JUL89	30JUN89	0
55	65	10	10	1	0		FORM, REIN. & POUR – COLUMN #3	3JUL89	17JUL89	3JUL89	17JUL89	0
60	65	10	10	1	0		PIER CAP #2	10JUL89	21JUL89	3JUL89	17JUL89	−4
65	70	10	10	1	0		PIER CAP #3	24JUL89	4AUG89	18JUL89	31JUL89	−4
70	75	0	0	1	0		DUMMY	7AUG89	4AUG89	8SEP89	7SEP89	23
70	85	2	2	1	0		STEEL – SPAN 1	7AUG89	8AUG89	1AUG89	2AUG89	−4
75	80	10	10	1	0		PAVE APPROACH #1	7AUG89	18AUG89	8SEP89	21SEP89	23
80	130	10	10	1	0		PAVE APPROACH #2	21AUG89	1SEP89	22SEP89	5OCT89	23
85	90	2	2	1	0		STEEL – SPAN 2	9AUG89	10AUG89	15AUG89	16AUG89	4
85	95	10	10	1	0		FORM, REIN. & POUR – SPAN 1	9AUG89	22AUG89	3AUG89	16AUG89	−4
90	95	0	0	1	0		DUMMY	11AUG89	10AUG89	17AUG89	16AUG89	4
90	100	2	2	1	0		STEEL – SPAN 3	11AUG89	14AUG89	11SEP89	12SEP89	20
95	105	10	10	1	0		FORM, REIN. & POUR – SPAN 2	23AUG89	6SEP89	17AUG89	30AUG89	−4
100	120	2	2	1	0		STEEL – SPAN 4	15AUG89	16AUG89	13SEP89	14SEP89	20
105	110	10	10	1	0		FORM, REIN. & POUR – SPAN 3	7SEP89	20SEP89	31AUG89	14SEP89	−4
105	115	5	5	1	0		CURBS & SIDEWALKS – SPAN 1	27SEP89*	30OCT89	15SEP89	21SEP89	−8
110	115	0	0	1	0		DUMMY	21SEP89	20SEP89	22SEP89	21SEP89	1
110	120	0	0	1	0		DUMMY	21SEP89	20SEP89	15SEP89	14SEP89	−4
115	125	5	5	1	0		CURBS & SIDEWALKS – SPAN 2	4OCT89	10OCT89	22SEP89	28SEP89	−8
120	125	10	10	1	0		FORM, REIN. & POUR – SPAN 4	21SEP89	4OCT89	15SEP89	28SEP89	−4
125	130	5	5	1	0		CURBS & SIDEWALKS – SPAN 3	11OCT89	17OCT89	29SEP89	5OCT89	−8
130	135	5	5	1	0		CURBS & SIDEWALKS – SPAN 4	18OCT89	24OCT89	6OCT89	12OCT89	−8
135	140	5	5	1	0		PUNCHLIST	25OCT89	31OCT89	13OCT89	19OCT89	−8
140	145	1	1	1	0		PROJECT COMPLETE	1NOV89	1NOV89	20OCT89	20OCT89	−8

Figure 6.13

PRED	SUCC	ORIG DUR	REM DUR	CAL	%	CODE	ACTIVITY DESCRIPTION	EARLY START	EARLY FINISH	LATE START	LATE FINISH	TOTAL FLOAT
105	115	5	5	1	0		CURBS & SIDEWALKS - SPAN 1	27SEP89*	3OCT89	15SEP89	21SEP89	-8
115	125	5	5	1	0		CURBS & SIDEWALKS - SPAN 2	4OCT89	10OCT89	22SEP89	28SEP89	-8
125	130	5	5	1	0		CURBS & SIDEWALKS - SPAN 3	11OCT89	17OCT89	29SEP89	5OCT89	-8
130	135	5	5	1	0		CURBS & SIDEWALKS - SPAN 4	18OCT89	24OCT89	6OCT89	12OCT89	-8
135	140	5	5	1	0		PUNCHLIST	25OCT89	31OCT89	13OCT89	19OCT89	-8
140	145	1	1	1	0		PROJECT COMPLETE	1NOV89	1NOV89	20OCT89	20OCT89	-8
1	5	10	10	1	0		MOBILIZATION	5MAY89	18MAY89	1MAY89	12MAY89	-4
5	20	5	5	1	0		PILES - PIER #1	19MAY89	25MAY89	15MAY89	19MAY89	-4
20	25	5	5	1	0		PILES - PIER #2	26MAY89	2JUN89	22MAY89	26MAY89	-4
20	30	5	5	1	0		PILE CAP #1	26MAY89	2JUN89	22MAY89	26MAY89	-4
25	30	0	0	1	0		DUMMY	5JUN89	2JUN89	30MAY89	26MAY89	-4
30	45	10	10	1	0		FORM, REIN. & POUR - COLUMN #1	5JUN89	16JUN89	30MAY89	12JUN89	-4
45	47	4	4	1	0		SHOP DRAWING DELAY	19JUN89	22JUN89	13JUN89	16JUN89	-4
47	60	10	10	1	0		PIER CAP #1	23JUN89	7JUL89	19JUN89	30JUN89	-4
60	65	10	10	1	0		PIER CAP #2	10JUL89	21JUL89	3JUL89	17JUL89	-4
65	70	10	10	1	0		PIER CAP #3	24JUL89	4AUG89	18JUL89	31JUL89	-4
70	85	2	2	1	0		STEEL - SPAN 1	7AUG89	8AUG89	1AUG89	2AUG89	-4
85	95	10	10	1	0		FORM, REIN, & POUR - SPAN 1	9AUG89	22AUG89	3AUG89	16AUG89	-4
95	105	10	10	1	0		FORM, REIN, & POUR - SPAN 2	23AUG89	6SEP89	17AUG89	30AUG89	-4
105	110	10	10	1	0		FORM, REIN. & POUR - SPAN 3	7SEP89	20SEP89	31AUG89	14SEP89	-4
110	120	0	0	1	0		DUMMY	21SEP89	20SEP89	15SEP89	14SEP89	-4
120	125	10	10	1	0		FORM, REIN. & POUR - SPAN 4	21SEP89	4OCT89	15SEP89	28SEP89	-4
45	50	10	10	1	0		FORM, REIN. & POUR - COLUMN #2	19JUN89	30JUN89	19JUN89	30JUN89	0
50	55	0	0	1	0		DUMMY	3JUL89	30JUN89	3JUL89	30JUN89	0
55	65	10	10	1	0		FORM, REIN. & POUR - COLUMN #3	3JUL89	17JUL89	3JUL89	17JUL89	0
30	35	5	5	1	0		PILE CAP #2	5JUN89	9JUN89	6JUN89	12JUN89	1
35	45	0	0	1	0		DUMMY	12JUN89	9JUN89	13JUN89	12JUN89	1
110	115	0	0	1	0		DUMMY	21SEP89	20SEP89	22SEP89	21SEP89	1
85	90	2	2	1	0		STEEL - SPAN 2	9AUG89	10AUG89	15AUG89	16AUG89	4
90	95	0	0	1	0		DUMMY	11AUG89	10AUG89	17AUG89	16AUG89	4
25	40	5	5	1	0		PILES - PIER #3	5JUN89	9JUN89	19JUN89	23JUN89	10
35	40	0	0	1	0		DUMMY	12JUN89	9JUN89	26JUN89	23JUN89	10
40	55	5	5	1	0		PILE CAP #3	12JUN89	16JUN89	26JUN89	30JUN89	10
90	100	2	2	1	0		STEEL - SPAN 3	11AUG89	14AUG89	11SEP89	12SEP89	20
100	120	2	2	1	0		STEEL - SPAN 4	15AUG89	16AUG89	13SEP89	14SEP89	20
70	75	0	0	1	0		DUMMY	7AUG89	4AUG89	8SEP89	7SEP89	23
75	80	10	10	1	0		PAVE APPROACH #1	7AUG89	18AUG89	8SEP89	21SEP89	23
80	130	10	10	1	0		PAVE APPROACH #2	21AUG89	1SEP89	22SEP89	5OCT89	23
5	10	5	5	1	0		CLEAR & GRUB APPROACHES	19MAY89	25MAY89	6JUL89	12JUL89	32
10	15	20	20	1	0		CONSTRUCT ABUTMENT #1	26MAY89	23JUN89	13JUL89	9AUG89	32
15	75	20	20	1	0		CONSTRUCT ABUTMENT #2	26JUN89	24JUL89	10AUG89	7SEP89	32

Figure 6.14

ACME CONSTRUCTION, INC.   PRIMAVERA PROJECT PLANNER   WEST STREET BRIDGE

REPORT DATE 17OCT89 RUN NO. 10   WEST STREET BRIDGE - CPM SCHEDULE UPDATE   START DATE 5MAY89 FIN DATE 20OCT89*
            12:55
TOTAL FLOAT SORT   DATA DATE 22JUN89 PAGE NO.   1

PRED	SUCC	ORIG DUR	REM DUR	CAL	%	CODE	ACTIVITY DESCRIPTION	EARLY START	EARLY FINISH	LATE START	LATE FINISH	TOTAL FLOAT
1	5	10	0	1	100		MOBILIZATION	5MAY89A	18MAY89A			
5	20	5	0	1	100		PILES - PIER #1	19MAY89A	25MAY89A			
20	25	5	0	1	100		PILES - PIER #2	30MAY89A	8JUN89A			
20	30	5	0	1	100		PILE CAP #1	5JUN89A	9JUN89A			
25	30	0	0	1	100		DUMMY	8JUN89A	8JUN89A			
30	35	5	0	1	100		PILE CAP #2	12JUN89A	16JUN89A			
30	45	10	5	1	50		FORM, REIN. & POUR - COLUMN #1	12JUN89A	28JUN89		16JUN89	-8
45	50	10	10	1	0		FORM, REIN. & POUR - COLUMN #2	29JUN89	13JUL89	19JUN89	30JUN89	-8
45	60	10	10	1	0		PIER CAP #1	29JUN89	13JUL89	19JUN89	30JUN89	-8
50	55	0	0	1	0		DUMMY	14JUL89	13JUL89	3JUL89	30JUN89	-8
55	65	10	10	1	0		FORM, REIN. & POUR - COLUMN #3	14JUL89	27JUL89	3JUL89	17JUL89	-8
60	65	10	10	1	0		PIER CAP #2	14JUL89	27JUL89	3JUL89	17JUL89	-8
65	70	10	10	1	0		PIER CAP #3	28JUL89	10AUG89	18JUL89	31JUL89	-8
70	85	2	2	1	0		STEEL - SPAN 1	11AUG89	14AUG89	1AUG89	2AUG89	-8
85	95	10	10	1	0		FORM, REIN. & POUR - SPAN 1	15AUG89	28AUG89	3AUG89	16AUG89	-8
95	105	10	10	1	0		FORM, REIN. & POUR - SPAN 2	29AUG89	12SEP89	17AUG89	30AUG89	-8
105	110	10	10	1	0		FORM, REIN. & POUR - SPAN 3	13SEP89	26SEP89	31AUG89	14SEP89	-8
110	120	0	0	1	0		DUMMY	27SEP89	26SEP89	15SEP89	14SEP89	-8
120	125	10	10	1	0		FORM, REIN. & POUR - SPAN 4	27SEP89	10OCT89	15SEP89	28SEP89	-8
125	130	5	5	1	0		CURBS & SIDEWALKS - SPAN 3	11OCT89	17OCT89	29SEP89	5OCT89	-8
130	135	5	5	1	0		CURBS & SIDEWALKS - SPAN 4	18OCT89	24OCT89	6OCT89	12OCT89	-8
135	140	5	5	1	0		PUNCHLIST	25OCT89	31OCT89	13OCT89	19OCT89	-8
140	145	1	1	1	0		PROJECT COMPLETE	1NOV89	1NOV89	20OCT89	20OCT89	-8
35	45	0	0	1	0		DUMMY	22JUN89	21JUN89	19JUN89	16JUN89	-3
110	115	0	0	1	0		DUMMY	27SEP89	26SEP89	22SEP89	21SEP89	-3
115	125	5	5	1	0		CURBS & SIDEWALKS - SPAN 2	27SEP89	3OCT89	22SEP89	28SEP89	-3
25	40	5	2	1	60		PILES - PIER #3	20JUN89A	23JUN89		23JUN89	0
40	55	5	5	1	0		PILE CAP #3	26JUN89	30JUN89	26JUN89	30JUN89	0
85	90	2	2	1	0		STEEL - SPAN 2	15AUG89	16AUG89	15AUG89	16AUG89	0
90	95	0	0	1	0		DUMMY	17AUG89	16AUG89	17AUG89	16AUG89	0
35	40	0	0	1	0		DUMMY	22JUN89	21JUN89	26JUN89	23JUN89	2
105	115	5	5	1	0		CURBS & SIDEWALKS - SPAN 1	13SEP89	19SEP89	15SEP89	21SEP89	2
5	10	5	5	1	0		CLEAR & GRUB APPROACHES	22JUN89	28JUN89	6JUL89	12JUL89	9
10	15	20	20	1	0		CONSTRUCT ABUTMENT #1	29JUN89	27JUL89	13JUL89	9AUG89	9
15	75	20	20	1	0		CONSTRUCT ABUTMENT #2	28JUL89	24AUG89	10AUG89	7SEP89	9
75	80	10	10	1	0		PAVE APPROACH #1	25AUG89	8SEP89	8SEP89	21SEP89	9
80	130	10	10	1	0		PAVE APPROACH #2	11SEP89	22SEP89	22SEP89	5OCT89	9
90	100	2	2	1	0		STEEL - SPAN 3	17AUG89	18AUG89	11SEP89	12SEP89	16
100	120	2	2	1	0		STEEL - SPAN 4	21AUG89	22AUG89	13SEP89	14SEP89	16
70	75	0	0	1	0		DUMMY	11AUG89	10AUG89	8SEP89	7SEP89	19

Figure 6.15

```
ACME CONSTRUCTION, INC.              PRIMAVERA PROJECT PLANNER              WEST STREET BRIDGE

REPORT DATE 23OCT89  RUN NO.   10      WEST STREET BRIDGE - CPM SCHEDULE UPDATE #3      START DATE  5MAY89  FIN DATE 20OCT89*
            14:14
TOTAL FLOAT SORT                                                           DATA DATE  30AUG89  PAGE NO.   1
```

PRED	SUCC	ORIG DUR	REM DUR	CAL	%	CODE	ACTIVITY DESCRIPTION	EARLY START	EARLY FINISH	LATE START	LATE FINISH	TOTAL FLOAT
1	5	10	0	1	100		MOBILIZATION	5MAY89A	18MAY89A			
5	20	5	0	1	100		PILES - PIER #1	19MAY89A	25MAY89A			
20	25	5	0	1	100		PILES - PIER #2	30MAY89A	8JUN89A			
20	30	5	0	1	100		PILE CAP #1	5JUN89A	9JUN89A			
30	35	5	0	1	100		PILE CAP #2	12JUN89A	16JUN89A			
30	45	10	0	1	100		FORM, REIN. & POUR - COLUMN #1	12JUN89A	28JUN89A			
25	40	5	0	1	100		PILES - PIER #3	20JUN89A	26JUN89A			
45	60	10	0	1	100		PIER CAP #1	28JUN89A	13JUL89A			
40	55	5	0	1	100		PILE CAP #3	29JUN89A	10JUL89A			
45	50	10	0	1	100		FORM, REIN. & POUR - COLUMN #2	29JUN89A	14JUL89A			
25	30	0	0	1	100		DUMMY	3JUL89A	3JUL89A			
35	45	0	0	1	100		DUMMY	3JUL89A	3JUL89A			
5	10	5	0	1	100		CLEAR & GRUB APPROACHES	5JUL89A	11JUL89A			
10	15	20	0	1	100		CONSTRUCT ABUTMENT #1	12JUL89A	8AUG89A			
60	65	10	0	1	100		PIER CAP #2	14JUL89A	27JUL89A			
50	55	0	0	1	100		DUMMY	17JUL89A	17JUL89A			
55	65	10	0	1	100		FORM, REIN. & POUR - COLUMN #3	17JUL89A	28JUL89A			
35	40	0	0	1	100		DUMMY	25JUL89A	25JUL89A			
65	70	10	0	1	100		PIER CAP #3	31JUL89A	11AUG89A			
15	75	20	0	1	100		CONSTRUCT ABUTMENT #2	10AUG89A	28AUG89A			
70	75	0	0	1	100		DUMMY	14AUG89A	14AUG89A			
70	85	2	2	1	0		STEEL - SPAN 1	30AUG89	31AUG89	1AUG89	2AUG89	-21
85	95	10	10	1	0		FORM, REIN, & POUR - SPAN 1	1SEP89	15SEP89	3AUG89	16AUG89	-21
95	105	10	10	1	0		FORM, REIN, & POUR - SPAN 2	18SEP89	29SEP89	17AUG89	30AUG89	-21
105	110	10	10	1	0		FORM, REIN, & POUR - SPAN 3	2OCT89	13OCT89	31AUG89	14SEP89	-21
110	120	0	0	1	0		DUMMY	16OCT89	13OCT89	15SEP89	14SEP89	-21
120	125	10	10	1	0		FORM, REIN, & POUR - SPAN 4	16OCT89	27OCT89	15SEP89	28SEP89	-21
125	130	5	5	1	0		CURBS & SIDEWALKS - SPAN 3	30OCT89	3NOV89	29SEP89	5OCT89	-21
130	135	5	5	1	0		CURBS & SIDEWALKS - SPAN 4	6NOV89	10NOV89	6OCT89	12OCT89	-21
135	140	5	5	1	0		PUNCHLIST	13NOV89	17NOV89	13OCT89	19OCT89	-21
140	145	1	1	1	0		PROJECT COMPLETE	20NOV89	20NOV89	20OCT89	20OCT89	-21
110	115	0	0	1	0		DUMMY	16OCT89	13OCT89	22SEP89	21SEP89	-16
115	125	5	5	1	0		CURBS & SIDEWALKS - SPAN 2	16OCT89	20OCT89	22SEP89	28SEP89	-16
85	90	2	2	1	0		STEEL - SPAN 2	1SEP89	5SEP89	15AUG89	16AUG89	-13
90	95	0	0	1	0		DUMMY	6SEP89	5SEP89	17AUG89	16AUG89	-13
105	115	5	5	1	0		CURBS & SIDEWALKS - SPAN 1	2OCT89	6OCT89	15SEP89	21SEP89	-11
90	100	2	2	1	0		STEEL - SPAN 3	6SEP89	7SEP89	11SEP89	12SEP89	3
100	120	2	2	1	0		STEEL - SPAN 4	8SEP89	11SEP89	13SEP89	14SEP89	3
75	80	10	10	1	0		PAVE APPROACH #1	30AUG89	13SEP89	8SEP89	21SEP89	6
80	130	10	10	1	0		PAVE APPROACH #2	14SEP89	27SEP89	22SEP89	5OCT89	6

Figure 6.16

After-the-Fact and Modified CPM Schedules

It was noted previously that the analyst must resist the temptation to create schedules after the fact. Analysts may want to create schedules because:

1. No schedule exists on the project.
2. The original schedule lacked detail.
3. The original schedule was incorrect.

None of these three situations constitutes a valid reason to create a new schedule. The analyst may argue that creating an after-the-fact CPM schedule will allow the analysis to be more precise. The analyst may even draft the after-the-fact CPM schedule with the help of the contractor's and/or the owner's personnel to back up the argument that the schedule reflects the actual initial plan for construction. Nevertheless, it must be remembered that after-the-fact CPM schedules are risky, mostly because there is more than one logical way to build a project, and the analyst may choose a different approach than that used by the original planner. Several CPM schedules might all accurately depict how one project could be built, but each may have a different critical path. Obviously, even a slight difference in the schedule can affect the outcome of the analysis.

The analyst who attempts to use an after-the-fact CPM schedule for delay analysis could easily be challenged by the following arguments.

- It is not the original schedule.
- It was not the way the project was planned.
- It is forcing the schedule to meet predetermined conclusions concerning delays.
- Another configuration would be more representative of the "real schedule.'

It is always best to use the contemporaneous schedule from the project. While the analyst may be allowed to make minor modifications to the original schedule to account for obvious errors, such changes must be made judiciously. The delay analysis methodology explained in Chapter 2 addresses most problems with the original schedule. The following example illustrates the pitfalls of using an after-the-fact schedule.

In a dispute between the Patham Construction Company and the Omaha District Corps of Engineers, the contractor created an after-the-fact CPM schedule, although a bar chart was used during the project. The analyst performed an impacted as-planned analysis on this after-the-fact schedule. The analysis was highly subjective, and thus questionable. In fact, the Board of Contract Appeals decided that the analyst's schedule did not represent the real schedule for the project.

Dollar-to-Time Relationships

Some analyses presented to support delay positions are based on the relationship between dollars and time. There is a widely-held, but mistaken belief that the dollar value of the work performed is directly related to the time progress of the job. Some arguments incorporating this method are as follows:

- **Contractor:** I was able to complete 90% of the work in ten months on the job. Then, because of the owner delays in inspection and punch list, it took four months to complete the last 10% of the work.
- **Owner:** During the period of the alleged delay to the contractor, he was able to perform 25% of the dollar value of his work on the project. The dollar value of work accomplished during that period reflected the same rate of progress as that before and after the delay. Therefore, we could not possibly have delayed the contractor.

While both of these arguments may appear acceptable from an initial quick reading, there is no quantifiable linear relationship between time progress and dollars on any project. The dollar value at each stage of the project depends on the nature and cost of the specific activities performed. Some high dollar value items of work may be performed in a short period of time. Other low dollar value items of work may take more time. Finally, the dollar value method does not identify and track the activities on the critical path of the project.

Again using the bridge example, the abutment/approach activities may have a low dollar value compared with the main bridge work. Yet, these items caused a delay to the project.

Unfortunately, some public owners have structured their contract documents to reflect the idea that time and dollar value have a linear relationship. For instance, some owners grant time extensions based on the dollar value ratio of a change order to the original contract amount. For example:

> Original contract amount: $100,000
> Dollar value of change: $10,000 (or 10% of original contract amount)
> Original contract duration: 100 days

Therefore, time extension granted is 10 days (10% of original contract time).

In fact, an owner could make a change that would increase the contract amount by ten percent, but would not affect the duration of the project. Likewise, the owner could make a change with a minimal (direct) dollar impact that could significantly delay the project.

"S" Curves

Some owners, such as the Corps of Engineers, have fostered this time-dollar relationship. The Corps of Engineers has, in the past, required contractors to provide "S" curves to show job progress. The contractor provides a bar chart of the major activities on the job and applies the dollar value from the schedule of values to the bar chart. By summing the dollars over time, an "S" curve is generated. Figure 6.17 is an example of a typical "S" curve for a project.

The contractor must then submit an updated "S" curve with each monthly pay request. Unfortunately, the monthly submission also has an entry for "progress to date," recorded as a percentage (see Figure 6.18). This update has often been used to measure the contractor's progress in time, which is very often misleading.

"S" curves developed from a contractor's total billing dollars do not measure the time progress of the project, but merely show the progress of billings over the course of time. There are several reasons why the author does not recommend use of this "S" curve for determining job progress.

- The original planned "S" curve might not be accurate due to "front end loading," or other factors.
- The updated "S" curve information might be misleading because of payments for stored materials and equipment.
- The contractor could be overbilling or "front end loading" and, therefore, portray more "progress" than is actually occurring.

Time-to-dollar relationships should not be used to establish delays on a project.

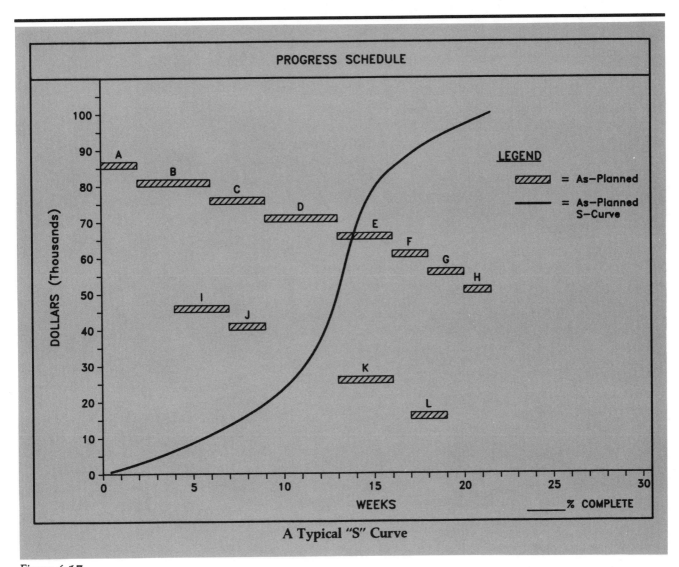

Figure 6.17

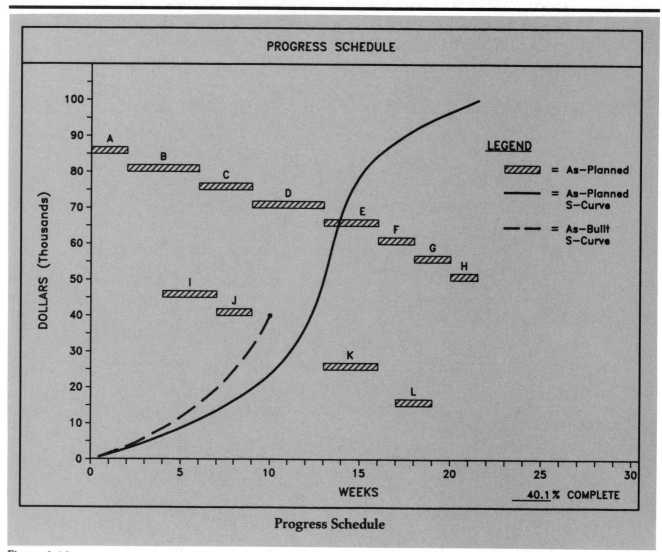

Figure 6.18

"But For" Schedules / Arguments

A school of thought exists that uses the "but for" approach to establish and, more often, to *refute* the cause of delays. In a "but for" argument, the analyst takes the position that, regardless of what occurred, there were other delays that would have had virtually the same effect. For example:

But for the owner's delay to the shop drawing process, the contractor would have been late anyway, since he had not mobilized his subcontractor on time.

This approach completely denies the concept of the critical path and float. It is normally the result of the analyst comparing the entire as-planned schedule with the overall as-built schedule. In this comparison, the analyst sees that several activities experienced delays. He then identifies each delay and argues that an owner-caused delay is offset by an apparent contractor-caused delay. This analysis fails to recognize the fact that the original owner-caused delay provided the contractor with float on other activities, which therefore, no longer had to be accomplished in the originally scheduled time frame.

For example, Figure 6.19 is a bar chart for a project showing the comparison between the original as-planned schedule and the actual as-built schedule. The contractor asserts that an activity was delayed because of a change by the owner. The owner responds that "but for" its change, the contractor would have been delayed anyway, since it did not start the activity until much later and therefore its delay was not related to the owner's change. The real situation is that once the contractor was delayed by the change order, he chose not to proceed, since the work could be done more efficiently by waiting until the change order work was accomplished.

Contractors

Contractors sometimes use a "but for" analysis when there is no contemporaneous schedule to support their delay position. The contractor may insert the owner delays into the original project schedule and then argue that "but for" these delays, he could have finished the work much sooner. The difference between the actual completion date and the "but for" schedule is then the measure of the delays caused by the owner. This method closely resembles the impacted as-planned analysis, almost in reverse. The difference is that this time, the analysis inserts the actual as-built durations, and subtracts out the so-called delays by the other side.

Using the "but for" approach, the party making the argument may even go so far as to admit that it is responsible for some of the delay. Purportedly, this adds credibility to the analysis ("if I admit that some of the delays are my fault, then I am being fair in my evaluation").

The "but for" approach relates back to the concept of concurrency discussed at the beginning of this book. It must always be kept in mind that the schedule is not static; it is dynamic, changing over the life of the project. What may be the measure of a delay one month may not be the accurate measure of a delay that occurs two months from that time. The schedule does not guarantee that the job will be built a certain way. It only provides a "road map" or guide for construction and for the durations of the activities.

Any time an analyst "freezes" the schedule to measure delays, he or she is asking for trouble and dispute. One cannot apply a static measure to a dynamic situation.

Collapsed As-Built Analysis

Another method of analysis is the collapsed or subtractive as-built. This approach is almost the reverse of the impacted as-planned analysis described previously.

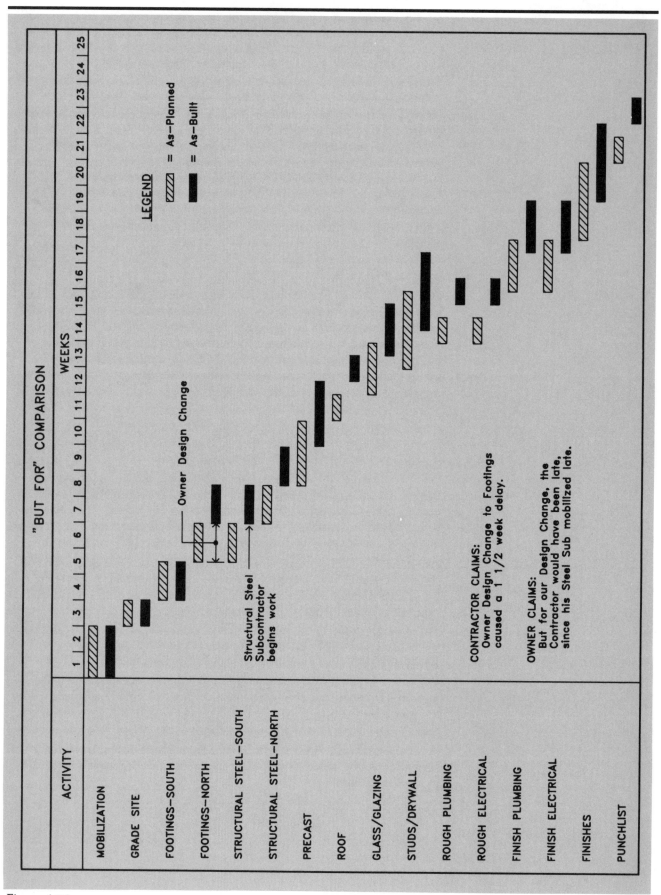

Figure 6.19

In the collapsed as-built, the analyst studies all of the contemporaneous documentation and constructs as detailed an as-built schedule as possible. Normally, this as-built is a CPM network drawn on a time scale. Next, the analyst "subtracts" or removes activities which he considers have impacted the project. If the removal of these activities or the shortening of these durations affects the schedule's end date, the difference in days between the as-built and the collapsed as-built end dates is considered to be the delay caused by the specific activities which were removed.

There are a few different variations of this approach. It is worthwhile to mention two of them and then note the fallacies in this approach.

Unit Subtractive As-Built

For simplicity, the first variation will be called a *unit subtractive as-built*. This method starts with the preparation of the overall as-built and subtracts one "impact" at a time to try to show a measurable number of days attributable to each item removed. Once alleged "impacts" are removed, the argument is made that the project should have finished earlier were it not for the impacts noted.

Gross Subtractive As-Built

The second variation is the gross subtractive as-built. This method starts with the preparation of the overall as-built and removes all possible impacts that may have caused a delay to the project. These potential impacts are both owner and contractor caused. The resulting schedule and duration supposedly represent the time the project would have taken if no problems had occurred.

The next step in the process adds specific problems back into the now "collapsed" as-built, one at a time. As the analyst re-inserts each impact, he or she attributes the corresponding increase in the project duration to the respective items.

Basic Flaws of the Collapsed or Subtractive As-Built Method

This overall method, regardless of the variation used, has several major problems. The three primary flaws are:

- The method requires the analyst to construct a CPM network diagram based on as-built information. This is extremely subjective and highly amenable to manipulation. With little effort, one can make the schedule support a predisposed conclusion.
- The method requires the analyst to determine specific "impacts" before performing any analysis. Not only is this subjective, it is impossible. The analyst is first reaching conclusions about what caused a delay, and is only using the analysis to attempt to prove it. This is the proverbial "tail wagging the dog."
- This method ignores the fact that the schedule is dynamic. It also "freezes" the critical path based on the as-built critical path constructed by the analyst. The path then changes depending on the "subtraction" made; these changes normally do not agree with what was actually taking place on the project.

Summary

While there are numerous approaches used to analyze delays, care must be exercised throughout the process. The method used must incorporate the available contemporaneous information, recognize the dynamic nature of a construction schedule and a critical path, and avoid after-the-fact hypotheses which do not reflect all the information available.

Chapter Seven

Owner Delay Damages

Chapter Seven
Owner Delay Damages

When a project is delayed, the owner, contractor, or both may suffer a loss. The entitlement of damages is based on the findings from the delay analysis and the determination of liability once the delays have been defined. This chapter addresses the types of damages that the owner may experience if it is shown that the contractor has caused the delay. In the broadest sense, the owner's damages are either *liquidated damages* or *actual damages*. Both of these categories are discussed in this chapter.

Liquidated Damages

Liquidated damages are predetermined prior to the execution of the contract. The exact amount of the liquidated damages is specified in the contract. A typical contract clause that incorporates liquidated damages appears in Figure 7.1.

Liquidated damages clauses can take many forms. The owner should seek the assistance of qualified counsel in structuring the wording of the clause and should carefully compute the damages it may reasonably sustain if a delay occurs to all or a portion of the project. One might ask why an owner would specify a liquidated damage amount in advance as opposed to seeking recovery for actual damages if a delay occurs. The answer is that liquidated damages are desirable when it is difficult or impossible to accurately determine the actual damages that the owner would experience in the event of a delay, particularly for public projects. Projects such as highways and transit systems have a value to the public, and delay damages for such cannot be accurately estimated. Therefore, the owner cites in the contract a liquidated damages amount to cover the estimated damages which will be sustained if the project is completed late. The owner should check with qualified counsel before calculating the amount of liquidated damages to ensure that the proper items (given the law in the owner's area of the country) are considered.

Many owners believe that the inclusion of a liquidated damages clause is a deterrent to lateness. In other words, fear of having to pay liquidated damages "motivates" the contractor to complete the project on time. In reality, liquidated damages clauses are not intended to deter lateness, and they do not have that effect. The vast majority of contractors are optimistic. They bid projects with the belief that they can and will finish on time. Generally, the inclusion of a liquidated damages clause does not affect their bids. Contractors recognize that with or without a liquidated damages clause, they are still liable for actual damages should they be late. Therefore, during project performance, the liquidated damages clause may not be a motivating factor. In fact, if a contractor falls behind schedule during the project, the liquidated damages clause allows him to determine whether acceleration efforts would be cost effective. For example, if a contractor is behind schedule by ten days on a project and the liquidated damages are $300 per day, the potential exposure is $3,000. If the cost of accelerating the work to make up the ten days is $7,000, then the cost effective decision is to finish late.

An owner should consider the following items when preparing an estimate of liquidated damages.

- Cost for project inspection
- Costs for continued design services
- Costs for the owner's staff
- Costs for maintaining current facilities
- Costs for additional rentals
- Costs for additional storage
- Lost revenues
- Costs to the public for not having the facility
- Additional moving expense
- Escalation costs
- Financing costs

While other costs may be included in the liquidated damages estimate, the list above provides a general idea of the types of costs to consider.

Estimating Liquidated Damages

A note of caution: liquidated damages are specific for each project. Unfortunately, owners often utilize standard tables for liquidated damages that may not reasonably reflect the damages they will sustain if a delay occurs on their project. For instance, many state departments of transportation have liquidated damages clauses similar to the one shown in Figure 7.2.

While the use of standard tables is convenient, the owner should ensure that the amounts in the table are valid and indeed were based on a reasonable estimate. Fortunately, the amount stated in the tables is most often low. Nevertheless, it is important that owners recognize that each project is different and will have specific amounts for liquidated damages.

Typical Liquidated Damages Clause

Should the contractor fail to complete the contract within the time allowed by the contract to include time extensions allowed by executed change orders, then for each calendar day of delay, the owner has the right to withhold the amount of $500 per calendar day as liquidated damages.

These liquidated damages are compensation to the owner for costs the owner may experience due to the contractor's delay, and are not to be construed as penalties.

Figure 7.1

Owners must recognize that liquidated damages do not necessarily bear a direct relationship to the contract amount. Two different projects of equal value can have very different potential damages. An owner who uses a standard table to figure liquidated damages may risk either understating the damages and thereby shortchanging himself, or overstating the damages and becoming susceptible to a successful legal challenge by the contractor.

The inaccuracy of a standard table for liquidated damages is demonstrated in the following example.

An owner and contractor execute a contract for the amount of $4,760,000. According to the table for liquidated damages in Figure 7.2, the amount of liquidated damages would be $1,150 per calendar day.

During the course of the project, the owner changes the contract requirements for the concrete mix design and requires that the contractor use a more expensive mix, for which the contractor receives a change order and will be paid. The amended contract amount is now in excess of $5,000,000. Therefore, the liquidated damages have increased to $1,350 per calendar day. In reality, however, the potential damages the owner would sustain in a delay have not changed. There are no additional inspection costs, moving expenses, etc. from the list of damage-type items previously noted.

Application to Project Milestones

Liquidated Damage Clauses can also be written to apply to milestone dates or events during the project. For instance, liquidated damages may be linked to phases of the work, such as building close-in or completion of a section of the

---

Liquidated Damages Clause for
State Department of Transportation

FAILURE TO COMPLETE ON TIME. For each calendar day that the work remains incomplete after the expiration of the contract time, the sum per day given in the following schedule shall be deducted from any monies due the Contractor. If no money is due the Contractor, the Department shall have the right to recover said sum from the Contractor, the surety, or both. The amount of these deductions is to cover estimated expenses incurred by the Department as a result of the Contractor's failure to complete the work within the time specified. Such deductions are liquidated damages and are not to be construed as penalties.

Daily Charge for Liquidated Damages
For Each Calendar Day of Delay

Original Contract Amount:

From More Than	To and Including	Daily Charge
$ 0	$ 100,000	$ 300
100,000	500,000	550
500,000	1,000,000	750
1,000,000	2,000,000	900
2,000,000	5,000,000	1,150
5,000,000	10,000,000	1,350
10,000,000	------	1,400

Figure 7.2

project. The amounts of these milestone liquidated damages may differ from the liquidated damages amount that applies to project completion. For instance, a project may involve the construction of several buildings. In the contract, the Liquidated Damages clause may specify separate damages for the completion of each building, as well as one liquidated damages amount for the overall completion of the project. A highway construction project may specify liquidated damages for the completion of each bridge and for project completion.

Hourly Fees

In some projects, liquidated damages are specified on an hourly basis. In certain critical highway projects, the owner has specified hourly liquidated damages for failing to open portions of the roadway to traffic at set times for each day of the project.

Graduated Damages

In some cases, liquidated damages may be graduated. For example, the liquidated damages may be $1,000 per day up to a certain date or for a defined number of days, and then may increase to $1,500 per day for delays beyond the date or in excess of the initial number of days. These graduated Liquidated Damages reflect the owner's increase in damages as the delay continues.

Bonus or Incentive Clause

In the construction industry it is often presumed that Liquidated Damages must also have a corresponding bonus or incentive. This is not true. There is no requirement that the owner must offer a bonus or incentive merely because the contract includes a Liquidated Damages clause. The lack of a bonus or incentive does not justify a challenge to the Liquidated Damages clause.

Amount of Bonus Clause

The owner may, in fact, include a Bonus or Incentive clause in the contract for early completion. If a bonus or incentive is used, it does not have to match the amount of the liquidated damages. The bonus can be higher or lower, and can have limitations. For example, the bonus in a contract could allow $1,000 per day for each day the contractor finishes the project earlier than the specified contract completion date, up to a limit of $50,000. Alternatively, the owner may allow a bonus for early completion that increases or decreases over time. For example, the owner will offer a bonus of $1,000 per day for early completion up to 50 days, and for every day that the project is finished early in excess of 50 days, the bonus may be reduced to $500.

Contract Completion Date

The bonus is computed from the *contract completion date*. Therefore, if the contract completion date is extended by a change order, the bonus is computed from the *new contract completion date*. In some instances, the benefit that the owner will realize from an early completion may evaporate after a certain calendar date. Therefore, this bonus clause may not apply if the completion date is changed by change order during the course of the project. In such cases, the owner should draft a clause that determines the bonus from a *specified calendar date*. In this case, regardless of the contract completion date, no bonuses will be paid if the contractor does not finish before the specified calendar date.

Such clauses can be difficult to write, and should be drafted by qualified counsel. Furthermore, the owner should make an extra effort to ensure that all bidders understand the intent of the bonus clause to minimize future claims.

Owner Delays and Bonuses

When a contract includes a bonus or incentive clause, the contractor may be eligible for the bonus if he is delayed by the owner during the course of the project. The contractor may argue that the owner's delay prevented an early finish. In such cases, the contractor may be entitled to the bonus for every day of the owner-caused delay.

Enforceability

One of the owner's major concerns when using a Liquidated Damages clause is whether or not it will be enforceable. A reasonable amount of case law exists and, with proper guidance by counsel, the owner should be able to structure a clause that will be upheld.

If a contractor completes a project late and is assessed liquidated damages by the owner, it is possible that the assessment may be challenged. There are two basic approaches that a contractor may use to overcome the assessment of the liquidated damages. First, he may attack the *propriety of the assessment* by disclaiming responsiblity for the delay. Second, the contractor may claim that the *specified amount of the liquidated damages is excessive* and consequently, more of a penalty than a damages compensation.

Propriety of Assessment

If a contractor challenges responsibility for a given delay, he must show through a delay analysis that the delays to the project were excusable delays and, therefore, warrant a time extension. If the delay analysis proves the assessment of the liquidated damages is inappropriate, the contractor may be granted relief from the damages. Similarly, the contractor may attempt to show only partial responsibility for delays to a project, arguing that the owner also caused some concurrent delays. As previously discussed, if it can be shown that delays were also caused by the owner, then the contractor may be granted relief from the assessment of some or all of the liquidated damages.

Magnitude of Damages

The second approach used to challenge liquidated damages is based on the magnitude of the damages specified. The contractor may argue that the amount specified was excessive and was, in effect, a penalty rather than a statement of the owner's loss. Some owners may feel that it does not matter whether the amount reflects a penalty or a loss, since the damages were clearly specified in the contract that bears the contractor's signature. However, in construction contract law in the United States, penalties in a construction contract are not enforceable. If it is found that the amount specified was too high, it may be judged as a penalty and not a liquidated damage. In such cases, the courts will not enforce the clause. For this reason, most knowledgeable attorneys carefully avoid the use of the word "penalty" anywhere in the contract. According to some construction attorneys, judges have been known to disallow clauses merely because the word "penalty" was used in the contract wording. Regardless of what one calls the damages an owner specifies in the contract for late completion, the courts will view them as liquidated damages as long as they are not referred to as a "penalty." By using the word "penalty," the owner may be taking a greater risk concerning the enforcement of the clause.

High Estimates: When the contractor challenges the amount of liquidated damages, the owner must substantiate the validity of the damages. This does not mean that the owner must demonstrate that actual damages are comparable to the liquidated damages specified in the contract. The issue that must be decided is whether or not the estimate for liquidated damages was reasonable at the time it was prepared. In other words, when the contract was drafted, given what was known at that time, was the estimate a reasonable one? Clearly, it is in the owner's best interest to maintain the documentation used to estimate the liquidated damages figure.

If it is determined that the owner's estimate was not reasonable, or did not reasonably approximate the liquidated damages amount specified, the clause may not be enforceable. For example, if the owner's estimate showed potential damages of $4,500 per day, but the liquidated damage amount specified in the contract was $10,000 per day, then the amount specified most likely would be construed as a penalty and not enforced.

Low Estimates: Most of the time, the amount of liquidated damages specified in a contract is too low. The owner's damages are often greater than the specified liquidated damages. Can the owner recover its damages when they are greater than the specified liquidated damages?

In most cases, the owner is limited to the liquidated damages amount specified. There are very few exceptions where an owner can recover more than the liquidated damages amount. The argument is that the owner wrote the contract and calculated the damages, and is not entitled to collect more than the specified amount. Because it allows the owner to recover his losses, but protects the contractor from excessive penalties, the Liquidated Damages clause is often referred to as the "owner's sword" and the "contractor's shield."

Once liquidated damages are in litigation, there are further issues to be addressed. Even if a contractor is successful in challenging the *amount* of the liquidated damages, it does not mean the owner is not entitled to *any* damages. It simply means that the owner must then prove the actual damages. Remember that a Liquidated Damages clause is often used because it was difficult to accurately calculate the actual damages. While the owner has the opportunity to recover actual damages, it may be very difficult to prove that he deserves damages above those specified in the Liquidated Damages clause.

Actual Damages

If the owner does not include a Liquidated Damages clause in the contract, or if the clause is deemed legally unenforceable, then the owner may seek actual damages for a delay caused by a contractor. When attempting to recover actual damages, the owner has the legal *burden* to prove the damages. The owner should seek qualified counsel to properly prepare the damage computations. In order to assess all the damages of a contractor-caused delay, the owner should document all damage items to the maximum extent possible. The items listed in Figure 7.3 should be considered during the process of damage calculations.

The last item of damages in Figure 7.3 is sometimes difficult to recover. The courts and boards look upon lost revenues and lost profits as being highly speculative and, therefore, not subject to exact quantification. Thus, it is difficult to recover compensation for lost revenues. That does not mean that they should not be claimed; the owner should simply understand the real chances of recovery. If the owner is able to show a measurable difference in the production rates of the old facility and the new facility, then the chances of recovery may be enhanced. This is possible primarily in situations where the project is a replacement facility, as opposed to a new product facility. Figure 7.4 is an example of an owner's calculation of actual damages sustained because of a delay caused by the contractor.

In general, actual damages are more difficult to recover since, by their nature, they may not be accurately quantified. Consequently, the owner must decide before the project begins whether or not it is most advantageous to utilize a liquidated damages clause or to seek actual damages if a delay occurs. The less amenable the damages are to accurate calculations, the more reason to utilize a liquidated damages clause.

Considerations for Making Damage Calculations

1. The owner should have its designer **keep separate records** which reflect those costs for inspection, site visits, etc., which are the result of the project having a longer duration.
2. The owner should assess if the delay caused an **increase in its moving costs**, such as escalation of moving costs, storage of items, temporary facilities, etc.
3. If the owner had to pay **additional rent** to occupy its previous facilities longer than planned, those costs should be carefully documented.
4. If the owner had staff involved with the construction project, then any **extended staff costs** should be documented.
5. Depending on the nature of the project, the owner may have increased cost associated with **temporary lodging** – particularly with respect to housing developments. These temporary lodging costs should be documented.
6. If the project is financed in some fashion, then the owner will be exposed to **additional interest expense** relative to the cost of financing. These costs must be tracked.
7. The owner may face damages from **other follow-on contractors** who have been delayed by the delay caused by the first contractor. These damages would then be a part of the owner's actual delay damages.
8. If the project is a production facility, the owner may claim the **lost revenues from not being able to produce its product**.

Figure 7.3

Statement of Actual Damages
ABC Corporation

As noted by our expert report prepared by Trauner Consulting Services, Inc., the project was delayed 150 calendar days, attributable to the contractor. Based on a delay of 150 calendar days, the following damages are claimed by the ABC Corporation.

1. *Additional Design Services*
   Based on the records of our design firm, the A/E made 22 more site visits than the number originally scheduled. The exact cost for these 22 site visits was $10,560.

2. *Moving Costs*
   Because of the delay, ABC Corporation was forced to renegotiate its contract with its moving company. The renegotiated contract was $6,520 higher than the original moving contract.

3. *Rental Costs*
   ABC Corporation was forced to stay in its previous facilities for an additional five months. The documented rental costs during this period were $617,000.

4. *Staff Costs*
   ABC Corporation's in-house construction staff remained active on the project for an additional 150 days. The staff costs based on salaries and benefits were $61,845.

5. *Temporary Lodging*
   ABC's plant start-up engineer moved to the project site based on a promised completion date (four months later than the original date) by the contractor. The contractor exceeded that date by 35 days. The lodging and subsistence paid to the start-up engineer during that 35-day period totalled $2,265.

6. *Finance Cost*
   ABC Corporation financed this project at an interest rate of .5% over prime. Because of the delay, ABC Corporation recorded additional financing costs of $792,000.

7. *Claims by Follow-on Contractor*
   ABC Corporation received a delay claim from its start-up contractor. The claim was settled for the amount of $29,000.

8. *Lost Revenues*
   Because of the delay, ABC Corporation was unable to benefit from the increased production capability of the new facility. Based on sales records, the lost revenues total $2,675,000.

Total Damages due ABC Corporation:
$4,174,190

Figure 7.4

Chapter Eight

Extended Field Costs

Chapter Eight
Extended Field Costs

The next few chapters deal separately with various kinds of damages to which contractors are entitled for excusable compensable delays. One type of damages that the contractor may claim is extended field costs. When a project has a delay, the field staff, materials, and equipment must be on site longer than scheduled. The field cost items in this chapter fall into three major categories: labor, equipment, and materials. This chapter explains how to calculate these kinds of damages to present a clear understanding of the impacts of a delay and the nature of delay damages.

Labor Costs

Supervisory Personnel

When a project experiences a delay, depending on the circumstances, the contractor might retain supervisory personnel in the field. This represents a direct labor cost to the contracting firm. Personnel such as the project manager, clerk, secretary, superintendent, and assistant superintendent, are in this category.

To calculate the cost, or damages, for retaining these people on site, add the daily salary to the burden and overhead, and then multiply that sum by the number of days of compensable delay.

Daily salary + burden & overhead × Number of days of
compensable delay
= Damages for supervisory personnel

This is a straightforward calculation; however, the analyst must justify the propriety of claiming supervisory personnel damages.

Propriety of Claiming Damages

To ascertain the propriety of claiming damages for extended retention of field staff, the analyst must review the contractor's normal accounting procedures for these costs. For example, if the contractor routinely *charges the project directly* for the project manager, then claiming damages for him would be appropriate. However, if the contractor routinely charges the project manager to *project overhead* or *home office overhead*, then claiming this cost as a direct field damage may be questionable. The owner would likely argue that the project manager's salary is an overhead item when resolving the delay damages. The same principle applies to the salary of any field supervisory personnel extended on the project because of the delay.

Union Supervisory Personnel

On certain projects, union agreements require that additional non-working personnel be at the job site while work is being performed — a master mechanic, shop steward, or some foreman levels. If there is a delay, these personnel also represent an extended labor cost. The contractor can provide copies of the union requirements to the analyst.

Idle Labor

Another category of labor costs that might arise during a delay is idle labor. If a project is delayed, suspended, or constructively suspended, the contractor's workers may be at the project site, but may be nonproductive. For this claim, the project daily reports must show that the laborers were on the site, but were not able to perform the work. The owner naturally questions why the contractor was unable to either shift those workers to other tasks or other jobs, or lay them off. The contractor should be prepared with project daily reports to substantiate an idle labor claim. If the owner does not retain such daily reports, there may be no basis for a challenge to the contractor's documented claim. For this reason, both the owner and the contractor should diligently maintain documentation of labor activity throughout the project. It should be noted that the contractor has an obligation to mitigate the damages when a delay occurs. Therefore, if he can shift his labor to other work during a delay, he should do so.

Escalation of Labor Costs

For some delays, the contractor may experience an escalation of labor costs. This may occur if the delay causes the wage scale to move into a more expensive time frame than that originally scheduled. This situation is sometimes referred to as *extended labor*, but should more appropriately be considered *escalation*.

The example below clarifies the idle and escalated labor costs.

A project is scheduled to start on a specified date and finish some 300 calendar days later. The contractor is using union labor contracted under a collective bargaining agreement that specifies pay increases at certain intervals. In the example, the pay increase for common laborers is to occur on day 150. The rate before the wage increase is $10 per hour; it escalates to $12 per hour after the increase.

In the third month of the project, the owner causes a ten-day delay to the project. The owner accepts responsibility for the delay so there is no question of liability or the magnitude of the delay. The project is extended by change order an additional ten days, and the contractor must assess the labor costs associated with the delay. (See Figure 8.1.)

The contractor's records show that during the delay, there were 200 man-hours of idle time for common laborers. To figure delay costs, the contractor multiplies the number of hours by the wage rate:

200 hours × $10 per hour = $2,000.

The contractor's records also show 300 man-hours for common laborers during the last ten days on the job, which occurred in a time frame later than that originally planned. The contractor seeks compensation for the additional $2 per hour for the 300 man-hours.

$2/hr. × 300 hrs. = $600

The total claim is for $2,600 — $2,000 for the idle labor and $600 for the extended labor. The contractor's approach, however, is incorrect. To correctly assess the situation, one must examine each piece of the damages separately.

The idle labor request of $2,000 is correct. This assumes, of course, that the contractor's records substantiate the idle labor and justify why it was impossible to channel the idle time to other activities.

The request for $600 for the extended labor is incorrect. If there had been no delay, the 300 man-hours worked at the end of the project would have been worked only ten days before the date they were actually worked. Therefore, these hours still would have been worked at a rate of $12 per hour. There is no impact to these last 300 hours. Instead, the contractor should be looking at the ten-day time period *immediately following the wage increase*. It is the labor hours in this time frame that were extended into a more expensive time period. The contractor's certified payrolls show that 400 man-hours were worked during the ten-day period after the wage increase. Therefore, the contractor would be entitled to an additional $800 for the delay.

$2/hr. × 400 man-hours = $800

The total contractor's damages were actually $2,800 for the direct labor costs caused by the delay. The contractor would naturally add the appropriate burden and overhead to this amount to calculate the total labor costs attributable to the delay.

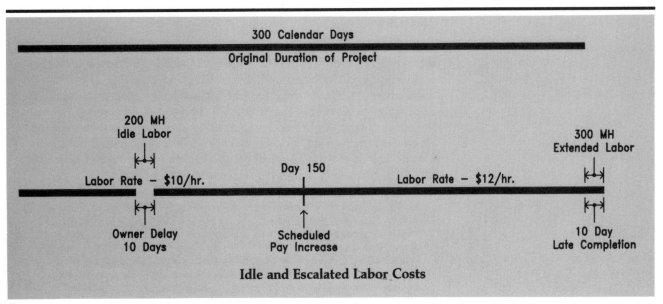

Idle and Escalated Labor Costs

Figure 8.1

This simple example illustrates that one should not estimate damages without first clearly understanding the impacts. Making such hasty conclusions leads to erroneous estimates. A more realistic and complex project might involve several trades with collective bargaining agreements with varying wage increases at different dates. A wage increase might extend over a period of more than a year for some trades. The contractor or owner must assess how the shift in the work performed by the labor force increased labor costs or exposed it to the escalated wage rate. The example just given is further simplified by the fact that no additional work was added by the delay. It also assumes that once the delay ended, the work was performed in the same sequence as originally planned. To show how a more complex situation would be handled, a more detailed example with more variables appears at the end of this chapter.

Alteration of the Work Sequence

What happens if the delay alters the work sequence or if a combination of the delay and other changes affects the labor distribution on the job? In these situations, the contractor must show the original planned distribution of labor versus the actual distribution. The following example illustrates this approach.

A project is scheduled for a duration of 300 calendar days. During the project, the contractor maintains a resource-loaded CPM schedule that shows the distribution of manpower by trade over time. Figure 8.2 shows the distribution of carpenter hours for the project on the original schedule; Figure 8.3 shows the actual distribution of carpenter hours on the project, based on the impact of the delay.

As can be seen from the figures, the wage increase took effect on day 150 for the carpenters. In the original schedule, the contractor anticipated that 720 carpenter man-hours would be expended after day 150, at the higher labor rate of $13 per hour. In the actual distribution of labor, the contractor expended 860 carpenter man-hours (140 more than anticipated) during the higher wage rate period. Therefore, 140 man-hours were subject to the increase of $2 per hour, and the contractor should calculate $280 for escalation of labor for carpenters.

860 actual hours − 720 planned hours = 140 man-hours
140 hrs. × $2/hr. wage increase = $280.00

In this example, it is assumed that the actual distribution of carpenter labor was caused solely by the owner's delay. If the owner can prove that this was not the case, then the delay damages would not include the extended labor calculations.

Comparison Using Bar Charts

Of course, not every project has a resource-loaded CPM schedule to allow a reasonably precise comparison between the planned and the actual distribution of labor. Without the CPM schedule, the analyst can estimate distribution of labor from the project bar charts. Then the analyst can match the documentation of the labor expended on the job (from the project daily reports), to the planned bar chart activities. The analyst then compares the planned bar chart with the actual bar chart to measure escalated labor. The following example illustrates this procedure.

A contractor plans to perform the work in accordance with the bar chart shown in Figure 8.4. As can be seen from the bar chart, no manpower is specified. Because of a delay caused by the owner, the contractor's work is performed later than originally planned. As a result, the contractor experiences escalated labor costs for the carpenters, as a rate increase (from $12 per hour to $13 per hour) went into effect on day 200 of the project. Figure 8.4 is the contractor's bar chart for the work as originally planned. Figure 8.5 shows the revised bar chart for the project, reflecting the delay. It also shows the actual carpenter man-hours worked on each activity. These man-hours were recorded on the project daily reports.

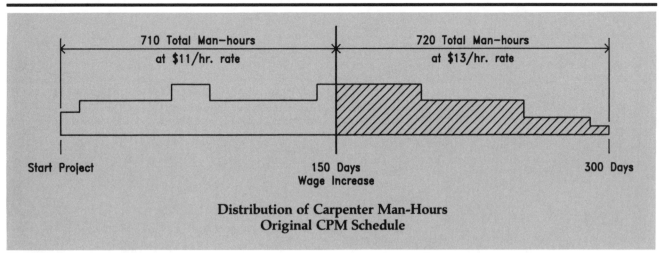

Distribution of Carpenter Man-Hours
Original CPM Schedule

Figure 8.2

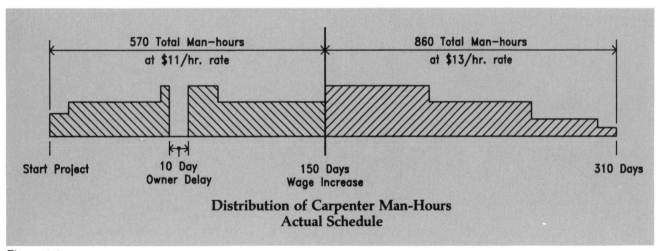

Distribution of Carpenter Man-Hours
Actual Schedule

Figure 8.3

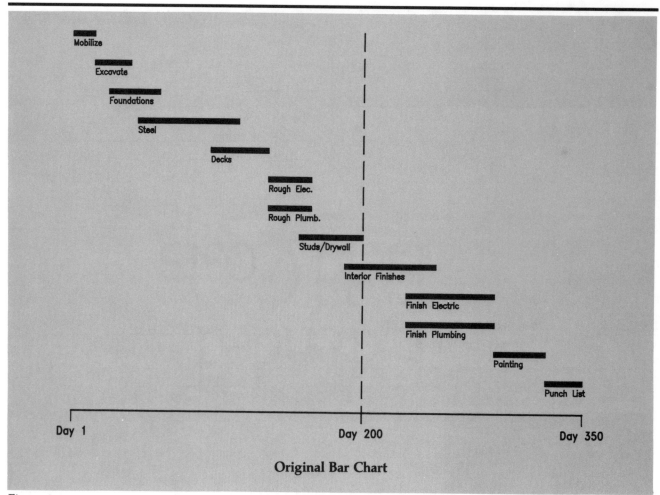

Mobilize
Excavate
Foundations
Steel
Decks
Rough Elec.
Rough Plumb.
Studs/Drywall
Interior Finishes
Finish Electric
Finish Plumbing
Painting
Punch List

Day 1   Day 200   Day 350

Original Bar Chart

Figure 8.4

130

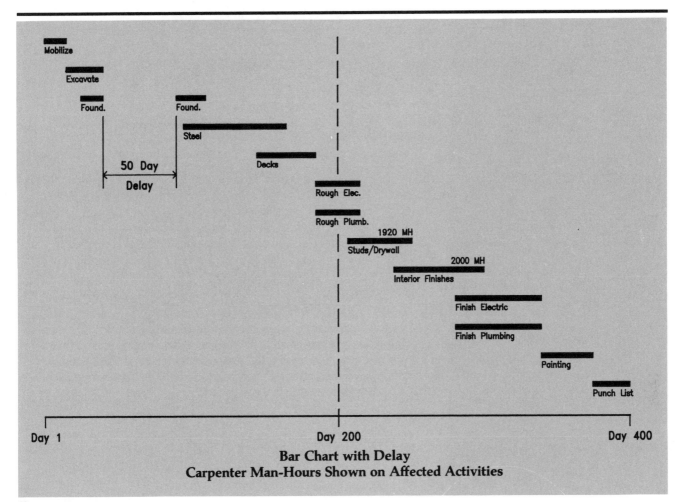

Bar Chart with Delay
Carpenter Man-Hours Shown on Affected Activities

Figure 8.5

In order to calculate the cost escalation, the contractor uses his original bar chart (Figure 8.4) and loads the actual carpenter man-hours onto it for the respective tasks. This is shown in Figure 8.6.

A comparison of Figure 8.5 and 8.6 shows that there were 2,740 carpenter man-hours shifted into the more expensive time frame. Therefore, the contractor's cost escalation for this trade is $2,740.

$1/hour × (1,920 man-hours & 820 man-hours) = $2,740

It should be noted that this conclusion assumes that the delay only shifted the work and that no inefficiency resulted.

Equipment Costs

Equipment costs on a job can also be affected by a delay. For example, delays may cause the equipment to be idle. The amount of damages that can be claimed for idle equipment depends on the wording of the contract. In some cases, the contract may address idle or standby equipment and allow only a reduced rate or no compensation at all. If this subject is not addressed by the contract, the contractor claims damages for the full cost of the equipment during the idle time. Once again, the contractor should record equipment activity in the project daily reports to show exactly when the equipment was idle and the duration of the idle time.

The owner generally questions whether the equipment was truly idle because of the delay. It may be worthwhile for the owner to verify the use of the equipment prior to and following the period of the delay. If the equipment was idle both before and after the delay period, then the owner may question whether any damages were, in fact, sustained.

Escalation Costs

As with labor costs, equipment may also be subject to escalation costs. If a contractor is using rented equipment, the rental rate could increase because of the delay. This situation can and should be documented with invoices.

Other Impacts

Other, more subtle impacts can also be associated with equipment in the event of a delay. For example, if a significant delay occurs to a portion of a project, the equipment originally planned for the work may no longer be available. The contractor could have originally planned to perform excavation using scrapers, but because of the delay, must now use loaders and trucks to excavate the material. The damages would be measured by a comparison between the cost of the two methods, the originally planned versus the actual. To some extent, this type of impact borders on inefficiencies, which will be addressed later in this book. In the purest sense, however, it does represent the impact of the delay on the equipment cost.

The following example illustrates both cost escalation and inefficiency in equipment use caused by a delay.

An owner is constructing an addition to a waste water treatment plant. The site is an inactive landfill. The excavation subcontractor is required to excavate approximately 200,000 cubic yards of waste and dispose of it at a nearby active landfill. Prior to beginning excavation, concerns are raised that the site may contain hazardous wastes. Consequently, the owner stops the excavation activity in order to perform toxicity testing. The testing takes three months to complete, at which time the excavation subcontractor is allowed to proceed with the work as originally specified. Because of the delay, however, the subcontractor experiences a change in his equipment cost and availability.

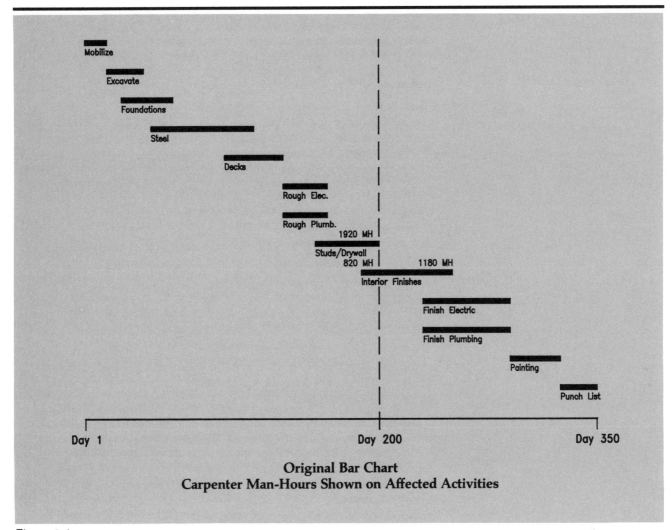

Original Bar Chart
Carpenter Man-Hours Shown on Affected Activities

Figure 8.6

133

Originally, the subcontractor planned to excavate 170,000 cubic yards with scrapers, and the remaining 30,000 cubic yards with a hydraulic excavator and 20-ton dump trucks. Because of the delay, the scrapers are no longer available, as they have been committed to another project. Consequently, the subcontractor now must perform all of the excavation without the use of scrapers. The subcontractor determines two impacts because of the delay. First, the excavators he intended to rent have increased in cost. Second, the unit cost for excavation is higher using the dump trucks than it would have been using the scrapers. Based on these factors, he calculates the following increased cost.

1. Escalation of rental equipment cost:
   Cat hydraulic excavator
      – quoted rate: $800/week (quote attached)
      – new rate: $850/week (invoice attached)
   Difference of $50/week
   Planned use is 10 weeks (2 excavators for 5 weeks)

   Extra cost: $50/week × 10 weeks = $500

2. Increased unit price of excavation:
   Excavation with scrapers: $4.50/cy
   (calculations attached)

   Excavation with dump trucks: $7.20/cy
   (calculations attached)

   Difference of $2.70/cy

   Extra cost: $2.70/cy × 170,000 cy = $459,000

Material Costs

The most common material impact caused by a delay is price escalation. Because of the delay, the contractor is forced to buy materials in a period when the price has increased.

The calculation of escalation cost for materials can be performed in the same manner as that for the escalation of labor cost. Basically, a comparison must be made between the quantity of each material that would have been purchased in the original schedule and the quantity of each material purchased under the delay schedule. The following example illustrates this method.

A project originally scheduled to take 300 calendar days experienced a 90-day delay. The delay occurred in the beginning of the project and forced the contractor to pay more for concrete. The contractor can demonstrate that he had a purchase order for concrete for $80 per yard from the beginning of the project until day 100. After day 100, the cost increased (by terms of the purchase order) to $85 per yard. Because of the delay, the contractor purchased more concrete at $85 per yard than originally scheduled.

A review of the schedule shows that the contractor planned to have constructed six of eight floors before the price increase. A takeoff of the quantities measures this as 2,000 yards of concrete. In the execution of the work, the contractor actually placed only 1,200 yards of concrete before the price increase. The increase is directly attributable to the excusable delay. Therefore, the damages would be $4,000, or $5 per yard for the 800 yards that experienced the escalated price.

2,000 yards planned — 1,200 actual = 800 yards
$5 additional cost/yard × 800 = $4,000 damages due to delay

Storage Costs

Material costs may also be affected by storage costs. The contractor may be forced to store materials either on or off the site as a result of a delay. The contractor must support claims for these costs with invoices. In some cases, the contractor may choose to purchase materials in advance and store them, as this may be less expensive than the increased cost of purchasing the materials at a later date. The contractor should notify the owner of this course of action.

Summary Example

The following summary example shows damage calculations, including the items described in this chapter. It is intended to help present a clear picture of the procedures for calculating delay damages for an excusable delay.

A project has a contract duration of 400 calendar days. The contractor estimates the construction schedule to last the full 400 calendar days, as shown in Figure 8.7. The project has a delay of 200 (calendar) days and finishes on day 600 (see Figure 8.8). Of the 200 days of delay, it has been determined that the owner caused 150 days of delay and the contractor is responsible for the remaining fifty days. The owner has issued a two-part change order for its delays. Part I issues a time extension of 150 days. Part II, the compensation to the contractor for the delay, is now in negotiation.

Figure 8.9, a summary of delays to the schedule, shows that the owner delayed the start of the project by suspending the work for fifty days. The next delay was also caused by the owner, who, by requesting design revisions, delayed the project an additional 100 days. The final delay was fifty days, attributable to the contractor for failing to mobilize a subcontractor to perform work.

The presentation shown in Figure 8.10 was made by the contractor to support the additional compensation requested.

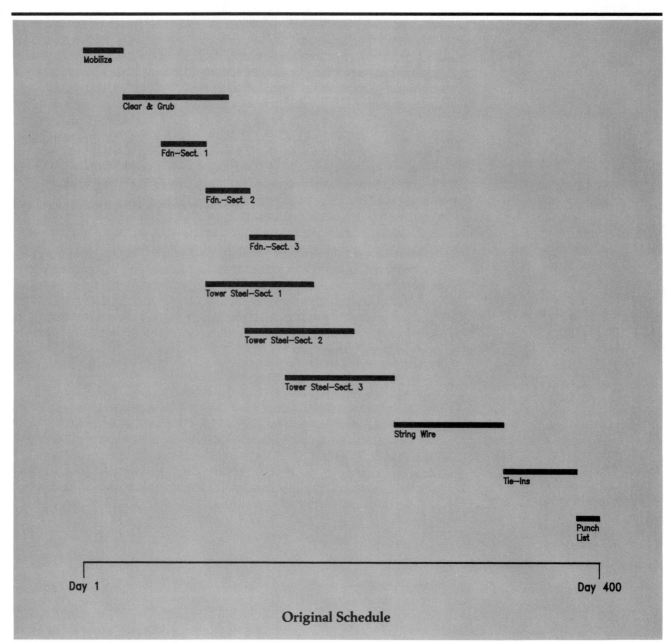

Figure 8.7

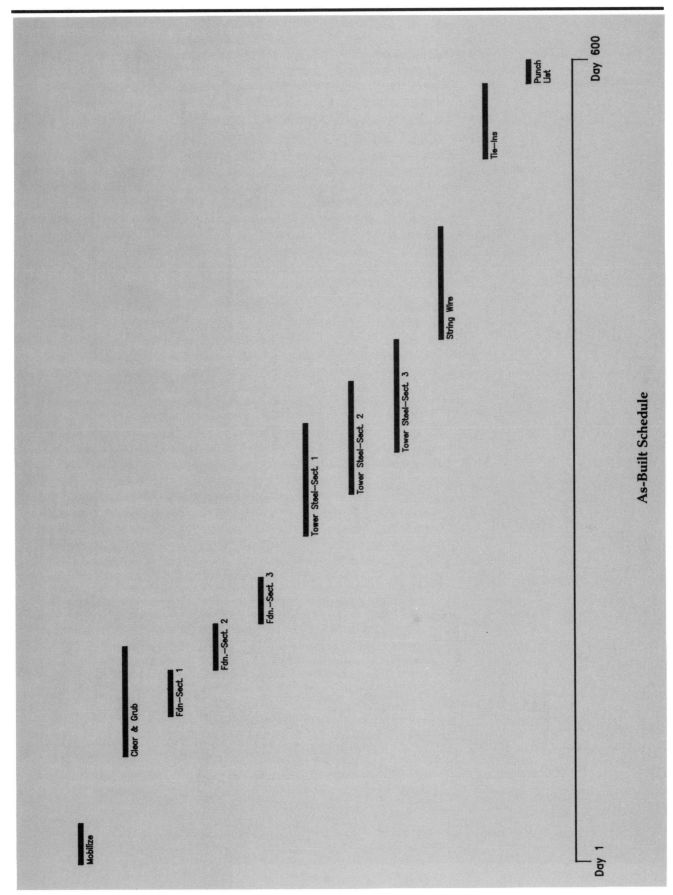

Figure 8.8

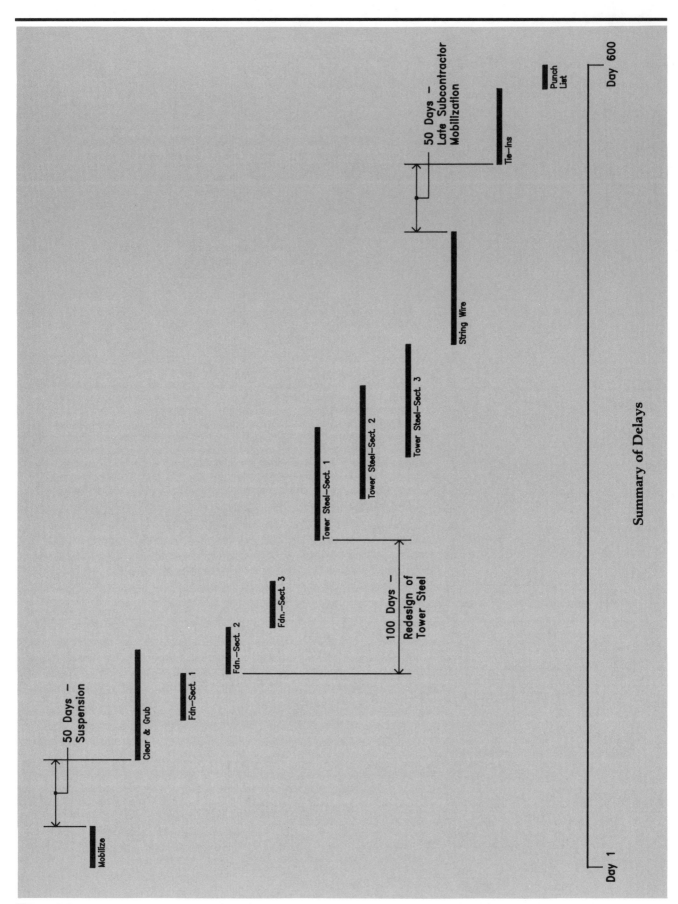

Figure 8.9

REQUEST FOR EQUITABLE ADJUSTMENT

Ace Construction Company hereby requests the following compensation for the 150 days of delay caused by factors beyond our control. In Part 1 of Change Order No. 7, the owner has granted a time extension of 150 calendar days. Because of this 150-day delay, Ace construction accrued the following extra costs.

Extended Field Overhead:

Labor:
Project Manager -- 150 days at $400/day for 25% of time = $15,000
Superintendent -- 150 days at $375/day   = $56,250
Clerk   -- 150 days at $125/day   = $18,750
Master Mechanic -- 150 days at $305/day   = $45,750
Subtotal Labor $135,750

Note: Certified payrolls attached. Project Manager is a direct job charge.

Equipment:
Superintendent's truck: 150 days at $5/day   = $750
Portable toilet: 5 mos. at $125/mo.   = $625
Project trailer: 5 mos. at $140/mo.   = $700
Tool Trailer: 5 mos. at $100/mo.   = $500
Subtotal Equipment $2,575

Note: Invoices attached for equipment.
         Superintendent's truck costed by normal company accounting
         practices.

General Conditions:
Utilities -- Electricity: 5 mos. at $130/mo.   = $650
              Water/sewer: 5 mos. at $75/mo.   = $375
Dumpsters -- two dumpsters: 5 mos. at $75 ea./mo. = $750
Copy machine: 5 mos. at $120/mo.   = $600
Office supplies: 5 mos. at $80/mo.   = $400
Scheduling updates: 5 mos. at $200/mo.   = $1,000
Subtotal General Conditions $3,775

Total Extended Field Overhead: $142,100

Figure 8.10

<u>Construction Equipment Costs:</u>

Extended Equipment
100-ton crane: 3 extra mos. at $4,000/mo.   = $12,000

Escalation of Equipment
D-7 dozer: 2 mos. at an increased rental rate of $200/mo. = $400

Idle Equipment
Scrapers for 327 hrs. at $35/hr.   = $11,445
D-7 dozer for 240 hrs. at $65/hr.   = $15,600

Note: Rental invoices attached.
          Company-owned equipment costed in accordance with normal
          company accounting practices.

Total Construction Equipment Costs   = $39,445

<u>Labor Costs:</u>

Idle Labor:
Carpenters -- 725 hrs. at $27/hr.   = $19,575
Laborers   -- 816 hrs. at $19.50/hr.   = $15,912
Ironworkers -- 420 hrs. at $29/hr.   = $12,180
Subtotal Idle Labor $47,667

Note: Applicable time sheets and certified payrolls attached.
          Union agreement and calculation of rates to include burden
          and overhead attached.

Escalation of Labor
Carpenters -- escalation: 700 hrs. at $1.10/hr.   = $770
Laborers   -- escalation: 250 hrs. at $.90/hr.
                      (1st increase)   = $225
           -- escalation: 320 hrs. at $1.00/hr.
                      (2nd increase)   = $320
Ironworkers -- escalation: 650 hrs. at $1.20/hr.   = $744
Subtotal Labor Escalation $2,059

Total Labor Costs $49,726

<u>Material Costs</u>

Escalation of concrete: 1,200 yds. at $2.00/yd.   = $2,400
Storage of rebar -- supplier charge   = $650

Total Material Costs $3,050

GRAND TOTAL ALL COSTS $234,331

Figure 8.10 *(continued)*

Chapter Nine

Home Office Overhead

Home Office Overhead

This chapter addresses the delay damages associated with home office overhead. The validity of claiming damages for home office overhead has been the subject of heated debate. Once it is established that such costs may represent a valid damages claim, one of several approaches can be used to calculate them.

Nature of the Damages

Home office overhead normally consists of the fixed costs of operating a home office. Such costs include:

- Rent
- Utilities
- Furnishings
- Office equipment
- Executive staff
- Support staff/clerical staff
- Project staff/estimators/schedulers
- Mortgage costs
- Real estate taxes
- Advertising
- Marketing
- Interest
- Accounting/data processing

In some manner, a contractor must pay for these costs through the projects it performs as a constructor. Normally, the contractor includes home office overhead costs in some part of the bid price for each project. Usually, the contractor calculates the final bid price by adding a percentage for markup to the direct cost bid amount. The exact markup depends on the amount of home office overhead costs the contractor incurs in a given period, usually one year. The number of projects the contractor has under construction at any one time also affects the markup. For instance, if a contractor works on only one project at a time, he would add to the direct project cost 100% of the home office costs for the period of construction. As the number of projects increases, the percentage allotted to each job is reduced as shown in Figure 9.1. Normally, the markup is a function of the dollar value of the job, and not just a fixed dollar markup for each project.

Effects of Delays on Home Office Costs

When a delay occurs, how are the contractor's home office costs affected? It is easiest to answer this question with a few examples.

One Project at a Time

For the contractor who performs one project at a time, the impact of a delay seems straightforward. For example:

> A contractor has home office costs of $48,000 per year and has a one-year contract for $1,000,000. The project experiences a one-month delay, and during that period, home office costs of $4,000 accrue. If the delay is the result of a compensable suspension of work, the contractor has the same contract amount of $1,000,000, but now has a total home office cost of $52,000, an increase of $4,000.
>
> **Contract amount:** $1,000,000
> **Yearly home office costs:** $48,000
>
> **Contract amount:** $1,000,000
> **New home office expense, including extending the project one month:** $52,000
>
> $52,000 − $48,000 = $4,000 increase in home office costs
>
> Therefore, the contractor may be entitled to receive $4,000 in damages to cover home office costs for the delay.

In this example, the contractor did not receive any additional compensation for any other extra work on any change order to offset the increase to the home office costs.

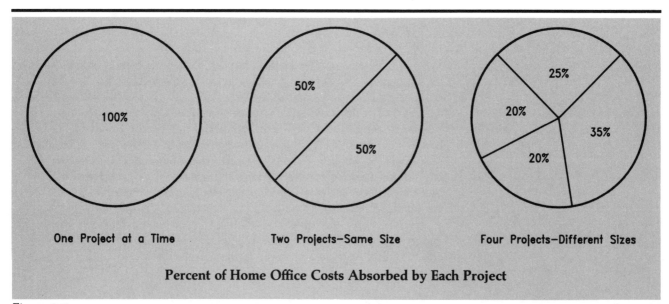

Percent of Home Office Costs Absorbed by Each Project

Figure 9.1

144

If the one month delay was the result of extra work with direct costs of only $10,000, and the overhead markup allowed by the contract was 10%, the contractor would receive $1,000 for overhead as compensation for the extra work. If, as in the previous example, actual home office overhead totals $4,000 per month, the contractor would be $3,000 short in compensation using the percent allowed in the contract. The difference between delays caused by a suspension and those that result from extra work are explained later in this chapter.

Multiple Projects

In the next example, the contractor has multiple ongoing projects.

> This contractor has home office overhead costs of $1,000,000 per year. He normally has four projects in progress at any one time, for a total yearly volume of $20,000,000. The contractor allocates home office costs by adding a five percent markup to each bid. Each of the five projects is valued at $5,000,000. What happens if one project experiences a delay?

> Originally, each project absorbs $250,000 of home office costs, or about $21,000 per month. If one project experiences a one-month delay, then the contractor receives no additional revenue to cover home office costs for that project, and therefore suffers a net loss of $21,000. If the delay is attributable to extra work, the contractor may receive compensation from the markup on a change order. If there is no extra work, the project experiencing the delay underabsorbs its share of the home office costs and the other projects must overabsorb some of the costs.

Clearly, the calculations become more difficult as the number of projects increases. Numerous articles have been written on this subject. Many authors distinguish between *extended home office overhead* and *unabsorbed home office overhead*. Normally, if a project is suspended, the contractor experiences extended home office overhead. If the project is extended without an official suspension of work, the damage is called *unabsorbed home office overhead*. The calculation of damages for each may differ.

The decisions of the courts and boards have not always maintained such a clear distinction. The analyst must establish the exact damages the contractor actually experiences, regardless of the nature of the delay. The remainder of this chapter presents some methods for calculating the delay damages associated with home office overhead costs.

Eichleay Formula

One method of calculating home office overhead costs for a delay is the Eichleay Formula. The formula originated from a decision by the Armed Services Board of Contract Appeals in 1960 (*Eichleay Corporation*, ASBCA 5183, 60-2 BCA 2688). In its appeal before the Board, the Eichleay Corporation proposed a formula for calculating its damages for home office overhead during a delay. The Board accepted this formula as a reasonable method of calculating the damages. This formula has since become known as the *Eichleay Formula*.

The Eichleay Formula is a simple three-step formula. First, the total contract billings are divided by the total company billings. The quotient is then multiplied by the total home office overhead to produce the *allocable overhead*.

$$\frac{\text{Total contract billings}}{\text{Total company billings}} \times \frac{\text{Total home}}{\text{office overhead}} = \frac{\text{Allocable}}{\text{overhead}}$$

Next, the allocable overhead is divided by the number of days of contract performance, including the delay. This produces the *daily allocable overhead rate*.

$$\frac{\text{Allocable overhead}}{\text{Number of days of contract performance}} = \frac{\text{Daily allocable}}{\text{overhead rate}}$$
$$\text{(including delay)}$$

Finally, the daily allocable overhead rate is multiplied by the number of days of compensable delay, to produce the home office overhead damages.

$$\text{Daily allocable overhead rate} \times \text{Number of days of compensable delay} = \text{Home office overhead damages}$$

The Eichleay formula is summarized in Figure 9.2.

A short example illustrates the formula. A company has a total billing of $50,000,000. The contract billings total $5,000,000. Total home office overhead = $1,000,000. The project duration totals 200 days. Compensable delays total 30 days.

The first calculation, to produce the allocable overhead is:

$$\frac{(\text{Contract billings})}{\text{Total Co. billing}} \times (\text{Home office overhead}) = (\text{Allocable overhead})$$

$$\frac{\$5,000,000}{\$50,000,000} \times \$1,000,000 = \$100,000$$

The next calculation produces the daily allocable overhead rate.

$$\frac{(\text{allocable overhead})}{(\text{No. of days of contract performance})} = \text{Daily allocable overhead rate}$$

$$\frac{\$100,000}{200 \text{ days}} = \$500/\text{day}$$

Finally, the daily allocable overhead rate is multiplied by the number of days of compensable delay to yield the home office overhead damages, $15,000.

$$\text{Daily allocable overhead} \times \text{No. of days} = \text{Home office overhead damages}$$

$$\$500/\text{day} \times 30 \text{ days} = \$15,000$$

Figure 9.3 summarizes this example.

Eichleay Formula

1. $\dfrac{\text{Total Contract Billings}}{\text{Total Company Billings}} \times \left(\begin{array}{c} \text{Total Home} \\ \text{Office Overhead} \end{array} \right) = \left(\begin{array}{c} \text{Allocable} \\ \text{Overhead} \end{array} \right)$

2. $\dfrac{\text{Allocable Overhead}}{\left(\begin{array}{c} \text{Number of Days of Contract Performance} \\ \text{(including delay)} \end{array} \right)} = \text{Daily Allocable Overhead Rate}$

3. $\left(\begin{array}{c} \text{Daily Allocable} \\ \text{Overhead Rate} \end{array} \right) \times \left(\begin{array}{c} \text{Number of Days of} \\ \text{Compensable Delay} \end{array} \right) = \left(\begin{array}{c} \text{Home Office} \\ \text{Overhead Damage} \end{array} \right)$

Figure 9.2

Problems with the Eichleay Formula

While the Eichleay Formula is simple to apply, one might reasonably question its accuracy. The Eichleay Formula is an estimated allocation and may, therefore, be somewhat inaccurate, yielding results that are either too high or too low. However, this formula is useful as a reasonable approximation of the damages sustained.

The Eichleay Formula has its basis in Federal contract disputes, and some state courts may not recognize it as an acceptable method for calculating damages for home office overhead. In many states, there is no established law or method like the Eichleay formula. In these cases, both the contractor and the owner must consult with counsel if the question of home office overhead damages occurs in a delay situation.

Certain courts and boards have generated numerous opinions concerning the Eichleay Formula and its application. For example, in *Excavation-Construction, Inc.*, ENG BCA 3851 (1984), the board recognized the use of the Eichleay Formula to determine the cost not only of a suspension of work, but also of a delay caused by extra work. The Engineering Board of Contract Appeals (ENG BCA) opinion is noted below.

> *"The Board believes in general that an Eichleay-type approach is the preferred way to determine home office overhead in a suspension situation and that a markup of direct costs is the preferred way to determine home office overhead for a change. However, no automatic approach can be applied in avoidance of a careful scrutiny of the facts. In this appeal, the changed work on the retaining walls is only part of the reason for extension of the contract period. Much of the delay and disruption occurred because the change was not timely made. The parties have agreed that the net effect was to extend the period necessary for performance by 99 days. Measurement of the effect on home office overhead by the costs alone is likely in these circumstances to understate the amount to which E-C is entitled. Therefore, the Board considers this appeal to be a proper one for application of the Eichleay Formula."*

Example of Eichleay Formula used to calculate home office overhead costs for 30 days of compensable delay	
Contract Billings	= $ 5,000,000
Total Billings	= $50,000,000
Home Office Overhead	= $ 1,000,000
Number of Days of Contract Performance	= 200
Compensable Delays	= 30 Days
1. $\dfrac{\$5,000,000}{\$50,000,000} \times 1,000,000$	= $100,000
2. $\dfrac{\$100,000}{200 \text{ days}}$	= $500/day
3. $500/day $\times$ 30 days	= $15,000

Figure 9.3

The board did, however, subtract from the Eichleay calculation the amount of overhead that was already being paid by virtue of the markup on the change order.

In *George E. Jensen Contractor, Inc.*, ASBCA no. 29772 (1984), the Armed Services Board of Contract Appeals noted:

> *"Finally, the Government argues that the home office or extended overhead costs are fixed costs which would have been incurred even if there had been no delay. Its argument continues that to allow relief by utilizing the Eichleay Formula would permit recovery of overhead costs much greater than the direct costs incurred during the periods of delay.*
>
> *This argument misses the point. Home office expenses are indirect costs usually allocated to all of a contractor's contracts based upon each contractor's incurred direct costs. When a government initiated delay causes a contractor's direct costs to decline greatly, that contract does not receive its fair share of the fixed home office expenses. The Eichleay Formula is one method approved by boards and courts over a long period of time which corrects this distortion in the allocation of these indirect expenses."*

The most common argument against the use of the Eichleay Formula is that the contractor receives compensation of home office overhead by virtue of the markup on a change. The obvious problem with this is that a contractor likewise receives this same markup whether or not the change causes a delay. Unless the markup clearly contains an allocation for home office overhead, the argument that Eichleay should not be used may not be valid. The ASBCA noted in *Shirley Contracting Corporation*, ASBCA No. 29848 (1984) that:

> *". . . We find no support for this position. The Corps' Area Engineer testified that he did not know the composition of the 15 percent allowed but nonetheless approved it as a matter of course. He also admitted that the 15 percent overhead was allowed even 'on modifications that involved no delay at all.'"*

This does not mean that the application of the Eichleay Formula is automatic. The contractor must reasonably demonstrate that during the delay period, he could not acquire additional work to absorb the overhead because of a limited bonding capacity or because of the specifics of the delay situation.

When to Apply the Eichleay Formula

By now the reader has probably recognized that the Eichleay Formula is a calculation applied at the end of the project after all work and delays are complete. If the parties attempt to resolve the question of home office overhead during the project, some form of a modified Eichleay Formula is applicable. The most realistic approach is to apply the Eichleay Formula from the beginning of the project up to the point of negotiations. Thus, the total contract billings, the total company billings, and the total number of days from the start of the project up to the approximate date of the calculation are used.

When using the Eichleay Formula in federal government cases, some costs (such as advertising, entertainment, interest, etc.) which are normally considered home office overhead, are not allowable. The government will normally disallow these costs during its audit procedures. In its contract, the federal government has the right to audit a contractor's records. For delay claims in excess of $100,000, the government normally will perform an audit. The various federal agencies have different internal guidelines mandating the dollar level at which an audit is required.

The use of the Eichleay Formula in other jurisdictions (such as at the state and municipal level) may or may not allow these costs. The contractor, on the other hand, might maintain that the owner cannot reduce the allowable costs unless specific case law so dictates. The non-federal owner should encourage that use of the Eichleay Formula follow federal guidelines, since its origins are in federal cases.

Home office overhead costs in a delay situation can represent a significant percentage of the overall delay damages. Owners should carefully consider this fact in drafting their construction contracts. Some owners prevent problems in this area by defining in the contract the allowable damages for delays, including a computation for home office overhead, if any.

Canadian Method

An alternative method of calculating home office overhead costs for a delay, used extensively in Canada, is known as the *Canadian Method*. The Canadian Method utilizes the contractor's actual markup for overhead in its calculation. This markup is based on either the project bid documents or an audit of the contractor's records. An audit would reveal the historical percentage markup for home office overhead applied to each project. The percentage markup is multiplied by the original contract amount, and then divided by the original number of days in the contract.

$$\frac{\text{Percentage Markup} \times \text{Original Contract Sum}}{\text{Original Number of Days in the Contract}} = \frac{\text{Daily Overhead}}{\text{Rate}}$$

This yields a daily overhead rate based on the amount the contractor bid. This rate is then applied to the number of days of compensable delay.

$$\frac{\text{Daily}}{\text{Overhead}} \times \frac{\text{Number of Days of}}{\text{Compensable Delay}} = \frac{\text{Compensation for Home}}{\text{Office Overhead}}$$

If the delay is significant (a couple of years, for example), then the daily rate may be escalated to account for an inflationary increase in overhead over time. For example, a project is bid for $5,000,000. The contracted duration is 500 days. Based on the original bid documents, the overhead markup is ten percent. Multiply the contract amount, $5,000,000, by the percent overhead, and divide by the number of days to determine the daily overhead rate, $1,000/day as shown in Figure 9.4. The daily overhead rate of $1,000/day is multiplied by 50 days, to determine the overhead for the delay period, $50,000.

The Canadian method is simpler than the Eichleay Formula, since normally, there is no consideration given to unallowable costs. Although this method is simple, it has not been widely used in the United States.

Calculation Based on Actual Records

Some owners are reluctant to include home office overhead costs in compensation for delays. This is particularly true when these damages are based on a formula (Eichleay or Canadian) which is an approximation. The contractor may strengthen his argument by maintaining accurate records in the home office that would support his specific claim for damages.

For example, a contractor has a home office staff of twenty people. The staff includes project managers, estimators, schedulers, clerical workers, and accountants. The company requires that all employees maintain accurate time sheets by activity, and by project. This documentation may be useful in supporting the contractor's request for home office overhead costs when a delay occurs.

In this approach, the contractor can use the records to determine the staff's percentage effort expended, either throughout the project or during the specific delay period, if appropriate. The time sheets show the hours the home office staff expended on the delayed project. This percentage can be applied to the other fixed home office costs to apportion those to this project. The example shown in Figure 9.5 illustrates this method.

Alternatively, the computation in Figure 9.5 could also be performed on a salary basis to generate the percentage of salary, as opposed to time.

Net Present Value Analysis

In lieu of, or in addition to, the preceding calculations for home office overhead damages, there is another type of damages associated with projects that are suspended or delayed. These are addressed by the Net Present Value Analysis, illustrated by the following example.

A contractor has five projects, A through E. Each project has a duration of one year to complete. The value of each contract is $1,000,000. The contractor's home office overhead costs are $100,000 per year. The contractor's direct expenses are expected to be 93% of revenues. He is given notice to proceed on all five projects, but shortly after starting the work, project C is halted for a year. Given this information, the contractor can formulate a budget and actual income statement for the period, as shown in Figure 9.6.

Figure 9.4

Example of the Canadian Method used to estimate overhead cost associated with a 50-day delay

Project bid	= $5,000,000
Contract duration	= 500 days
Overhead from bid papers	= 10%
Compensable delay	= 50 days

$$\text{Daily Rate} = \frac{10\% \times \$5,000,000}{500 \text{ days}} = \$1,000/\text{day}$$

$$\text{Damages} = \$1,000/\text{day} \times 50 \text{ days} = \$50,000$$

Figure 9.5

Calculation Based on Actual Records

A project is suspended for 50 calendar days. The home office staff consists of eight people, including the CEO who does not maintain a time sheet. Staff time for this project during the delay was:

Position	Project Hours	Total Hours
Secretary	25	288
Estimator	24	288
Accountant	96	288
Project Manager	288	288
Project Manager	0	288
General Super	40	288
Clerk	10	288
	543	2016

$$\frac{543}{2016} = 26.9\%$$

Home office costs during suspension = $51,000

$$26.9\% \times \$51,000 = \$13,719$$

As shown, the delay of project C results in an unfavorable variance of $70,000 in the income from operations for the period.

The next year, the contractor wins five more contracts (F through J) valued at $1,000,000 each. His cost and overhead data remain the same as in year 1. However, the suspension of project C is lifted and he completes that project in year 2, along with contracts F through J. The budgeted and actual income statements for year 2 are shown in Figure 9.7.

Whereas the contractor showed an unfavorable variance of $70,000 in year 1 of project C's underabsorption, the contributions from project C in year 2 create a favorable balance because of project C's overabsorption in that year. As a result, the contractor's cash flow (in year 1) is adversely affected by the delay. The contractor can also calculate the cost of this impact.

Discounted Cash Flow

The Net Present Value Analysis (NPVA) not only considers the amount of cash that flows in and out of a project, but also the time value of cash flows. A dollar received sometime in the future is not worth as much as the dollar received and available for reinvestment today. The NPVA can measure the indirect impact of delays, such as cash flow problems. In this way, NPVA is also known as the Discounted Cash Flow Method.

Contractor's Budgeted and Actual Income Statements for _____			
	Budget Income Statement	Actual Income Statement	Variance
Revenues	$5,000,000	$4,000,000	
Costs	4,650,000	3,720,000	
Gross profit	350,000	280,000	
Home office overhead	100,000	100,000	
Income	$ 250,000	$ 180,000	$70,000 (unfavorable)
Net Present Value Analysis Example			

Figure 9.6

Contractor's Budgeted and Actual Income Statements for Year 2			
	Budget Income Statement	Actual Income Statement	Variance
Revenues	$5,000,000	$6,000,000	
Costs	4,650,000	5,580,000	
Gross profit	350,000	420,000	
Home office overhead	100,000	100,000	
Income	$ 250,000	$ 320,000	$70,000 (favorable)
Net Present Value Analysis Example			

Figure 9.7

The only difficulty in using NPVA is choosing the appropriate rate for discounting the cash flow. The most objective rate to use in performing the NPVA analysis is the contractor's cost of capital. For publicly held corporations, this is the Weighted Cost of Capital (WCC). The WCC is a weighted average of the component costs of debt, preferred stock, and common equity. The WCC is determined by using the Capital Asset Pricing Model (CAPM). CAPM is a formula that considers:

- The firm's rate of return
- The risk-free rate of return
- The firm's "beta" value (a measure of a firm's inherent risk)

The Cost of Capital

The CAPM yields a WCC value for contractors that is slightly higher than the prime interest rate. Since the WCC calculation is based partly on equity markets, it is not the most accurate discount rate for privately held contractors to use for short-term borrowing. This rate is determined by a lending institution's loan officer instead of the capital markets. As with the WCC rates, the private contractor's short-term borrowing rate will be slightly higher than the prime interest rate.

Example Estimate for Indirect Impact

In this section, the Net Present Value Method will be used to indicate the indirect impact on the contractor. Using the previous example, recall that the contractor has an unfavorable variance of $70,000 in year 1 because of project C's underabsorption. In contrast, the contribution from project C in year 2 creates a favorable balance in that year. To simplify the example, revenues and expenses are assumed to be realized and paid in twelve equal monthly segments (see Figure 9.8).

At this point, both years 1 and 2 as-budgeted and actual cash flows are discounted back to the present to determine the impact of the delay on the cash flows. This is shown in steps 1 through 3 below.

> Note: Texts dealing with construction/engineering economics provide tables for the time value of money for various periods and different interest rates. **Contractor's Business Handbook** by Michael S. Milliner (R.S. Means, 1988) is an excellent source of information on construction accounting, financial planning, tax management, and cost control.

The example assumes that the contractor's cost of capital is twelve percent.

Step 1

Determine present value of budgeted cash flows. The year 1 and year 2 projects, as budgeted, forecast a monthly net cash flow to the beginning of the year that yields a present value of $234,477.50. Discounting the second year cash flows back to the beginning of year 2, and then discounting that sum as a lump sum back to the beginning of year 1 yields a present value of $209,364.96. The sum of these two present values is the Net Present Value of the budgeted or as-planned cash flow for years 1 and 2.

Present Value of budgeted cash flow for year 1	+	Present Value of budgeted cash flow for year 2	=	Net Present Value of budgeted cash flows for years 1 and 2

In the example, this amounts to $443,842.46. Calculations are shown in Figure 9.9. "PVIFA" stands for Present Value Interest Factor of an Annuity.

Step 2

Calculate the Net Present Value of actual cash flow. As shown earlier, because of the delay to project C, the contractor's monthly net cash flows were reduced in year 1, but increase in year 2. The same procedure is followed in this step as in Step 1. First, year 1 actual monthly net cash flows are discounted to present at a twelve percent cost of capital. Next, year 2 cash flows are twice discounted as in Step 1 to arrive at a present value for the year 2 actual monthly net cash flows. Calculations are shown in Figure 9.10.

Step 3

Determine the indirect impact to the contractor resulting from disrupted cash flows. This step involves simply subtracting the NPV of the actual cash flow from the NPV of the budgeted cash flows, to determine the impact to the contractor's cash flow (see Figure 9.11).

NPV budgeted − NPV actual = Impact to contractor's cash flow

	Net Cash Flows		
	Year 1		
Time Period	**Budgeted**	**Actual**	**Variances**
Each Month	$20,833	$15,000	− $5,833
	Year 2		
Time Period	**Budgeted**	**Actual**	**Variances**
Each Month	$20,833	$26,667	+ $5,833

**Indirect Impact on the Contractor using
Net Present Value Analysis**

Figure 9.8

**Estimating Contractor's Indirect Impact
Using Net Present Value Analysis**

Step 1: Determine Present Value Budgeted Cash Flow

    Year 1 Cash Flow:

$$PV^1 = \$\ 20{,}833 \times PVIFA$$
$$PV^1 = \$\ 20{,}833 \times 11.2551$$
$$PV^1 = \$234{,}477.50$$

    Year 2 Cash Flow:

$$PV^2(a) = \$\ 20{,}833 \times PVIFA$$
$$PV^2(a) = \$\ 20{,}833 \times 11.2551$$
$$PV^2(a) = \$234{,}477.50$$
$$PV^2(b) = PV^2(a) \times PVIF$$
$$PV^2(b) = \$234{,}477.50 \times .8929$$
$$PV^2(b) = \$209{,}364.96$$

Net Present Value (as budgeted) = $PV^1 + PV^2(b)$
NPV = $234,477.50 + $209,364.96
NPV = $443,842.46 (as budgeted)

Figure 9.9

Figure 9.10

**Estimating Contractor's Indirect Impact
Using Net Present Value Analysis**

Step 2: Calculate Net Present Value of Actual Cash Flow

Year 1 Cash Flow:

$PV^1 = \$15,000 \times PVIFA$
$PV^1 = \$15,000 \times 11.2551$
$PV^1 = \$168,826.50$

Year 2 Cash Flow:

$PV^2(a) = \$26,667 \times PVIFA$
$PV^2(a) = \$26,667 \times 11.2551$
$PV^2(b) = PV^2(a) \times PVIFA$
$PV^2(b) = \$300,139.75 \times .8929$
$PV^2(b) = \$267,994.78$

Net Present Value (actual) $= PV^1 + PV^2$
NPV $= \$168,826.50 + \$267,994.78$
NPV $= \$436,821.28$ (actual)

Figure 9.10

**Estimating Contractor's Indirect Impact
Using Net Present Value Analysis**

**Step 3: Determine Indirect Impact to the contractor resulting
from disrupted cash flows**

Indirect Impact $=$ NPV budgeted $-$ NPV actual
$= \$443,842.46 - \$436,821.28$
$= \$ 7,021.18$

Figure 9.11

**Calculating Contractor's Indirect Impact
Using Net Present Value Analysis**

Step 4: Determine Current Value of Indirect Impact

Indirect Impact per year 1 dollars $= \$7,021.18$
(from Steps 1–3)
Current Value $= \$7,021.18 \times$ CVIF (1.12×1.12)
$= \$7,021.18 \times 1.2544$
$= \$8,807.37$

Figure 9.12

Step 4

Determine the current value of indirect impact. The indirect cash flow impact calculated in steps 1 through 3, $7,021.18, represents the cost to the contractor of disrupting the cash flow. This impact is valued in pre-year 1 dollars. The final step of this process involves calculating the current value of the pre-year 1 dollars. In this example, settlement is made at the end of year 2 (see Figure 9.12).

This $8,807.37 represents the indirect cost to the contractor for the project suspension in year 1. Note that this figure cannot be calculated if the delay is analyzed using a pure accounting approach, since it would not consider the time value of money.

Of course, this is a very simple example, but the technique is equally applicable to more complex situations. In some cases, a contractor can project a cash flow using a computerized, cost-loaded, CPM schedule that becomes the as-planned part of the analysis. The pay requisitions the contractor submits serve as the as-built schedule cash flow data. The analyst can calculate variances using these two pieces of data.

The next step is to evaluate these variances in light of the as-planned versus as-built schedule analysis described above. The schedule analysis will show the liability for variances. From this information, the financial (direct cost) extent of the liability for schedule variances can be analyzed. The final step in this process is the calculation of the indirect impact using Present Value Analysis, as shown earlier. The following example illustrates this approach.

> A contractor has an as-planned cost-loaded CPM schedule for a project. Based on this schedule, the following cash flow is projected:
>
> > Year 1: $1,360,000
> > Year 2: $2,540,000
> > Year 3: $950,000
>
> Because of delays and changes by the owner, the project is performed later than planned, and in a different sequence. The actual cash flow based on the pay requests shows the following:
>
> > Year 1: $900,000
> > Year 2: $2,000,000
> > Year 3: $1,950,000

Using the same method shown earlier, the variance in years 1, 2, and 3 can be calculated and the NPVA performed to establish the impact to the contractor.

It should be recognized that the impact would occur only in the areas of overhead and profit. Costs for labor and materials, although shifted in time, would not result in any impact to the contractor, in that he merely passes along these dollars and does not have beneficial use of them.

Summary

This four-step process can also be used in situations where a contractor's progress is not delayed across the board, but rather, some work activities are halted. Once again, the schedule analysis, along with the project documents, form the basis for assessing liability for the delays. Delays that extend throughout the project duration, but are not compensated for by change orders, are evaluated on the basis of their effect on the project cash flow. Of course, there is a difference between a partial delay and a complete suspension of work. The effect on cash flow must be analyzed either way. It may be necessary to apply the present value analysis to cash flow from different pay items to calculate the indirect impact of delays. The procedure for the line-by-line analysis for a partial delay remains the same as for a full suspension of work. However, this analysis is more complex.

The bottom line in recovering delay damages is still **proof of damages**. To provide acceptable "proof," the contractor must do two things:

1. First, the contractor must show that *the performance period was extended because of factors beyond its control* (excepting excusable/non-compensable delays, such as labor strikes). A comparison of the as-planned and as-built project schedules, along with an analysis of project schedules and documentation, will accomplish this first step.

2. Second, the contractor must accurately prove the *amount of the damages*. This is done by computing the direct cost increases (such as field office overhead), and indirect impact costs (by Eichleay or Net Present Value Analysis). Should the owner agree to pay for these increases by a change order, all added costs are included in the change order price.

When it becomes necessary to present a claim for added compensation in litigation or arbitration, the contractor must present all costs incurred (both direct and indirect), as well as substantiation for each item claimed, to fully recover damages.

Inefficiency Costs Caused by Delays

Chapter Ten
Inefficiency Costs Caused by Delays

In addition to the direct and indirect impacts and damages presented in previous chapters, there are other types of impacts and damages that may occur. Most important on this list is a decrease in the contractor's efficiency due to delays. The delay and impact may occur in two stages. The delay may not directly cause the inefficiency, but initially causes some other impact which then leads to the inefficiency.

This chapter is not intended to explain every type of inefficiency or present techniques for measuring productivity. Rather, it will show how a delay can impact the productivity of the job, and how that impact can be measured, as long as accurate, contemporaneous records are maintained.

Shifts in the Construction Season

A delay to a project can shift work originally scheduled for one season into a different season. For example, work scheduled for late summer and early fall may be pushed into the winter months by a delay. The effect of the delay on the contractor's efficiency depends on the type of work. Several examples follow.

Example # 1
A contractor plans to complete all concrete operations before the winter season. A delay forces the contractor to continue concrete work through the winter months in a cold weather environment. As a consequence, the concrete crews do not work as efficiently as they would under ideal conditions and the contractor experiences an increase in the unit cost for placing concrete. The contractor is also forced to change the concrete mix design to include accelerators, which further increases the unit cost, in this case, for materials. Finally, the contractor must use winter concrete placing techniques, including extra winter protection and steam curing in some instances. All of these impacts were the direct result of the shift in season caused by the initial delay to the project.

Example # 2
A highway contractor plans to complete all paving operations before the winter, which marks the seasonal shutdown of local asphalt plants. The project is initially delayed and, as a result, the contractor cannot finish paving before the winter begins. Because the asphalt plants shut down and the owner's specifications do not allow paving from November 1 to April 1, the initial delay is compounded by the winter shutdown period. The contractor

must now finish the work during the next season. In this case, there may not be a direct inefficiency in the contractor's labor or equipment productivity, but the contractor experiences additional demobilization and remobilization costs. It is also possible that some loss of efficiency may result since new workers may have to be trained and, initially, may have a less productive period before reaching peak productivity levels. (See Figure 10.1 for a chart showing typical time frames required to bring a new crew up to the expected productivity rate.)

Example # 3

A contractor performing a heavy earth moving operation is delayed so that work that was to be performed during a relatively dry season is forced into a wetter season. The earth moving operation is adversely affected by muddy conditions in the cut and fill areas. In wet weather, the overall productivity of cubic yard per crew/equipment day is reduced.

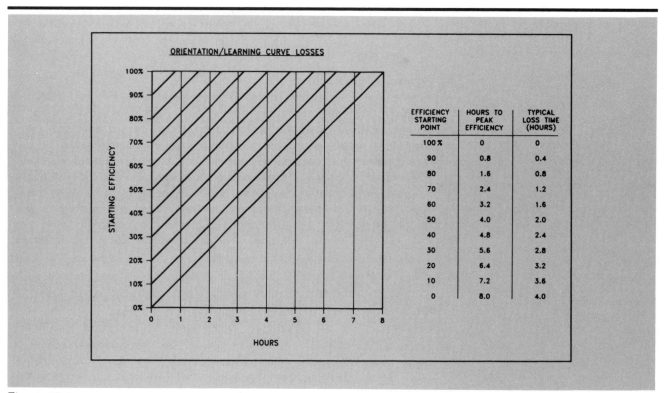

Figure 10.1

Example # 4

An HVAC contractor is scheduled to install the heating system in a building to be operational by March. Because of some initial delays, the work is resequenced and the HVAC contractor must accelerate the work to ready the system for operation by the end of November. Since the project is in a cold weather climate and the subsequent crews will be working inside by December 1, the building will now be a heated structure in which to work, which would not have been the case according to the original schedule. The result should be an increase in productivity.

Numerous other scenarios could develop from the shift of work from one season to another. Season-related impacts resulting from a delay are sometimes referred to as a *ripple effect*. The important issue for the delay analyst is to assess whether a delay caused the operations to shift into another season, and if that shift had any impact on productivity.

Availability of Resources

At times, delays can affect the availability of resources in the areas of manpower, subcontracts, or equipment. The following examples illustrate the effects of unavailable resources.

Example # 1

A general contractor plans to complete a project in April. Because of a delay, the work extends into the summer. However, because the construction workload in that location is at its peak during the summer, there is less available labor from which to draw. Therefore, the contractor may not be able to obtain enough labor to finish the work by the revised schedule for completion. This is particularly true of weather-related work such as exterior painting, site work, and landscaping.

Example # 2

An earth moving contractor plans to excavate several hundred thousand cubic yards of material using scrapers. The project is delayed at the beginning. By the time it gets under way, the scrapers are committed to another project and are no longer available. Consequently, the contractor must either rent equipment at a higher cost than the use and maintenance of his owned equipment, or use loaders and dump truck to move the material. The productivity resulting from the use of loaders and dump trucks is significantly lower than that originally planned based on the use of scrapers, and therefore, the operation is more costly.

Example # 3

A contractor constructing a bridge must schedule a portion of the work during a specific interval because of the availability of certain equipment, for instance, the use of a snooper crane. Because of a delay to the project, the work shifts and the equipment is no longer available. The contractor must now perform the work using a new method, thereby increasing project cost.

When a delay occurs, the analyst must look closely at exactly what the impacts are on resources such as equipment and manpower and how to quantify that impact.

Manpower Levels and Distribution

Certain types of delays affect the level of manpower and its distribution on a project. These changes may occur in the form of additional manpower, erratic staffing, or variations in preferred/optimum crew size. Any of these situations may affect the level of efficiency of the work.

Additional Manpower

Delays to specific activities may force the contractor to work on more activities than planned at one time, and to increase the levels of manpower significantly for a specific trade. Depending on the union rules, additional manpower may also require more foremen or master mechanics.

Also, as the contractor increases the crew size, it is not uncommon for the added personnel to be less productive than the original crew. Contractors often say that as they draw more personnel from the union hall, they see a decline in the level of productivity.

Erratic Staffing

In the face of a delay, a contractor may staff a project erratically in order to address specific needs as they arise. Theoretically, a contractor would like to staff a project in a bell curve fashion — starting out with a small crew, building up to optimum size, and then tapering down toward the end of the project. (See Figure 10.2)

Constant fluctuations in the size of the crew on the site are clearly not desirable. However, the contractor may in some circumstances be forced to man the project erratically in order to achieve budgetary and schedule goals. In such situations, there may be a measurable reduction in efficiency.

To demonstrate the negative effect of a forced change in labor distribution, the contractor would be well advised to plot the original schedule to graphically portray the planned distribution of labor, and then plot the actual distribution of labor caused by the delay and compare the two.

Preferred/Optimum Crew Size

Another factor that should be considered is preferred/optimum crew size. For example, a finish contractor has a standing force of eight carpenters employed through the year. Because the crew works together throughout the year, they have established a smooth and efficient routine. If a delay now causes that contractor to accelerate his work and increase his staff above his optimal crew, there can be some measured loss of efficiency, as the original crew assimilates the new personnel, and brings them "up to speed."

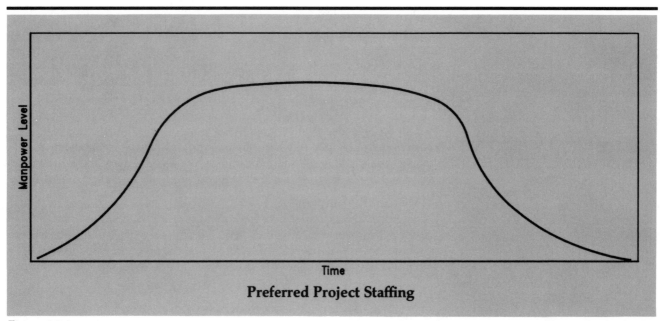

Preferred Project Staffing

Figure 10.2

Sequencing of Work

Delays to critical and non-critical activities can also force a contractor to re-sequence the work. The re-sequencing itself is not a problem, but its effects may reduce the contractor's productivity in a number of ways. The contractor's crew may be hampered in their work by the presence of another trade, or the crew may be obstructed by material stockpiled in the work area. With such interferences, workers inevitably experience some reduction in productivity.

Measuring Inefficiency

There are many ways in which a contractor's work can be affected because of changes to the work schedule. The delays may cause these problems directly or indirectly. The delays may be to critical or non-critical items.

The contractor must be able to measure and demonstrate how the delays adversely affected the workers' productivity if he is to be compensated in the form of damages. There are several methods for quantifying productivity loss. The delay analyst should be aware of each of these options. The following list ranks the different methods by their accuracy in measuring losses in productivity.

1. Compare unimpacted work with impacted work.
2. Compare similar work on other projects with the impacted work on the project in question.
3. Use statistically developed models.
4. Use expert testimony.
5. Refer to industry published standards.
6. Use the total cost.

Compare Unimpacted with Impacted Work

The impacted vs. unimpacted method is the preferred method to measure losses in productivity, particularly where no direct cause and effect can be measured for each delaying event. The contractor must show a comparison between unimpacted and impacted work. For example, if a contractor's work is shifted into a cold weather season, he should compare it with productivity during the less favorable weather. Of course, the comparison must be made on the same type of work. A more specific example:

> A contractor plans to set reinforcing steel during the summer. A delay pushes this activity into the winter months. The contractor's records show that during the favorable weather, the work crews were able to set two tons per crew-day. During the less favorable weather, however, the same crews are able to set only 1.5 tons per crew-day. Hence, the loss of productivity was 25%.

To measure productivity in this manner, all information must be recorded in a form that can be converted into productivity units.

The other methods mentioned become less accurate as one progresses down the list. Total cost is the least desirable, as can be seen in the following comparison between the total cost method and the demonstrated productivity method.

Total Cost Method

In the total cost method, a contractor argues that he estimated a certain cost for his work. Because of the delay and the subsequent inefficiency of a shift in work seasons, the actual cost was higher. Therefore, the contractor claims the difference in damages. This method is carried out as follows.

Actual cost of paving operation:	$1,975,000
Estimated cost of paving operation:	$1,250,000
Damages claimed because of inefficiency:	$ 725,000

This method assumes that the contractor's estimate was accurate. It also assumes that the contractor in no way contributed to the reduced efficiency and that all additional costs are solely attributable to the delays cited. Both of these assumptions may be easily challenged.

Demonstrated Productivity Method

The demonstrated productivity method does not suffer from the shortcomings of the total cost method. If the contractor is responsible for some loss of efficiency, this is factored in and accounted for in the calculation for the demonstrated productivity. Likewise, there is no reliance on an estimate, but rather on actual demonstrated productivity for specific work.

As long as the contractor is comparing the same type of work, and no other intervening factors affect the work except the shift in season, then the demonstrated productivity calculation should be reasonably accurate.

This chapter is not intended to be a treatise on the subject of inefficiency or on the techniques for measuring productivity. Rather, the intent is to point out that a delay may adversely affect productivity on the project. Also, it must be recognized that detailed, accurate, and contemporaneous information must be maintained in order to measure productivity impacts associated with a delay.

Chapter Eleven

Other Categories of Delay Damages

Chapter Eleven

Other Categories of Delay Damages

As the reader may now understand, the calculation of delay damages is as much an art as a science. The appropriate damage calculations are project specific and situation specific. No book can address every combination and permutation. This chapter addresses certain points which, while not obvious, are important in defining damages related to delays. Included are some situations that frequently occur, but are not well understood.

Damages Associated with Non-Critical Delays

Thus far, this book has focused on delays to the critical path or delays that affect the overall completion date of the project. Normally, most damages are associated with a delay to the overall project. That does not mean, however, that delays to non-critical activities may not also cause damages. Activities not on the critical path can be delayed and can have damages without ultimately affecting the completion date. The following example illustrates this concept.

A contractor has a contract for the construction of a hospital complex. The complex consists of three buildings. Two buildings (A & B) already exist and must be renovated. The third (C) is new construction.

The contractor schedules the project using the critical path method. The schedule shows that the critical path of the overall project is controlled by the construction of the new building, C. The other two buildings need only be completed within that overall duration and have twelve months of float. (See Figure 11.1)

Early in the project, the owner discovers asbestos in buildings A and B. The contractor cannot proceed until the project architects develop a method for the safe removal of the asbestos. The hold on the two buildings remains in effect for ten months, at which time an acceptable method is devised and the contractor is released to continue work. In the interim, the contractor works on the construction of building C.

The owner and contractor meet to negotiate a change order for the delay and the extra work associated with removing the asbestos in buildings A and B. The direct cost of the asbestos removal is a straightforward calculation. The owner and contractor can agree on the work involved and the cost of the work. The contractor, however, requests additional compensation for the delay to buildings A and B. The owner argues that the overall project was delayed and, therefore, the contractor is not due any delay damages or any extra cost associated with the delay.

Did the contractor experience any damages from the delayed start of these two buildings? To answer this question, the contractor must establish the impact of the delay and the corresponding damages.

The contractor explains that the work sequence in the original schedule would have been more efficient and that the delay affects these three areas:

1. Escalation of Labor
2. Additional Supervision
3. Reduced Efficiency

Escalation of Labor

The contractor had originally planned to work each trade through the three buildings in a consecutive sequence. For instance, the drywall crew was to work building A first, then move to building B, and then move into building C. This same sequence was planned for electrical, HVAC, plumbing, millwork, flooring, and painting.

Because of the delay, the contractor now must work several crews in all three buildings at the same time to meet the project completion date, instead of moving the same crew from building to building. As a result, the distribution of labor shifts to a later time frame. The contractor can document a wage increase of $1.25 per hour for his sheetrockers. The shift in labor is plotted on a graph as shown in Figure 11.2. The graph shows that 1,560 man-hours have been shifted to a later time frame.

For sheetrock, the contractor claims damages of $1,950 (an increase of $1.25 per hour for labor for 1,560 man-hours). The contractor performs the same analysis for each trade affected by the change in sequence. These calculations would be similar to that shown for the sheetrockers in Figure 11.2.

Additional Supervision

To allow for the inclusion of supervision costs, the contractor explains that when crew sizes increase, additional non-working foremen must be added. The contractor calculates additional supervision for the affected trades and summarizes the claim as shown in Figure 11.3.

Reduced Efficiency

Finally, the contractor argues that if he had been able to use the same crew throughout all the buildings, they would have absorbed the initial mobilization and learning curve to become most productive. Because each crew had to go through the mobilization/learning curve, the result is a lower productivity level than that originally planned. The contractor argues that reduced productivity represents an increase in cost.

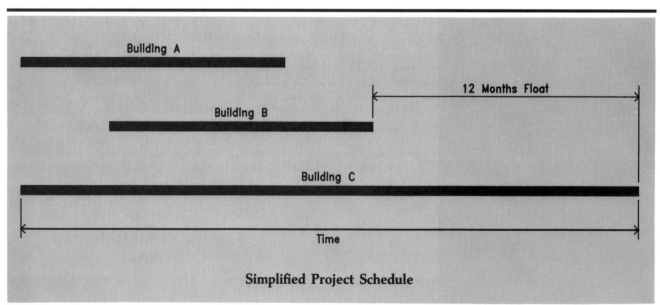

Simplified Project Schedule

Figure 11.1

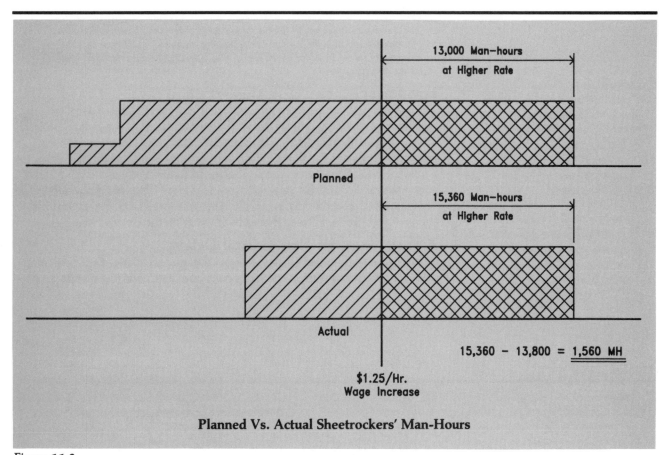

Planned Vs. Actual Sheetrockers' Man-Hours

Figure 11.2

Unfortunately, productivity is a very difficult item to document. In order to raise the owner's level of confidence, the contractor has used his best crew for each trade as a benchmark to measure the learning curve/start-up effect and the difference in productivity caused by added crews. Figure 11.4 is an example the contractor developed for the drywall crews.

Equipment

The preceding example shows how a delay to a non-critical activity can significantly affect the cost of the work without delaying the overall project. The cost of work may also go up due to a change that affects equipment usage, yet does not involve a critical path activity. For example, if a delay to a non-critical activity forces the contractor to mobilize an additional piece of equipment, the contractor can claim compensation. Only the mobilization and demobilization costs would be a valid damage, since the cost of using that equipment (once mobilized) should be included in the contract sum.

A Final Word on Non-Critical Delays

Many owners argue that the concept of damages associated with non-critical delays is really an argument of "who owns the float." Most contracts do not

---

Additional Supervision

Trade: Sheetrockers
Crews planned: 2
Duration planned: 23 Months
Therefore, 1 non-working foreman for 23 months

Crews actual: 4
Actual duration: 15 Months
Therefore, 2 non-working foremen for 15 months each

Additional Supervision:
30 man months - 23 man months = 7 man months

Damages: 7 man months × $2,950/month = $20,650

Figure 11.3

Loss of Efficiency – Drywall

Demonstrated productivity by benchmark crew:	1200 s.f. per crew day (Based on daily reports and labor tickets)
Productivity of additional crews:	1000 s.f. per crew day (Based on daily reports and labor tickets)
Loss of efficiency:	1200 − 1000 = 200 s.f. per crew day $\frac{200}{1200} = 16.7\%$
Additional crews gross costs:	$9,600/mo. × 28 months = $268,800
Damages:	16.7% × $268,800 = $44,890

Figure 11.4

address who "owns" the float or the consequences if float is used by the owner. In reality, the contract owns the float and either party may use it as long as it does not financially affect the other party. Some owners claim they own the float and, if they use it, the contractor will receive no additional compensation. This is a form of a *no damages for delay* clause. The owner should hire qualified counsel to review such a clause before inserting it into the contract.

Legal / Consulting Costs

In general, the costs for attorneys and consultants are not recoverable in a claim situation. This does not mean that they will not be collected in a settlement, but they are not usually awarded in litigation or arbitration. The party asserting the claim should include legal/consultant costs as valid elements of its claim, recognizing the limited chance of recovery.

Lost Profits / Opportunity Costs

Both contractors and owners may submit claims for damages associated with lost profits and/or lost opportunity. In general, these are not recoverable damages.

The owner without a *liquidated damages* clause may claim that a contractor's delay caused lost profits. It may argue that the facility could have produced a certain amount of money if it had been completed on time. Unfortunately, most courts consider lost profits as highly speculative and, therefore, are reluctant to award them. The astute owner carefully considers this fact while drafting the contract with the help of qualified counsel. If, in fact, significant damages might result from lost profits, the owner should consider including a Liquidated Damages clause in the contract, rather than relying on recovery through litigation.

Contractors' chances for success in receiving compensation for lost profits are no better than owners' chances. Some contractors claim damages to other projects are the result of delays to a specific project. For example, a contractor may claim that because of a delay to project # 1, he was unable to utilize equipment on project # 2 which began on the scheduled completion date of project # 1. As a result, it was necessary to rent additional equipment at increased cost. While this argument may seem viable, these types of costs are not usually recoverable because these damages are not reasonably contemplated by the owner as a consequence of the delays caused. Therefore, they are not awarded. The contractor is more likely to receive compensation for using rented equipment if he employs it on project # 1 and instead uses his owned equipment on project # 2.

Other Impacts

Delays on a construction project may cause a myriad of different impacts. These may include items such as:

- Temporary utility and facility costs
- Extended warranties
- Maintaining and protecting work during delays
- Stacking of trades
- Increased bond costs

Normally, all of these items fit into one of the general categories such as field overhead, inefficiency, etc. The individual structuring the claim must carefully assess all of the impacts to the project occasioned by the delay. In this way, items such as these will be included.

Constructive Acceleration

When an excusable delay occurs on a project, either compensable or noncompensable, the owner should at least grant a time extension (via change order). Otherwise, the owner may be inviting a claim for constructive acceleration.

Constructive acceleration exists when the following conditions occur:
1. There is an excusable delay to the project.
2. The contractor requests a time extension for the excusable delay.
3. The request for a time extension is either directly or effectively denied by the owner.
4. The contractor is told to finish on time – in other words, according to the then-existing contract completion date.
5. The contractor actually accelerates his work.
6. The contractor sustains additional costs.

If all six of these conditions exist, the contractor has a valid claim for damages for constructive acceleration. Note that there is no requirement in the list above that the contractor finish on time. To illustrate acceleration, consider the following example.

A contractor experiences an excusable delay of fifteen calendar days, notifies the owner, and requests a time extension. The owner agrees, grants a time extension, and issues a change order accordingly. The owner then directs the contractor to accelerate the project, finishing it fifteen calendar days earlier (or by the original date specified in the contract). This is a clear case of directed acceleration, in which the owner assumes liability for any increased costs. In constructive acceleration, the owner does not grant the time extension, but still requires the project to be completed on the originally-scheduled date.

Reluctance to Grant Time Extensions

Many delay claims today have an element of constructive acceleration, since owners are generally reluctant to grant time extensions. Owners often prefer to wait until the end of the project before granting a time extension, in case the contractor is able to make up the time. This is not an advisable tactic. The owner may well be setting himself up for a constructive acceleration claim. If there is a valid excusable delay, it is best for the owner to grant the time extension as quickly as possible.

Contractor's Position

If the owner refuses to grant a time extension, the contractor should notify the owner that the directive to finish the project by the existing contract completion date is considered a directive to accelerate, since the contractor is entitled to a time extension for excusable delays.

As was noted at the beginning of this chapter, delay damages are as much an art as a science. Consequently, the analyst must carefully and meticulously consider and assess all possible impacts associated with delays. Merely because a delay does not affect the overall completion date of the project does not mean that no damages were sustained. Delays to non-critical activities and changes in sequence can also give rise to increased costs.

Chapter Twelve

Risk Management

Chapter Twelve
Risk Management

Construction is a business fraught with risk. One of the greatest areas of risk is controlling time and the cost of time. All parties can exercise better risk management in this area. By recognizing and planning, risks can be minimized and controlled. This chapter addresses some risk management considerations for each of the parties in the construction project.

All parties in a construction project must be keenly aware of the importance of good project documentation. The analysis procedures presented in this book cannot be performed if the required documentation does not exist. At the top of the list are *daily reports*. Also important are photographs/videos taken periodically over the course of the project. Finally, detailed documentation on costs must be maintained and must be amenable to segregation of discrete issues.

Owner Considerations

The owner's considerations for risk start at the project inception. First, the owner must consider external constraints concerning time. Must the facility be completed to meet a critical production date? Must the project finish by a certain date for political reasons? These factors influence the way in which the owner pursues the project. For example, certain time requirements and other factors may indicate a fast-track approach to the project.

The owner must consider the realities of finishing the project within the required time frame. Merely because external considerations require that a project be completed by a certain date does not mean that the project can, in fact, be completed by that date. The owner should consult with knowledgeable advisors to determine a reasonable duration to specify in the contract documents. Bidders should themselves thoroughly investigate the time constraints, but the owner should point out any special considerations up front. For example, if the required duration can only be achieved by an accelerated effort such as multiple shifts and seven-day work weeks, these elements should be in the contract or at least discussed during the pre-bid meeting. The owner is far better off alerting bidders to an urgent situation.

When the contract is being drawn up, the owner should also decide whether to include a *liquidated damages* clause. At this time, the owner should carefully consider the potential damages if the project is delayed. When writing a *liquidated damages* clause, the owner should determine not only the *amount* of potential damages, but also whether to include *milestone liquidated damages.* (See Chapter 10 for coverage of liquidated damages and milestone dates.)

In drafting the contract, the owner should also consider establishing time limits for the filing of claims by the contractor. In other words, the contract should clearly specify that claims for additional compensation must be submitted to the owner or his representative within a set number of days after the event that gave rise to the claim. A period of between 20 and 90 days is generally considered a reasonable time frame for the submission of claims. The clause should further state that if the required claim information is not submitted within the time specified, then the contractor forfeits the right to recover any additional compensation.

Not only should the contract specify a time limit for the filing of claims, but it should also specify exactly the information that the contractor must submit when asserting a claim. Such information would include:

- A clear statement of what is being claimed.
- An explanation of why the claim item differs from that already required by the contract.
- References to the specific contract clauses that apply.
- An explanation of the cause (or liability) for the claim.
- A clear definition of the specific impacts associated with the claim (i.e., extra work, overtime, delay, etc.).
- A detailed breakdown of the damages or extra costs with supporting information.

Scheduling Clauses

To control the project's duration, the owner must have a viable schedule. To ensure that the desired schedule is used, the contract must specify the requirements for both a viable schedule and periodic updates. Depending on the owner's degree of participation, different scheduling requirements may be dictated by the contract. Figure 12.1 is a sample scheduling specification that clearly requires the construction contractor to perform all the mechanics of the schedule production process.

Contractors are not always well versed in CPM scheduling. Some may provide the absolute minimum documentation to meet the contract requirements, but never really use the schedule as a management tool. If that potential exists, the owner may consider including in the contract a specification such as that shown in Figure 12.2. This specification allows the owner to provide the mechanics of the schedule, ensures a good schedule, and allows the owner to update at desired intervals.

In both the scheduling clauses, there is a requirement for manpower, equipment, and cost loading. These requirements are invaluable tools, both for the contractor and the owner. A manpower, equipment, and cost-loaded schedule allows the owner to analyze the planned schedule for feasibility.

Such a schedule also enhances work monitoring during the project. Checking the required productivity against the loaded resources will help determine whether or not an activity can be performed within the time scheduled. The scheduling requirement should also specify schedule updates during the project and daily progress reporting of specific activities identified on the CPM schedule.

SAMPLE SCHEDULING SPECIFICATION

(Contractor Performs Mechanics)

The construction of this project will be planned and recorded with a conventional Critical Path Method (CPM) schedule. The schedule shall be used for coordination, monitoring, and payment of all work under the contract including all activity of subcontractors, vendors, and suppliers.

CONTRACTOR is responsible for preparing the initial schedule in the form of an activity on arrow diagram. All costs incurred by CONTRACTOR in preparing the schedule shall be borne by CONTRACTOR as a part of its responsibility under this contract.

A.   60-Day Preliminary Schedule

Before proceeding with any work on site, CONTRACTOR shall prepare, submit, and receive OWNER'S approval of a 60-day Preliminary Schedule. This schedule shall provide a detailed breakdown of activities scheduled for the first 60 days of the project and shall include mobilization, submittals, procurement, and construction.

No contract work may be pursued at the site without an approved 60-day Preliminary Schedule or an approved CPM schedule.

B.   Preparation of Initial Schedule
Within 30 calendar days of the contract award, CONTRACTOR shall submit for the OWNER'S approval a detailed initial schedule. The schedule shall meet the requirements set forth in Section C.

The construction time, for the entire project or any milestone, shall not exceed the specified contract time. In the event that any milestone date or contract completion date is exceeded in the schedule, logic and/or time estimates will be revised.

Following the OWNER'S review, if revisions to the proposed schedule are required, the CONTRACTOR shall do so promptly. The schedule must be finalized within 60 days of the Notice to Proceed. Failure to finalize the schedule by that date will result in withholding all contract payments until the schedule is finalized.

Figure 12.1

C. <u>Schedule Requirements</u>

All activity on arrow diagrams shall include:

    1.   Activity nodes

    2.   Activity description

    3.   Activity duration

The activity on arrow diagram shall show the sequence and interdependence of all activities required for complete performance of all items of work under this contract, including shop drawing submittals and approvals and fabrication and delivery activities. All network "dummies" are to be shown on the diagram.

No activity duration shall be longer than 15 work days without OWNER'S approval.

OWNER reserves the right to limit the number of activities on the schedule.

The activities are to be described so that the work is readily identifiable and the progress of each activity can be readily measured. For each activity, CONTRACTOR shall identify the trade or subcontractor performing the work, the duration of the activity in work days, the manpower involved by trade, the equipment involved, the location of the work, and a dollar value of the activity. The dollar value assigned to each activity is to be reasonable and based on the amount of labor, materials, and equipment involved. When added together, the dollar value of all activities are to equal the contract price.

CONTRACTOR shall also provide the following information: work days per week, holidays, number of shifts per day, number of hours per shift, and major equipment to be used.

Any activity on arrow diagram submitted by the CONTRACTOR may be hand drawn or computer plotted. Regardless of the type of diagram, the network must be legible, readable, and understandable. Network diagram will be standard D size sheets (24" x 36"), and not a continuous diagram.

All network diagram submissions by the CONTRACTOR must include one reproducible sepia and three copies.

For both the initial schedule and all updates, the CONTRACTOR will provide the following:

Figure 12.1 (*continued*)

1. Computerized sorts by:
    I-J
    Total Float
    Early Start
    Area Sort
    Trade responsibility

2. 60-day look ahead bar charts by early start.

3. A narrative explaining progress to date on the
    project, work required in the succeeding update
    period, a description of the critical path, and
    comments concerning potential problem areas.

4. CONTRACTOR will submit four copies of each of
    the above.

D. Schedule Updates and Progress Payments

Job site progress meetings will be held monthly by OWNER
and CONTRACTOR for the purpose of updating the project work
schedule and determining the appropriate amount of partial
payment due CONTRACTOR. Progress will be reviewed to verify
finish dates of completed activities, remaining duration of
uncompleted activities, and any proposed logic and/or time
estimate revisions. CONTRACTOR will report progress on a
daily basis in accordance with the attached form.

CONTRACTOR will revise activity on arrow diagrams for
the following: delay in completion of any critical activity;
actual prosecution of the work which is, as determined by
OWNER, significantly different than that represented on the
schedule; or the addition, deletion, or revision of activities
required by contract modification. The contract completion
time will be adjusted only for causes specified in this
contract.

As determined by CPM analysis, only delays in activities
which affect milestone dates or contract completion dates will
be considered for a time extension.

If CONTRACTOR does seek a time extension of any
milestone or contract completion date, it shall furnish
documentation as required by OWNER to enable OWNER to
determine whether a time extension is appropriate under the
terms of the contract.

It is understood by OWNER and CONTRACTOR that float is
a shared commodity.

The principles involved and terms used in this section are
as set forth in the Associated General Contractors of America
publication, "The use of CPM in Construction, a manual for
General Contractors and the Construction Industry," Copyright
1976.

Figure 12.1 *(continued)*

SAMPLE SCHEDULING SPECIFICATION

(Owner Performs Mechanics)

The construction of this project will be planned and recorded with a conventional Critical Path Method (CPM) schedule. The schedule shall be used for coordination, monitoring, and payment of all work under the contract, including all activity of subcontractors, vendors, and suppliers.

CONTRACTOR is responsible for preparing the initial schedule in the form of an activity on arrow diagram. OWNER will provide a scheduling expert to work with the CONTRACTOR in preparing the initial schedule. OWNER is responsible for providing computer processing of the schedule data provided by CONTRACTOR. All costs incurred by CONTRACTOR in preparing the schedule shall be borne by CONTRACTOR as part of its responsibility under this contract.

A. 60-Day Preliminary Schedule

Before proceeding with any work on site, CONTRACTOR shall prepare, submit, and receive OWNER'S approval of a 60-Day Preliminary Schedule. This schedule shall provide a detailed breakdown of activities scheduled for the first 60 days of the project, and shall include mobilization, submittals, procurement, and construction.

No contract work may be pursued at the site without an approved 60-Day Preliminary Schedule or an approved CPM schedule.

B. Preparation of Initial Schedule

Within 10 calendar days of the contract award, CONTRACTOR shall meet with the OWNER'S expert to begin developing the initial schedule. Within 30 days of the Notice to Proceed, CONTRACTOR will complete development of the initial schedule and present to OWNER an activity or arrow diagram depicting its schedule for computer processing by OWNER.

Following computer processing and within 14 calendar days of submission of the diagram, OWNER and CONTRACTOR shall meet for joint review, correction, and adjustment of the schedule. The construction time, as determined by the schedule, for the entire project or any milestone, shall not exceed the specified contract time. In the event that any milestone date or contract completion date is exceeded in the schedule, logic and/or time estimates will be revised.

Figure 12.2

After any changes in the logic and/or time estimates have been agreed upon, another computerized schedule will be generated. The process will be repeated, if necessary, until the schedule meets all contractual requirements. However, the schedule must be finalized within 60 days of the Notice to Proceed. Failure to finalize the schedule by that date will result in withholding all contract payments until the schedule is finalized.

Once the initial schedule has been finalized and is within contract requirements, CONTRACTOR shall submit a signed copy of the schedule to OWNER.

C.   Schedule Requirements

All activity on arrow diagrams shall include:
1.   Activity nodes
2.   Activity description
3.   Activity duration

The activity on arrow diagram shall show the sequence and interdependence of all activities required for complete performance of all items of work under this contract, including shop drawing submittals and approvals, and fabrication and delivery activities. All network "dummies" are to be shown on the diagram.

No activity duration shall be longer than 15 work days without OWNER'S approval.

OWNER reserves the right to limit the number of activities on the schedule.

The activities are to be described so that the work is readily identifiable and the progress of each activity can be readily measured. For each activity, CONTRACTOR shall identify the trade or subcontractor performing the work, the duration of the activity in work days, the manpower involved by trade, the equipment involved, the location of the work, and a dollar value of the activity. The dollar value assigned to each activity is to be reasonable and based on the amount of labor, materials, and equipment involved. When added together, the dollar value of activities is to equal the contract price.

CONTRACTOR shall provide the following information: work days per week, holidays, number of shifts per day, number of hours per shift, and major equipment to be used.

Any activity on arrow diagram submitted by the CONTRACTOR or prepared by the OWNER'S expert, may either be hand drawn or computer plotted. Regardless of the type of diagram, the network must be legible, readable, and understandable. Network diagram will be on standard D size sheets (24" x 36") and not a continuous diagram.

Figure 12.2 (*continued*)

Any network diagram submitted by the contractor must include one reproducible sepia and three copies.

For both the initial schedule and all updates, the OWNER'S expert will provide the following:

1. Computerized sorts by:
   I-J
   Total Float
   Early Start
   Area Sort
   Trade responsibility

2. 60-day look ahead bar charts by early start.

3. A narrative explaining progress to date on the project, work required in the succeeding update period, a description of the critical path, and comments concerning potential problem areas.

4. CONTRACTOR will be provided with four copies of each of the above.

D. Schedule Updates and Progress Payments

Job site progress meetings will be held monthly by OWNER and CONTRACTOR for the purpose of updating the project work schedule and determining the appropriate amount of partial payment due CONTRACTOR. Progress will be reviewed to verify finish dates of completed activities, remaining duration of uncompleted activities, and any proposed logic and/or time estimate revisions. It is CONTRACTOR'S responsibility to provide OWNER with the status of activities at this meeting. The CONTRACTOR will report progress on a daily basis in accordance with the attached form. OWNER will process schedule updates based on this information once it has been verified.

CONTRACTOR will submit revised activity on arrow diagrams for the following: delay in completion of any critical activity; actual prosecution of the work which is, at determined by OWNER, significantly different than that represented on the schedule; or the addition, deletion, or revision of activities required by contract modification. The contract completion time will be adjusted only for causes specified in this contract.

As determined by CPM analysis, only delays in activities which affect milestone dates or contract completion dates will be considered for a time extension.

Figure 12.2 (continued)

If CONTRACTOR does seek a time extension of any milestone or contract completion date, it shall furnish documentation as required by OWNER to enable OWNER to determine whether a time extension is appropriate under the terms of the contract.

It is understood by OWNER and CONTRACTOR that float is a shared commodity.

The principles involved and terms used in this section are set forth in the Associated General Contractors of America publication, "The Use of CPM in Construction, A Manual for General Contractors and the Construction Industry", Copyright 1976.

Figure 12.2 (continued)

Change Orders

During the course of the project, the owner must carefully monitor the management of change orders. Every change order has two parts: time and money. Every change order should state whether or not additional time is warranted. Obviously, this task is far easier if an up-to-date CPM schedule is maintained throughout the project.

Delay Damages Clauses

A final risk management consideration for the owner is the area of delay damages. The owner can insert a *no damage for delay* clause in the contract, thus attempting to shift the burden of risk for delays to the contractor. However, the use of this type of exculpatory language is no guarantee that a dispute over delays will be prevented. The owner should research the use of a *no damage for delay* clause with qualified counsel before including it in the contract.

An alternative approach is to specify limits to what *types* of damages are allowable in the event of a delay. Some government agencies use this approach. An example clause appears in Figure 12.3. (This specific clause is presently used by the Pennsylvania Department of Transportation.)

General Contractor Considerations

Like the owner, the general contractor also must assess the risks of delays to the contract completion. These considerations parallel those of the owner, with a slightly different perspective.

Assess the Time Allowed in the Contract

The contractor should assess the time allowed by the contract to determine if enough time is provided to perform the work without the use of extraordinary resources. The contractor must include in his bid, the cost for additional effort (such as overtime) required to meet the contract completion date.

Assess Exculpatory Language

If the contract is rampant with exculpatory language, especially if in the area of *no damages for delay*, the contractor should carefully consider accepting the risks involved. Some projects are not worth the risk of bidding. The contractor should consult with qualified counsel before entering into a highly restrictive contract with *liquidated damages* or any other damage clause. Again, if the risk is too great, the contractor may consider not bidding on this project.

Not only must contractors assess the risk of exculpatory language in a contract, but they must also read, understand, and comply with the contract provisions, particularly with respect to changes and claims. For instance, the contract may specify a time limit for issuing notice of a change or for filing a claim. The contractor must comply with these requirements. Also, the contractor should make sure to submit all information and documentation required by the contract.

CPM Schedules

Like it or not, construction has changed; contractors are now being forced to truly manage construction projects. Consequently, the contractor must use CPM schedules as management tools.

Section III – Delay Claims

111.01 COMPENSABLE DELAYS – The Department is responsible for delay damages arising only from delays created by its negligent acts or omissions. Unless otherwise specified, assume the risk of damages from all other causes of delay.

111.02 GENERAL CONDITIONS CONCERNING DELAY CLAIMS – Because of the nature and extent of damages arising out of work that has been delayed; of the need for the Department to be aware of potential delay claims promptly after the cause or causes of delay have arisen so that record-keeping can begin; and of the parties' intent to have all such claims as fully documented as possible, strict adherence to the provisions of this section is an essential condition precedent to filing a delay claim with the Board of Claims.

The following items of damage cannot be included in any delay claim against the Department:

- profit;
- loss of profit;
- labor inefficiencies;
- home office overhead, including but not limited to costs of any kind for home office personnel; and
- consequential damages, including but not limited to loss of bonding capacity, loss of bidding opportunities, and insolvency.

111.03 NOTIFICATION OF DELAY CLAIM – Notwithstanding the provisions of Section 105.01, within 10 days of any negligent act or omission of the Department, notify the Inspector-in-Charge that operations have been or will be delayed and that a claim for delay damages either is going to or might be filed with the Board of Claims. Confirm such notification in writing to the District Engineer within 10 days of such notification to the Inspector-in-Charge.

111.04 PROCEDURES – Upon notifying the Inspector-in-Charge as provided above, keep records, on a daily basis of all non-salaried labor, material and equipment expenses for all operations that are affected by the delay. Identify in such daily records each operation and the station or stations thereof affected by the delay. Daily records of all non-salaried labor, equipment and materials used on operations affected by the delay also will be kept by the Department's forces. On each Monday, compare the previous week's daily records with those kept by the Department and review for accuracy. Report to the District Engineer within 10 days of each such review all disagreements with such records. Refusal or repeated failure to meet to review the Department's records or to report disagreements with such records will create an irrebuttable presumption in favor of the Department that its records are accurate. Claim no delay costs of any kind allegedly incurred, prior to notifying the Inspector-in-Charge that operations have been delayed.

On a weekly basis, prepare and submit to the Inspector-in-Charge written reports containing the following information:

(a) Number of days behind schedule.

(b) Identification of all operations that have been delayed, or are to be delayed.

Figure 12.3

(c) Explanation of how the Department's negligent act or omission delayed each operation, and estimation of how much time is required to complete the project.

(d) Itemization of all extra costs being incurred, including:

- an explanation as to how those extra costs relate to the delay and how they are being calculated and measured;
- identification of all non-salaried project employees for whom costs are being compiled; and
- identification of all manufacturer's numbers of all items of equipment for which costs are being compiled.

Upon completion of the project, submit to the Inspector-in-Charge and the District Engineer copies of a report containing the following information:

- an itemization and explanation of the measurement and basis of all extra cost being sought, including all reports certified by an accountant;
- a description of the operations that were delayed, and how they were delayed, including the reports of all scheduling experts or other consultants, if any; and
- an as-built chart, CPM scheme or other diagram depicting in graphic form how the operations were adversely affected.

The District Engineer will review the submission and any reports prepared by the Inspector-in-Charge. If, in the opinion of the District Engineer, the Department is not responsible for any delay, a written decision will be given. Comply with the provisions of Section 105.01 if the District Engineer's decision is disputed.

If the District Engineer determines that operations were delayed by the Department, a review of the damages claimed will be made and a written decision will be made by the Department. Comply with the provisions of Section 105.01 if the District Engineer's decision is disputed.

Only expenses for extra non-salaried labor, material, and equipment costs will be considered by the Department in the event it is determined that operations were delayed by the Department. To these costs will be added 10% to cover allocable home office overhead. Likewise, in the event a delay claim is filed with the Board of Claims, only the foregoing expenses may be claimed.

When measuring additional equipment expenses (i.e. ownership expenses) arising as a direct result of a delay caused by the Department, do not use the Blue Book or any other rental rate book similar thereto. Use actual records kept in the usual course of business, and measure increased ownership expenses pursuant to generally accepted accounting principles.

Figure 12.3 *(continued)*

CPM schedules consider not only time, but resources. It is the efficient use of resources that will allow the contractor to maximize his profits. Contractors should not hesitate to utilize resource-constrained schedules to determine the critical path. If delays arise on the project, the CPM schedule is probably the most effective tool the contractor has to demonstrate the delays that occurred and their impacts, to both critical and to non-critical activities.

Risk to Subcontractors

The general contractor may pass some requirements on to its subcontractors. The percentage of risk and responsibility is dictated to some extent by the terms of the contract. Passing risk to the subcontractors is not always as easy as including a general *pass-through clause*. This type of clause incorporates by reference all the conditions of the general contract into the subcontract agreement. With a general *pass-through clause*, if a subcontractor delays a project, the damages assessed against the subcontractor may be limited to the liquidated damages amount specified in the general contract. Yet the general contractor is liable for that same amount of liquidated damages to the owner, plus its own additional costs. For example, a subcontract may include the following general language:

> "All of the conditions of the contract between the owner and the general contractor are incorporated herein by reference and are binding upon the subcontractor."

If the general contract has a liquidated damages amount of $200 per calendar day, the incorporation by reference of the general contract may effectively limit any subcontractor's liability for delays to the $200 per day.

Consider Early Finish

General contractors should try to complete projects earlier than the time allowed in the contract. By reducing time on the site, the contractor reduces general conditions costs and thereby realizes greater profit. At the planning stage, the general contractor should approach every contract with the intent of early completion. If the contractor plans to finish the project early, the project schedule should so state. There is no sense in having two schedules on the job — one for the early completion (the actual schedule), and one that is shown to the owner reflecting the full contract duration.

Subcontractor Considerations

Normally, the general contractor dictates the subcontractor's schedule. At times, the schedule requirements incorporated into subcontract agreements may be undefined or unreasonable. For example, subcontract agreements commonly state that the subcontractor will perform his work in accordance with the general contractor's schedule and will adjust accordingly so as not to delay the job. Since this statement leaves the work period undefined, the subcontractor may have to accelerate his work for the entire duration of the job.

Specific Schedule

To reduce risks associated with acceleration costs, the subcontractor should clearly communicate to the general contractor the time and schedule to which the bid applies. The subcontractor should insist that schedules be included in the terms of the subcontract agreement.

The subcontractor should always submit a formal schedule for the work with the bid. Subcontractors sometimes insist that specific language be included in the contract recognizing the schedule. They may even include the specific sequence of work the subcontractor will follow during the project. While the general contractor may not always agree to such an inclusion, the subcontractor should attempt to incorporate it. Clearly, the subcontractor is better off addressing the schedule up front than arguing it after having worked in a completely disrupted sequence during the project.

Contract Language

Subcontractors should seriously consider whether to bid on contracts with extensive exculpatory (general contractor-protective) language. As noted before, some jobs are not worth bidding.

Subcontractors must become thoroughly familiar with all clauses in their contracts. For instance, it is common to see clauses that state that for subcontractor claims, the general contractor will "pass through" the claim to the owner. The subcontractor will accept whatever damages the general contractor is able to collect and will also share in any costs for litigation or arbitration. Clauses of this nature may not sound "fair," but they are common.

It is also common to see clauses which state that if the subcontractor is delayed by another subcontractor, he must seek compensation directly from that subcontractor. Obviously, the clause is not desirable and creates legal problems for the subcontractor who suffers the loss, vis-a-vis privity of contract.

Clearly, the general contractor may not always be motivated to act in the subcontractor's best interests. Therefore, the subcontractor should attempt to include the following in its agreement with the general contractor:

- An equitable breakdown of awards or settlements for claims involving more than just the respective subcontractor.
- The right to pursue damages only against the general, and not the other subcontractors.
- Proportional legal and administrative costs in claims actions.

Designer Considerations

Normally, the designer provides input on the duration of the project. Such observations should not be formed or communicated casually. It is a subject that should be analyzed in a careful, detailed manner to determine the time required to perform the work considering the project, the site, the weather, etc.

Designer as Owner's Representative

Designers who act as the owner's representative during construction should require the contractor to submit a detailed schedule for construction. The designer then reviews the schedule submitted by the contractor and monitors progress during construction. It is advisable to establish procedures ahead of time with the contractor for schedule monitoring.

Changes

If the designer as the owner's representative makes a change to the project because of owner decisions or errors and omissions in the plans and specifications, he or she should assess the time impact of that change on the project. Designers should resist the tendency to deny any time impact simply because they fear it might negatively reflect upon them. If a change necessitates a valid extension to the duration of the job, the problem can be resolved much sooner and usually at far less cost if assessed (fairly and impartially) as soon as it arises.

Early Completion Schedules

Early completion schedules were briefly noted in the discussion of the general contractor's considerations. They are of considerable importance and are worthy of additional coverage.

Most construction contracts specify the *maximum* time allowed for the contractor to perform the work. Few, if any, contracts require a minimum duration. A contractor has every right to finish a project early if possible.

Some contractors request damages for *not* finishing early, if the owner is responsible for damages or obstacles that prevented an early finish. In such cases, the owner may be liable for the damages associated with the delay. This is another argument for showing the early finish, if intended, on the official schedule. Clearly, if a contractor planned to finish early, but the schedule does not reflect this plan, it is extremely difficult to convince the owner or the courts that this was the case.

Some contractors choose to use the early completion schedule for themselves and for their subcontractor(s), but give the owner a schedule that reflects the full contract time. The rationalization for this approach is that if the contractor falls behind schedule, he will not suffer any consequences. This does not make sense for the following reasons.

If a contract has a required duration of 300 calendar days and the contractor plans to complete the project in 200 calendar days, the schedule should show 200 calendar days. If a *liquidated damages* clause is included in the contract, the damages do not start to run until day 301. Therefore, even if the contractor is late (exceeds the 200-day schedule) through his or her own fault, he or she has no greater exposure to the damages.

Utilizing two different schedules is counterproductive and can cause greater problems than it may seem to "solve." For example, how does a general contractor explain this situation to a subcontractor who has been given the shorter schedule but who sees the 300-day schedule posted in the owner's trailer?

If a dispute arises over delays, the contractor may lose credibility when attempting to explain why there are two schedules and which one is "real." He may find himself answering questions from an attorney such as, "When were you lying, when you drafted the 300-day schedule or when you drafted the 200-day schedule?" Obviously, this is a no-win question for the contractor.

Some owners will not accept schedules that show a duration less than the contract duration. While this may occur, there is no basis in the contract for the owner to insist on such a requirement. The contractor should ask the owner to show him where in the contract the minimum time is specified. Even then, some owners may still insist on having a schedule that uses all the contract time. In those cases, the contractor should submit the same early completion schedule, but add one activity at the end that makes up the difference between the early planned finish date and the contract duration, and call that activity "contractor contingency." This schedule should be accompanied by a letter that clearly explains that the contractor plans to finish early and has added the contingency activity only to get the schedule approved. The letter should further note that the contractor expects to receive compensation if he is delayed from finishing early because of the owner's actions.

Owners should not panic when they receive early completion schedules. The owner (or owner's representative) should, however, review the schedule carefully to ensure that the logic is correct and the durations are reasonable, given the contractor's resources. The owner should not presume that he is being "set up" for a delay damage claim. He should, however, be alert to the fact that management of the schedule is very important for this particular project.

Index

Index

U

W

Z